IC User's Casebook

HOWARD W. SAMS & COMPANY/HAYDEN BOOKS

Related Titles

For the retailer nearest you, or to order directly from the publisher, call 800-428-SAMS. In Indiana, Alaska, and Hawaii call 317-298-5699.

IC User's Casebook

Joseph J. Carr

HOWARD W. SAMS & COMPANY

A Division of Macmillan, Inc.

11711 North College, Suite 141, Carmel, IN 46032 USA

International Standard Book Number: 0-672-22488-7
Library of Congress Catalog Card Number: 88-60061

Acquisitions Editor: *Greg Michael*
Editor: *Louis Keglovits*
Illustrators: *Sally Copenhaver, William D. Basham*
Cover Graphic: *Linda Simmons*
Compositor: *Shepard Poorman Communications Corp.*
Word Processor: *David Ann Gregson*

Printed in the United States of America

Contents

Chapter 11

Solid-State Audio Circuits: Transistor and IC 127

Chapter 12

Instrumentation and Other Circuits 161

Chapter 13

Active Filters 191

Chapter 14

Digital Electronics: An Introduction for Hobbyists 201

Chapter 15

TTL IC Devices 221

Chapter 16

CMOS IC Devices 229

Preface

Electronics has been a fascinating field ever since the earliest days of radio. Electronics and radio hobbyists have always been activists who experiment with practical circuits, design their own projects, and build everything from simple "one-evening" jobs to complex systems that take months to complete. This book is designed for those electronics hobbyists, and others who enjoy learning about or building fundamental electronic circuits.

At one time all electronic projects were composed of discrete components such as resistors, capacitors, transistors, and vacuum tubes. But in the early 1960s a great change in circuit construction occurred with the advent of integrated circuitry. The first commercial ICs (integrated circuits), devices such as the $\mu A709$ operational amplifier, MC800-series RTL digital circuits, and the $\mu A703$ FM IF amplifier, are now considered to be over the hill. Those devices are small scale integration, and are primitive compared with products we have today . . . but in 1967 they were the latest and greatest.

Since those early days we have progressed through several orders of integration, where we now commonly see medium scale integration (MSI), large scale integration (LSI) and very large scale integration (VLSI) devices sold through nonindustrial distributors such as Jameco and Radio Shack. On the horizon are very high speed integrated circuits (VHSIC) and monolithic microwave integrated circuits (MMIC). The latter are even now appearing on the market in the form of devices such as the Mini-Circuits Laboratories MAR-1 through MAR-8, and the Signetics NE-5205 devices.

The purpose of this book is to give you some insight into how practical ICs work in actual circuits. Both analog (linear) and digital circuits are covered. Because of their widespread popularity, operational amplifiers (op amps) figure heavily in our presentation (although other types are not overlooked). The idea is to allow you to design and configure your own circuits, and the material is presented with that goal in mind.

Whatever else this book is, it is intended to be a workshop aid. Although most authors probably like to see their works given a place of honor in their reader's homes, on the bookshelf in the living room for instance, it is my fervent desire that this book be kept on your workbench, get folded over from long and hard use, and (of course) amply solder-splashed. If so, then it will have fulfilled its purpose. Enjoy.

Joseph J. Carr

Chapter 1

Linear IC Amplifiers

In 1966 I worked as an electronics technician repairing stereo amplifiers and receivers. One day, while working on an H. H. Scott receiver (one of the better brands in those days), I came across a series of semiconductor components in the FM IF stage that had a funny look about them. They looked like plastic epoxy transistors with six "dead bug" legs sticking up in the air. At first perplexed, my mind snapped into gear as it remembered an article on the then-new "integrated circuit" (IC). What I was looking at was one of the earliest examples of a μA703 IF/RF gain block IC device. Shortly thereafter I discovered the first IC operational amplifier, the μA709 (which cost $80 then, and goes five for a buck now) . . . the μA709 was truly revolutionary.

There are few who would not agree that the integrated circuit (Fig. 1-1) has revolutionized the entire electronics industry. Virtually unknown a couple decades ago, the IC "chip" brought us both the extreme miniaturization of electronics circuits, and previously unheard of component densities (Fig. 1-2). It is unlikely that the miracles of modern electronics—from "smart" cardiac pacemakers to the moon landing program, from consumer entertainment electronics to the most massive fifth generation supercomputers—would have been possible without the little chip.

Device performance also was improved by IC construction. Consider thermal drift of DC amplifiers, for example. Even low-cost modern IC operational amplifiers are several orders of magnitude better off than traditional vacuum tube or discrete transistor models because in ICs all of the semiconductors and internal resistors (the main sources of drift) share the same thermal environment. In discrete circuits, those components are spread out over several square inches of circuit board and thus do not share the same thermal environment—so drift is more pronounced.

Lower cost is another great advantage of the integrated circuit. Early transistor and vacuum tube operational amplifiers were not only

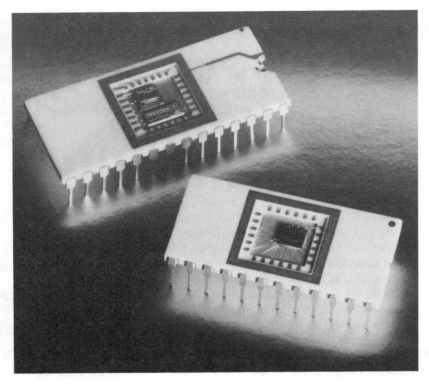

Fig. 1-1. The integrated circuit.

larger and ran hotter than their modern IC counterparts, but they were more costly as well. In addition, those early amplifiers only poorly approximated the performance of the ideal textbook version of the amplifier (see Chapter 2). Modern IC operational amplifiers (especially premium types) come so close to the ideal that textbook authors no longer look like habitual liars to those students who try to translate the theory into workbench practice.

The first ICs appeared in the mid-1960s, and were low-density devices (for example, the μA703 mentioned previously). But as industry familiarized itself with IC construction, the number of active devices on the chip skyrocketed. Today, medium scale integration (MSI) and large scale integration (LSI) are the norm, and superscale integration devices loom on the horizon as the frontiers of technology crumble to the onslaught of the quantum cooks of Silicon Valley.

The principal subject of the first section of this book is the operational amplifier, or op amp as it is commonly referred to. While our

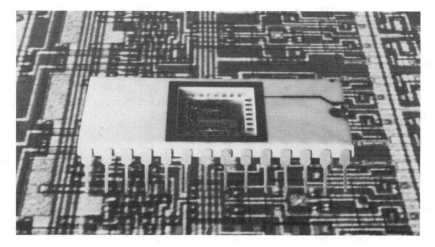

Fig. 1-2. Photomicrograph of an IC chip.

overall topic is ICs in general, op amps loom large and useful to most readers. We will also consider digital devices and other linear analog devices, such as the operational transconductance amplifier (OTA) and current difference amplifier (CDA), also called the Norton amplifier. But first, let's take a short look at amplifier basics.

Amplifier Fundamentals

Amplifiers are classified according to several schemes: conduction angle, transfer function, and so forth. The conduction angle method of classification places the amplifier into one of several different classes labeled A, B, C, and AB (which is a combination of class A and B type characteristics, and is further subdivided into AB1 and AB2). The different classes are divided according to the conduction angle of the active device, be it tube, transistor, or whatever. The conduction angle is the number of degrees of a sine wave input signal over which output current flows. In a transistor amplifier, for example, we examine the collector current to determine classification. The requirements for the various classes follow.

Class-A

Output current flows for all 360 degrees of the input sine wave cycle. This class of amplifier is said to be *linear* because the output waveform is merely a larger (i.e., amplified) version of its input waveform. Typical class-A amplifiers conduct current regardless of the input signal level. When the input signal is zero, then the power developed in the output circuit (e.g., transistor collector) is dissipated as heat rather than as signal applied to the load. Class-A amplifiers are often used as power amplifiers in consumer low-cost audio and radio receiver circuits. Mostly, however, class-A amplifiers are used as low-level current and voltage amplifiers or audio preamplifiers.

Class-B

In this class of amplifier output current is conducted over 180 degrees (i.e., one-half) of the input sine wave cycle. Thus, only 50 percent of the input signal is reproduced in the output load circuit. A single-ended class-B amplifier is therefore nonlinear (i.e., the output signal is distorted), but can be made linear if two class-B amplifiers drive the same load 180 degrees out of phase. Typically, the two amplifier outputs will be connected to the load in parallel, and their respective input signals are derived from 180-degree out-of-phase sources. Such an amplifier is said to be a *class-B push-pull amplifier*. Although more hardware is needed by class-B amplifiers when operating in the linear mode as compared with class-A amplifiers, class-B amplifiers are more efficient with respect to the consumption of DC power. When used as a linear power amplifier, a class-A amplifier is typically 30 to 40 percent efficient (i.e., only 30 to 40 percent of DC power consumed is delivered as audio to the load, and 60-70 percent is converted to heat). The class-B amplifier, on the other hand, operates at efficiencies of from 50 to more than 70 percent.

Class-AB

This combination class provides some of the better attributes of class-A and class-B amplifier circuits. Output current flows more than 180 degrees of the input sine wave cycle, but less than the full 360 degrees. When two stages are combined in a push-pull configuration, the class-AB amplifier is capable of linear operation at better efficiency than class-A. In subclass AB1, no base current flows on signal peaks, while in subclass AB2 a small amount of base current does flow.

Class-C

In the class-C amplifier output current flows for considerably less than 180 degrees of the input sine wave cycle (120 degrees is common). This form of amplifier is never linear, but it is capable of very high efficiency. The class-C amplifier is used only in RF power amplifier circuits in radio transmitters that are either high-level amplitude modulated, frequency modulated (where the distortion of amplitude peaks does not offend the modulation of the transmitter), CW on-off telegraphy, or unmodulated (which group includes industrial inductive heating and medical diathermy). Single-sideband and low-level AM modulated radio transmitters cannot use a class-C amplifier in the signal chain, so they will use one of the other classes.

The *transfer function* of an electrical circuit (including amplifiers) is the ratio of the output function over the input signal function. For example, a voltage amplifier transfer function, indicated by the symbol A_v, is the ratio of output voltage over input voltage: V_o/V_{in}. There are several transfer functions used in common amplifier configurations: power, voltage, current, transresistance, and transconductance.

The power amplifier transfer function is of the general form:

$$A = \frac{P_o}{P_{in}} \qquad \textit{[Eq. 1-1]}$$

where

    A   is the power gain,
    P_o is the output power,
    P_{in} is the input power

Related forms of transfer function relate output power to input current (P_o/I_{in}) or input voltage (P_o/V_{in}). The latter applies to audio amplifiers, for example, in which an input signal voltage (usually expressed in millivolts) drives a loudspeaker load to a given power level (expressed in watts).

The voltage amplifier, which includes most operational amplifiers, has a transfer function that relates output signal voltage to input signal voltage:

$$A_{vol} = \frac{V_o}{V_{in}} \qquad \textit{[Eq. 1-2]}$$

where

    A_{vol} is the voltage gain,
    V_o is the output voltage,
    V_{in} is the input voltage

It is important that input and output functions be expressed in terms of the same units (volts, millivolts, etc). If the input potential is expressed in millivolts, then we must either convert it to volts or express the output signal in millivolts also. For example, assume that a 10-millivolt input signal produces a 2 volt output signal. The gain of this amplifier is correctly expressed as $2/.010 = 200$, not $2/10 = 0.2$.

The current amplifier relates the output current to the input current, and has a transfer function of the form:

$$A_i = \frac{I_o}{I_{in}} \qquad \text{[Eq. 1-3]}$$

where

A_i is the current gain,
I_o is the output current,
I_{in} is the input current

Again, we must remain consistent regarding units (amperes, milliamperes, microamperes, etc).

The transconductance and transresistance amplifiers offer transfer functions that look a little weird. While the amplifier types previously mentioned had dimensionless transfer functions (volts/volts is dimensionless because the "volts" units cancel out mathematically), the transresistance amplifier has its transfer function expressed in units of resistance. Similarly, the transconductance amplifier has its transfer function units in mhos, millimhos, or micromhos (all units of conductance, the reciprocal of resistance). For the transresistance amplifier the transfer function is:

$$A_r = \frac{V_o}{I_{in}} \qquad \text{[Eq. 1-4]}$$

where

A_r is the gain in ohms,
V_o is the output potential in volts,
I_{in} is the input current in amperes

The transconductance amplifier is the inverse of the transresistance amplifier. Recall by Ohm's law, resistance R is the quotient V/I. Conductance (G) is the reciprocal of resistance ($G = 1/R$), so conductance is expressed by I/V in units called *mhos*. The transfer function of a transconductance amplifier (of which, we will look at an IC version later on) relates an output current to an input voltage:

$$A_g = \frac{I_o}{V_{in}} \qquad \text{[Eq. 1-5]}$$

where
- A_g is the gain in mhos,
- I_o is the output current,
- V_{in} is the input signal potential in volts

Of the various classes of amplifiers, most useful to us in this text are voltage, current, and transconductance.

Operational Amplifiers

The op amp (operational amplifier) is the most commonly used linear IC amplifier in the world. Originally, the first vacuum tube op amps were designed to calculate mathematical operations in old-fashioned analog computers, hence the name *operational amplifiers* sticks today. The IC form of op amp today is so widely used that it no longer has any significant role in the all but totally obsolete analog computers of yesteryear. The range of other applications for the op amp is, however, truly awesome— it has become a mainstay of more audio, communications, TV, broadcasting, instrumentation, control, and measurement circuits than anyone can imagine.

The circuit symbols for the operational amplifier are shown in Fig. 1-3. The symbol shown in Fig. 1-3A is by far the most commonly used, and will be used in this book unless otherwise specified. This same symbol could also be used to represent any amplifier with differential inputs, but here it will be used as the only proper symbol for op amps.

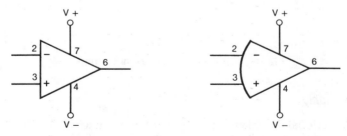

(A) Commonly used modern symbol.   *(B) Original and technically correct symbol.*

Fig. 1-3. Operational amplifier symbols.

The symbol shown in Fig. 1-3B is also seen occasionally, and some people regard it as the only proper symbol for operational amplifiers. The IEEE standard for circuit symbols, as well as industrial semiconductor companies such as Burr-Brown Corporation, specify the symbol of Fig. 1-3B.

There are two input pins on the typical op amp. The inverting input (−) produces an output signal that is 180 degrees out of phase with the input signal (Fig. 1-4A). Here we see a positive input signal produces a negative output signal, and vice versa. The noninverting input (+) produces an output signal that is in phase with the input signal (Fig. 1-4B). In the various applications shown in this book we will use either or both inputs. An amplifier that uses only the inverting input is called an *inverting follower*, while the amplifier that uses only the noninverting input is called a *noninverting follower*. An amplifier that uses both inputs might be a summing amplifier in some cases, but it is more likely to be a differential amplifier. That is, it produces an output signal that is a function of its gain and the difference between two input signal potentials.

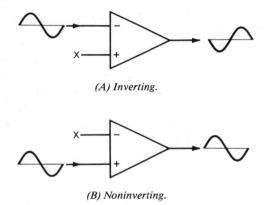

(A) Inverting.

(B) Noninverting.

Fig. 1-4. Operating modes of an op amp.

Power Supply

The operational amplifier normally operates from a bipolar DC power supply, such as shown in Fig. 1-5 (the pin numbers in this figure are for the so-called *industry standard* 741 device). This circuit shows that the two DC power supplies are independent of each other. The V+ power supply is positive with respect to common (or ground), while the V−

supply is negative with respect to the common. The operational amplifier manufacturer will specify minimum and maximum values for V− and V+. Typically, the maximum voltages will be on the order of −18 volts and +18 volts, with some offering −22 and +22 volts (or in at least one advertised case −40 volts and +40 volts).

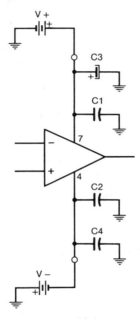

**Fig. 1-5. Configuration for bipolar power supply,
with correct decoupling.**

There may be certain limitations on the maximum supply voltages that do not show up at first glance, especially in the short-form specification or data sheets that hobbyists are usually given. For example, the most common limitation is the V− to V+ potential. The manufacturer will specify that the voltage between (V+) and (V−) does not exceed a certain potential, say 30 volts. On some 741 devices, for example, the V− and V+ ratings are both 18 volts. This means that the potential difference between the two is 36 volts. The pin-to-pin supply voltage is not to exceed 30 volts. Since the potential difference between +18 VDC and −18 VDC is 36 volts, operating both supply terminals at their maximum voltage is not permitted. Let's look at a practical example. Suppose we wanted to operate V+ at 18 volts. What's the maximum value permitted of V− that will not exceed the pin-to-pin limit?

$$(V+) − (V−) = 30$$
$$+18 \text{ VDC} − (V−) = 30$$
$$(V−) = 30 − 18$$
$$(V−) = 12$$
$$(V−)_{max} = 12 \text{ volts}$$

Because most practical circuits operate with equal bipolar DC power supplies, it is also true that most of those using popular operational amplifiers with the 30-volt limit also limit the (V−) and (V+) DC power supplies to not more than 15 volts each.

Single Supply Operation The operational amplifier is intended for dual or bipolar power supply operation. There are, however, many applications where only one polarity DC power supply is available. In order to operate the op amp in these cases we must either supply the missing potential, or devise a method for getting around the need for the missing potential.

It is reasonably easy to supply a missing potential. All we need is to add a DC-to-DC converter circuit that provides the needed voltage from the existing voltage. There are quite a few devices on the market that will produce either −15 volts from +15 volts (or 12 volts, as the case may be), or will produce isolated − and + 15-volt potentials from an existing nonisolated +15-volt potential. A popular version of this type of circuit is seen in hobbyist magazines from time to time. It uses a 555 IC timer device operated at or near 100 kHz, and a rectifier/filter circuit to produce a negative voltage. Of course, a voltage regulator can be added if needed. Typically, negative regulators will be in the 79xx or LM320xx series.

Another method for using a single DC power supply is shown in Fig. 1-6. Here we use a resistor voltage divider, R1–R2, to bias the noninverting input of the operational amplifier to some potential between ground and V+. The V− terminal of the op amp is grounded. The bias voltage on the noninverting input also appears on the output terminal as a DC offset potential. Unless the following circuit somehow doesn't care about this offset potential, the output must be capacitor coupled. The value of the bias voltage is found from:

$$V1 = \left(V+\right)\left(\frac{R2}{R1 + R2}\right) \qquad \text{[Eq. 1-6]}$$

The capacitor shown in Fig. 1-6 is used to place the noninverting input at, or near, ground potential for AC signals, while retaining the DC level produced by the resistor voltage divider. This capacitor sometimes causes noisy operation of the op amp, so it is often omitted in practical circuits. The value of the capacitor is such that it has a capacitive reactance of less than R2/10 at the lowest frequency of operation. For example, if the amplifier is designed to work down to 10 hertz, and the value of R2 is 2200 ohms (a typical value in real circuits), then the value of C1 must be such that it has a reactance of 220 ohms (2200/10) or less, at 10 Hz. This requirement evaluates to:

$$C1 = 1,000,000/(2\pi f X_c)$$
$$C1 = 1,000,000/((2)(3.14)(10 \text{ Hz})(220 \text{ ohms}))$$
$$C1 = 1,000,000/13,816$$
$$C1 = 73 \ \mu F$$

Because 100 μF is the next higher standard value capacitor, most designers will select 100 μF for C1 instead of 73 μF.

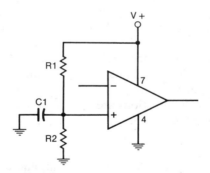

Fig. 1-6. Op amp operation from a single polarity DC supply.

Current Difference (Norton) Amplifiers

A relatively recent form of IC linear amplifier is the Norton amplifier, also known as the current difference amplifier (or CDA). The CDA produces an output voltage that is proportional to the difference between two input currents. The operation of the CDA is not exactly analogous to the op amp (i.e., with the input voltages replaced by input currents), so will not be detailed here. Chapter 10 deals with CDA devices in detail.

The symbol for the CDA differs from the normal op amp symbol in order to distinguish its unique operation. The CDA symbol shown in Fig. 1-7 is the regular differential amplifier symbol with a current source symbol added along one edge to let the reader know that current mode is intended.

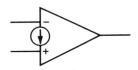

Fig. 1-7. Symbol for current difference amplifier (CDA), also called the Norton amplifier.

Operational Transconductance Amplifiers (OTA)

Another form of linear IC amplifier, different from either op amp or CDA, is the operational transconductance amplifier, or OTA. This type of amplifier has a transfer function that relates output current to input voltage. Since the transfer function expression has the units amperes/ volts (or subunits thereof), the transfer function *gain* can be expressed in the units of conductance, (mhos), or the subunits millimhos or micromhos. Since these are units of conductance, I/V, we call the amplifier a transconductance amplifier. The name operational conveys the idea that some of the functions are similar to those of the operational amplifier. Chapter 9 deals with the OTA in detail.

Protecting Linear IC Amplifiers

Operational and other linear IC amplifiers are sensitive to problems on the DC power supply. The amplifier may oscillate if not properly decoupled. Furthermore, variations and noise placed on the DC power supply lines in one stage can affect the other stages—power supply rejection is not absolute.

We also find one other problem, especially in breadboarding and in portable (battery operated) equipment—reverse polarity DC power supplies. The results will be catastrophic in that case! An operational amplifier with reversed DC power supplies will be destroyed instantly. Let's see how these problems can be avoided in practical circuits.

The problems with noise and oscillation are cured with decoupling capacitors on the amplifier power supply terminals. Capacitors C1 and C2 (each 0.1 μF) in Fig. 1-8 are used to decouple high frequencies, while the low frequency decoupling is provided by C3 and C4 (each 4.7 μF or higher). Now why do you suppose that two forms of capacitors are needed at each op amp power supply terminal? That seems a bit odd, doesn't it? Why not just use the 4.7 μF capacitors—they are very much higher in value than the 0.1 μF units, after all.

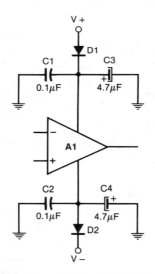

Fig. 1-8. Reverse-polarity protection for bipolar power supply.

The higher value capacitors (C3 and C4) are typically aluminum or tantalum electrolytics. The performance of these capacitors drops drastically as frequency increases, and may well be zero at higher frequencies that are nonetheless within the range of most IC operational and other linear amplifiers. At those elevated frequencies the typical electrolytic capacitor is about as effective as a block of wood. For this reason we also use a smaller value capacitor, but one that is of a type that will work at higher frequencies (e.g., mylar, mica, ceramic, etc). This situation is changing a little bit, however, as certain new forms of capacitor are now able to offer high frequency operation as well as high capacitance.

One rule of thumb ensures the success of the circuit in regard to noise and oscillation: place those capacitors as close as physically possible to the body of the amplifier. The 0.1-μF capacitors (C1 and C2) are more important than the higher value capacitors, so they should be closest to the IC amplifier body.

The fix for reverse-polarity conditions (apart from not doing it in the first place) is shown in Fig. 1-8 also. Diodes D1 and D2 are placed in series with each DC power supply line. Under normal operation these diodes are forward biased, so they will conduct current to the amplifier. If someone should accidentally connect one or both DC supplies backwards, then these diodes will be reverse biased and will not conduct current. Thus, the series diodes protect the amplifier IC from wrong power supply polarity. Typical diodes for this application are any of the 1N400x series (1N4001–1N4007).

For reverse-polarity protection of a single polarity DC power supply only a single diode is needed, as shown in Fig. 1-9. Again, a 1N400x diode is both low cost and effective. In both cases (Figs. 1-8 and 1-9), it is imperative that the capacitors be used as well as the diodes.

A brute force method of protecting the amplifier is shown in Fig. 1-10. In this case, a zener diode is placed across the two DC power supply terminals of the amplifier. The zener potential must be greater than the maximum value of potential difference between V+ and V−. For a

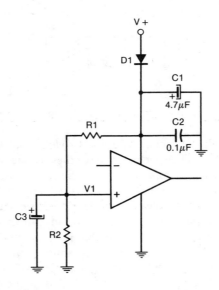

$X_{C3} \leqslant R2/10$ @ Lowest Frequency of Operation

Fig. 1-9. Reverse-polarity protection for single-polarity supply.

case where DC power supplies of −12 VDC and +12 VDC are used, then this value is 24 volts. A 28-volt zener diode would be adequate, provided that the power supply voltages are reasonably stable. Under these conditions, with V_{zener} greater than the voltage between the terminals, zener diode D1 is reverse biased at a value lower than the zener potential. Thus, it is not used in normal operation.

In reverse-polarity operation, diode D1 becomes forward biased in the nonzener mode. It will pass current around the amplifier harmlessly—hopefully. The big maybe is whether or not the zener diode will be destroyed. One solution is to use a zener diode with very high value of power dissipation. Another solution is to place a series resistor in the line with D1. All in all, it is better to use the alternative circuits using series diodes, but Fig. 1-10 is provided for the truly bold reader.

The protection of multiple amplifier stages is shown in Fig. 1-11. There are two alternatives shown in this figure. In one case, we could place 1N400x-series diodes across the power supply lines and series current-limiting resistors to prevent them from burning up. The diodes are normally reverse biased but when one or both DC power supplies are reversed, these diodes become forward biased—and short the line to ground.

The second alternative is to place the diodes in series with the line at

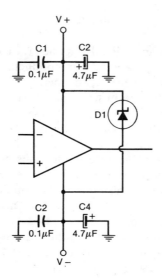

Fig. 1-10. Reverse-polarity protection using a zener diode between V− to V+.

the power supply terminals (shown in dotted lines in Fig. 1-11). This method is analogous to the method of Fig. 1-8, except that it serves more than one amplifier.

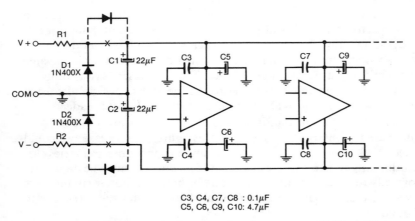

C3, C4, C7, C8 : 0.1μF
C5, C6, C9, C10: 4.7μF

Fig. 1-11. Reverse-polarity protection for a group of DC supplies.

Conclusion

We have discussed the operational amplifier, the current difference Norton amplifier, and the operational transconductance amplifier. We have also covered amplifiers in general, and methods of protecting IC amplifiers. Now let's get down to business and find out how some of these circuits actually work. First, we will examine the ideal operational amplifier in Chapter 2, and then follow up with several chapters on operational amplifier applications. We will conclude the linear IC amplifier portion of this book with general applications. Starting in Chapter 14 we will introduce digital electronics.

The approach used in this book is the popular cookbook style. It was selected not only because it is popular, but also because it is easy to follow. Each case will be presented not just as a simple circuit that you could build (which you can if you want to), but also with the design steps laid out so that you can follow the logic and modify the circuit to fit your own needs. Please feel quite free to change and modify as it suits you.

Chapter 2

The Ideal Operational Amplifier

When you study any form of electron device, be it vacuum tube, transistor, or integrated circuit, it is wise to start with an ideal representation of that device and then proceed to practical devices. In some cases, the practical and ideal devices are so far apart that you might wonder at the wisdom of this approach. In engineering and technical schools the students often take laboratory classes to put into practice what was learned in the theory classes. When they study their lab workbook sheets they often wonder if the theory instructor wasn't fantasizing—the experiments often fail to come close to predicted theoretical behavior. But for IC operational amplifiers, the modern commercial product so nearly approximates the ideal op amp of textbooks that the lab experiments actually work. The analysis method thus becomes extremely useful for learning the technology, designing new circuits, or doping out how someone else's circuit works.

In Chapters 3 and 4 we will discuss the inverting and noninverting operational amplifier configurations, respectively. In those discussions we will derive the design equations that you can use to make your own circuits—or understand mine. We will use a simplified analysis method that uses ordinary arithmetic rather than elegant engineering math. While lacking the elegant mathematical rigor of an engineering textbook presentation, this method is nonetheless sufficiently powerful to permit you to understand and design other forms of circuit. The usefulness of our simplified approach proceeds directly from the correspondence of the ideal and practical operational amplifier IC devices.

Properties of the Ideal Op Amp

Our ideal op amp is characterized by several unique properties. From this short list of properties we can deduce circuit operation and design equations. Also, the list gives us a basis for examining nonideal operational amplifiers and their defects (plus solutions to the problems caused by those defects). The basic properties of the op amp include:

1. Infinite open-loop voltage gain.
2. Infinite input impedance.
3. Zero output impedance.
4. Zero noise contribution.
5. Zero DC output offset.
6. Infinite bandwidth.
7. Both differential inputs stick together.

Let's take a look at these properties to determine what they mean in practical terms. You will find that real op amps only approximate these ideals, but in premium grade devices (and some lower-cost units as well) the approximation is quite good.

Property No. 1. Infinite Open-Loop Gain

The *open-loop* gain of any amplifier (operational or not) is simply its gain without negative or positive feedback. Positive feedback is found in oscillators, but only in some amplifiers. For our purposes it is the negative feedback that is of concern. By definition, negative feedback is a signal fed back to the input, 180 degrees out of phase with the input. In operational amplifier terms this means feedback between the output and the inverting input.

Negative feedback has the effect of reducing the loop gain by a factor (called B) that depends upon the transfer function and properties of the feedback network. Fig. 2-1 shows the basic configuration for any negative feedback amplifier. The *transfer equation* for any circuit is the output function divided by the input function. For example, the transfer function of a voltage amplifier is V_v/V_{in}. In Fig. 2-1 the term A_{vol} represents the gain of the amplifier element only, i.e., the gain with the feedback network disconnected. The term B represents the transfer function of the feedback network (without the amplifier). The overall transfer function of this circuit, i.e., with both amplifier element and feedback resistor in the loop, is defined as:

$$A_v = \frac{A_{vol}}{1 - A_{vol}B} \qquad \textit{[Eq. 2-1]}$$

where
A_v is the closed-loop gain,

A_{vol} is the open-loop gain,

B   is the transfer equation for the feedback network

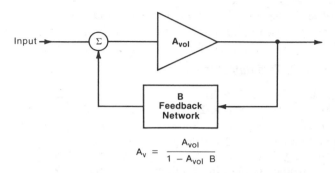

$$A_v = \frac{A_{vol}}{1 - A_{vol}\,B}$$

Fig. 2-1. Equivalent circuit for a feedback amplifier.

In the ideal op amp A_{vol} is infinite, so the voltage gain is a function only of the feedback network. Remember this fact, for it is important enough to commit to memory very early in the game. In real op amps, the value of the open-loop gain is not infinite, but it is quite high. Typical values range from 20,000 in low-grade consumer models to more than 2,000,000 in premium units.

Property No. 2. Infinite Input Impedance

This property implies that the op amp input will not load the signal source. The input impedance of any amplifier is defined as the ratio of the input voltage and the input current: $Z_{in} = V_{in}/I_{in}$. When the input impedance is infinite, therefore, we must assume that the input current is zero. Thus, an important implication of this property is that the operational amplifier inputs neither sink nor source current. In other words, it will neither supply current to a circuit, nor accept current from an external circuit. We will depend upon an implication of this property— $I_{in} = 0$—to make our circuit analysis in Chapters 3 and 4.

Real operational amplifiers have some finite input current other than zero. In low-grade devices this current can be substantial (1 milliampere), and will cause a large output offset error. The primary source of this current is the base-bias currents from the NPN and PNP transistors used in the input circuits. Certain premium grade op amps that feature bipolar inputs reduce this current to scores of picoamperes. In op amps that use field effect transistors in the input circuits, the input impedance is quite high due to miniscule bias or leakage currents. The JFET input devices are typically called *BiFET* op amps, while the MOS-FET types are called *BiMOS* devices. The RCA CA3140 device is a BiMOS op amp in which the input impedance approaches 1.5 terraohms (i.e., 1.5×10^{15} ohms), which is near enough to infinite to make the inputs of those devices approach the ideal.

Property No. 3. Zero Output Impedance

A voltage amplifier (of which class the op amp is a member) ideally has a zero output impedance. Fig. 2-2 represents any voltage source (amplifier or otherwise) and its load or external circuit. Consider V to be a perfect voltage source with no internal resistance (resistor R1 represents the internal resistance of the source), and R2 to be the load. Because the internal resistance (which in amplifiers is usually called *output resistance*) is in series with the load resistance, the output voltage V_o that is available to the load is reduced by the voltage drop across R1. Thus, the output voltage is:

$$V_o = V \left(\frac{R2}{R1 + R2} \right)$$

It is clear from the preceding equation that the output voltage will equal the source voltage only when the output resistance of the amplifier (R1) is zero. In that case, $V_o = V \times (R2/R2) = V$. Thus, in the ideal voltage source or the ideal op amp, we get the maximum output voltage (and the least error) because no voltage is dropped across the internal resistance of the amplifier.

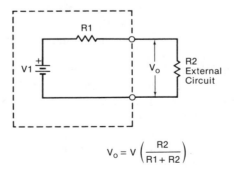

$$V_o = V \left(\frac{R2}{R1 + R2} \right)$$

Fig. 2-2. Resistance R1 represents the output resistance of the amplifier.

Real operational amplifiers do not have a zero output impedance. The actual value is typically less than 100 ohms, and many times in the neighborhood of 50 ohms. Thus, for typical voltage amplifier inputs driven by the operational amplifier, the output can be taken as if it were ideal.

A rule of thumb used by designers is to make the input resistance of any device that is driven by a nonideal output to be at least ten times the device output impedance. We see this situation in Fig. 2-3. Amplifier A1 is a voltage source that drives A2. In this situation, R1 represents the output resistance of A1 and R2 represents the input resistance of amplifier A2. In practical terms, we find that the circuit where R2 > 10R1 will yield results acceptably close to *ideal* for most purposes. In some cases, the rule R2 > 100R1 must be followed, but these instances are rare and are only for those circuits that require precision.

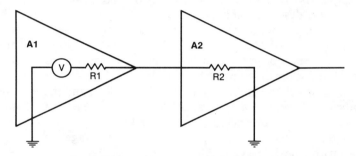

Fig. 2-3. Equivalent circuit for cascade amplifiers.

Property No. 4. Zero Noise Contribution

All electronic circuits, even simple resistor networks, produce noise signals. An example of electronic noise can be seen by shorting together the antenna input terminals of your FM receiver and then turning the volume control all the way up. The hiss that you hear is the noise that is generated inside the electronic circuitry of the receiver. If the noise increases when the antenna is connected, then the increase represents atmospheric or natural noise.

In the ideal operational amplifier, all noise voltages produced are external to the op amp. Thus, any noise in the output signal must have been in the input signal as well. Except for amplification, the output noise voltage will be exactly the same as the input noise voltage. In other words, the op amp contributed nothing extra to the output noise.

Practical op amps do not approximate the ideal, except for certain high cost models. Even a simple resistor creates noise due to the movement of electrons within it. For all resistive circuits, the noise contribution is:

$$V_{noise} = (4KTBR)^{1/2} \qquad \qquad [Eq.\ 2\text{-}2]$$

where
    K   is Boltzman's constant,
    T   is the temperature in degrees Kelvin,
    B   is the bandwidth in hertz,
    R   is the resistance in ohms

As you can easily see, the noise voltage produced by a resistor varies with the square root of its resistance.

Amplifiers use semiconductor devices that create not merely resistive noise (as described above), but also create special noise of their own. There are a number of internal noise sources in semiconductor devices, and any good text on transistor theory will give you more information on them. For present purposes, however, assume that the noise contribution of the op amp can be considerable. Premium op amps are available in which the noise contribution is very low, and these are usually advertised as *low-noise* types. Others, such as the RCA CA3140 device, will offer low-noise performance when the DC supply voltages are limited to − 5 volts and + 5 volts, and the metal package of the op amp is fitted with a flexible TO-5 style heatsink.

Property No. 5. Zero Output Offset

The output offset voltage of any amplifier is the output voltage that exists when it should be zero. The voltage amplifier sees a zero input voltage when both inputs are grounded. This connection should produce a zero output voltage. If the output voltage is not zero, then there is said to be an output offset voltage present. In the ideal op amp, this offset voltage is zero volts, but in real op amps this just isn't so.

In practical op amps the output offset voltage is nonzero, although it can be quite low in some cases. There are several methods for dealing with output offset voltage, and these will be discussed at length in Chapter 5. Most readers of this book are electronic hobbyists or students of one type or another, and often buy components from certain "bargain" sources. Be aware that many of the "bunches of op amps for less than a buck" deals are possible only because these op amps are factory seconds (bought wholesale for pennies per shovelful). In one famous chain's offering I found that six of the ten 741 op amps had more than 1 volt of output offset potential. Always test those cheapie op amps (or other IC chips) before using them; in that way you'll be able to distinguish a bad circuit or construction error from a bad op amp device.

Property No. 6. Infinite Bandwidth

The ideal op amp will amplify all signals from DC to daylight—clearly a ridiculous claim for real op amps. In real op amps the bandwidth is sharply limited. There is a specification called the *gain bandwidth product (GBP)*, which is symbolized by F_t. This rating is simply the frequency at which the gain drops to unity (1). The maximum available gain is found by dividing the maximum required frequency into the gain-bandwidth product. If the value of F_t is not sufficiently high, the circuit will not behave in classical op amp fashion at some frequencies.

Some practical op amps have GBP products in the 2 to 10 MHz range; others, on the other hand, are quite limited. The 741 family of devices is very limited, such that the device will perform as an op amp for only a few kilohertz. Above that range, the gain drops off considerably. But in return for this apparent limitation, we obtain unconditional stability. Such op amps are said to be *frequency compensated*. It is the frequency compensation of those devices that kills off the GBP. Noncompensated op amps will have a wider frequency response, but at the expense of certain instabilities. Those op amps may oscillate at some frequency without any special encouragement (see Chapter 5).

Property No. 7. Both Differential Inputs Stick Together.

Although differential inputs are not part of the definition of operational amplifiers, and indeed at least one major manufacturer offers op amps with only an inverting input; most op amps have two inputs, one inverting ($-$) and the other noninverting ($+$).

By "stick together" I mean that a voltage applied to one of these inputs also appears at the other input. This voltage is real, and is not merely some theoretical device used by engineers to evaluate circuits. If you apply a voltage to, say, the inverting input, and then connect a voltmeter between the noninverting input and the power supply common (or ground), then the voltmeter will read the same potential on noninverting as on the inverting input.

The implication of this property is that we must treat both inputs the same mathematically. This fact will make itself felt in Chapter 3 when we discuss the needlessly confusing concept of *virtual* as opposed to actual grounds, and again in Chapter 4 when we deal with the noninverting follower circuit configuration.

Conclusion

Our discussion thus far has not dealt with the problems caused by the departures from the ideal properties offered by real, practical, "kind you can actually buy" operational amplifiers. For that discussion you may turn to Chapter 5. In the meantime, however, we will want to first develop the two major configurations of the operational amplifier: inverting follower (Chapter 3) and noninverting follower (Chapter 4).

The inverting follower produces an output signal that is 180 degrees out of phase with its input signal. These circuits are covered in detail in Chapter 3. The noninverting follower, as you might expect, produces an output signal that is in phase with its input signal. These circuits are covered in Chapter 4. Almost all other operational amplifier circuits are variations on either the inverting or noninverting follower. Understanding these two configurations will help you to understand, and design or modify, a wide variety of different circuits.

Chapter 3

Inverting Follower Operational-Amplifier Circuits

The inverting follower is an op amp configuration in which the output signal is 180 degrees out of phase with the input signal. To accomplish this neat trick we use the inverting (−) input of the operational amplifier.

Fig. 3-1 shows the basic configuration for inverting-follower (also called inverting-amplifier) circuits. The noninverting input is not used, so it is set to ground potential. There are two resistors in this circuit. Resistor R2 is the negative feedback path from the output to the inverting input, while R1 is the input resistor. In a moment we will examine R1/R2 in order to determine how gain is fixed in this type of circuit. But first, let's take a look at the implications of grounding the noninverting input in this type of circuit.

What Is a Virtual Ground

The concept of *virtual ground* sounds like a ground that only pretends to be a ground, and in a funny kind of way that's not an unreasonable description. Unfortunately, that type of terminology is confusing and leads to an implication that the virtual ground doesn't really function as a ground. Let's clear up that little mess, OK?

In Chapter 2 you learned about the properties of the ideal operational amplifier. One of those properties tells us that differential inputs "stick together." Put another way, this property means that a voltage applied to one input appears also on the other input. In the arithmetic of op amps, therefore, we must treat both inputs as if they were at the same potential. This is not merely a theory. If you actually apply a potential, say 1 volt DC, to the noninverting input the same 1-volt DC potential will also be measured with a real voltmeter at the inverting input (try it).

In Fig. 3-1, the noninverting input is grounded, so it is at zero volts potential. This fact, by the properties of the ideal op amp means that

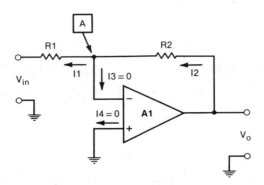

Fig. 3-1. Inverting-follower circuit.

the inverting input of the op amp is also at ground potential (zero volts). Since the input is at ground potential, but has no physical ground connection, it is said to be at a *virtual* (as opposed to a physical) ground.

The choice of the term virtual ground was unfortunate, for the idea of a virtual ground is actually quite simple even though the terminology makes it sound a lot more abstract.

Developing the Transfer Equation for the Inverting Follower

The *transfer equation* of a circuit is merely the output function divided by the input function. For an operational amplifier used as a voltage amplifier, the transfer function describes the gain, and is:

$$A = \frac{V_o}{V_{in}}$$ *[Eq. 3-1]*

where
    A is the voltage gain (dimensionless),
    V_o is the output signal potential,
    V_{in} is the input signal potential (V_o and V_{in} in the same units)

In the op amp inverting-follower circuit (Fig. 3-1) we find that the gain is set by the two resistors, R1 and R2. Let's make a step-by-step analysis to see if we can figure out what this relationship is. The method we use is simplified, but is valid for most op amp circuits so you might want to pay as much attention as to how we do it as to the result.

Example:

What is the voltage gain if 100 mV (0.100 volt) at the input produces a 10-volt output potential?

$$A = V_o/V_{in}$$
$$A = 10/0.100$$
$$A = 100$$

Consider the currents flowing in Fig. 3-1. The input bias currents, I3 and I4, are assumed to be zero. In a real op amp they are nonzero and have to be accounted for. But in the analysis case we use ideal textbook op amps rather than the kind you can buy on the hobbyist and amateur markets. Thus, in the analysis that follows we can ignore I3 = I4 = 0.

Remember that the summing junction (point A) is at ground potential because the noninverting input is grounded. Because of this fact, current I1 is a function of only the applied input voltage, V_{in}, and the resistance R1. By Ohm's law, then, the value of I1 is:

$$I1 = V_{in}/R1 \qquad \textit{[Eq. 3-2]}$$

Further, we know that current I2 is also related by Ohm's law to the output voltage, V_o, and the feedback resistor R2 (again, because the summing junction is grounded):

$$I2 = V_o/R2 \qquad \textit{[Eq. 3-3]}$$

How are I1 and I2 related? These two currents are the only currents entering or leaving the summing junction (recall that I3 = 0), so by Kirchhoff's current law we can assume:

$$I2 = -I1 \qquad \textit{[Eq. 3-4]}$$

We begin to home in on the transfer function by substituting Eqs.[3-2] and [3-3] into Eq.[3-4]:

$$I2 = -I1 \qquad \textit{[Eq. 3-4]}$$

$$\frac{V_o}{R2} = \frac{-V_{in}}{R1} \qquad \textit{[Eq. 3-5]}$$

Rearranging Eq.[3-5] yields the formal version of the transfer equation:

$$\frac{V_o}{V_{in}} = \frac{-R2}{R1} \qquad \textit{[Eq. 3-6]}$$

According to Eq.[3-1], the gain (A) is V_o/V_{in}, so we may write Eq.[3-6] in the form:

$$A = \frac{-R2}{R1} \qquad \textit{[Eq. 3-7]}$$

Example:

What is the gain of an op amp inverting follower if the input resistor (R1) is 10 kilohms, and the feedback resistor is 1 megohm?

$$A = -R2/R1$$
$$A = -1,000,000/10,000$$
$$A = -100$$

Thus, we have shown that the voltage gain of an op amp inverting follower is merely the ratio of the feedback to the input resistor ($-R2/R1$). The minus sign indicates that a 180 degree phase reversal takes place. Thus, a negative input voltage produces a positive output voltage, and vice versa.

We often see the more practical form of the transfer equation [3-6] written to express output voltage in terms of gain and input signal voltage. The two expressions are:

$$V_o = -AV_{in} \qquad \textit{[Eq. 3-8]}$$

and,

$$V_o = -V_{in}\left(\frac{R2}{R1}\right) \qquad \textit{[Eq. 3-9]}$$

Example:

What is the output voltage from an inverting follower in which V_{in} = 100 mV (0.100 V), R2 = 100kΩ, and R1 = 2kΩ?

$$V_o = -V_{in}(R2/R1)$$
$$V_o = -(0.100 \text{ V})(100k/2k)$$
$$V_o = -(0.100)(50)$$
$$V_o = -5 \text{ volts}$$

In the example above the voltage gain (A) is;

$$R2/R1 = 100k/2k = 50.$$

Summary

The following equations are used for inverting followers, and should be memorized:

$$A = -R2/R1 \qquad \text{[Eq. 3-10]}$$

$$V_o = -AV_{in} \qquad \text{[Eq. 3-11]}$$

$$V_o = -V_{in}\left(\frac{R2}{R1}\right) \qquad \text{[Eq. 3-12]}$$

Frequency-Response Tailoring

We can tailor the upper-end frequency response of the operational amplifier with a capacitor shunting the feedback resistor (see Fig. 3-2). This capacitor, acting on the value of R2, sets the frequency at which the upper-end frequency response falls off to −3 dB below the low-end gain. The gain at frequencies higher than this −3 dB frequency falls off at a rate of −6 dB/octave (an octave is a 2:1 frequency ratio), or −20 dB/decade (a decade is a 10:1 frequency ratio).

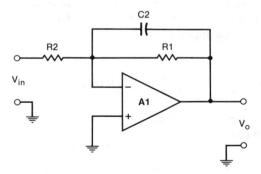

Fig. 3-2. Capacitor rolls off the high-frequency response.

The value of capacitor C2 is found by:

$$C2 = \frac{1,000,000}{2\pi R2F} \qquad \text{[Eq. 3-13]}$$

where
>   C2 is the capacitance in microfarads (μF),
>   R2 is in ohms,
>   F   is the upper -3 dB frequency in hertz (Hz)

Example:

Find the value of capacitance required to shunt across R2 in Fig. 3-2 in order to achieve a -3 dB frequency of 3000 Hz when the feedback resistor is 470 kilohms.

$$C2 = 1,000,000/(2\pi R2F)$$
$$C2 = 1,000,000/((2)(3.14)(470,000 \text{ ohms})(3000 \text{ Hz}))$$
$$C2 = 1,000,000/8.85 \times 10^9$$
$$C2 = 0.0001 \ \mu F = 100 \text{ pF}$$

The low-frequency response is controllable by placing a capacitor in series with the input resistor, which also makes the inverting follower an AC-coupled amplifier.

AC-Coupled Inverting Followers

Fig. 3-3 shows the circuit for an AC-coupled inverting follower. Capacitor C2 limits the upper -3dB frequency response point. Its value is set by the method discussed above. The lower -3dB point is set by the combination of R1 and input capacitor C3. This frequency is set by the equation:

$$C3 = \frac{1,000,000}{2\pi R1F} \qquad \textit{[Eq. 3-14]}$$

where
>   C3 is in microfarads (μF),
>   R1 is in ohms,
>   F   is the lower -3 dB point in hertz (Hz)

The circuit of Fig. 3-3 is an AC-coupled amplifier. In some cases we will want to also AC-couple the output circuit (although this is optional in most cases). Capacitor C1 is used to AC-couple the output, thus preventing any DC component on the op amp output from affecting the following stages. Resistor R3 is used to keep capacitor C1 from being

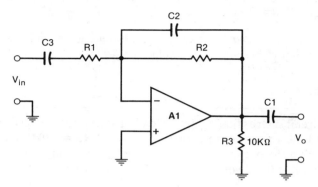

Fig. 3-3. AC-coupled inverting follower.

charged by the offset voltage from op amp A1. The value of capacitor C1 is set to retain the lower −3 dB point, using the resistance of the stage following as the R1 of equation [3-14].

Multiple-Input Inverting Followers

We can accommodate multiple inputs on an inverting follower by using a circuit such as seen in Fig. 3-4. There are a number of applications for such circuits: summing amplifiers, audio mixers, and so forth (for example). The output voltage transfer function for this type of amplifier is as follows:

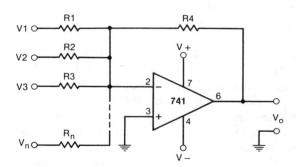

Fig. 3-4. Multiple-input inverting follower;
also called a summing amplifier.

$$V_o = R4 \left(\frac{V1}{R1} + \frac{V2}{R2} + \frac{V3}{R3} + \ldots + \frac{V_n}{R_n} \right) \quad \text{[Eq. 3-15]}$$

The terms V_n and R_n refer to the nth voltage and nth resistance. Let's consider a three-input example.

Example:

A circuit such as that in Fig. 3-4 has a 100kΩ feedback resistor (R4), and the following input resistors: R1 = 10kΩ, R2 = 50kΩ, and R3 = 100kΩ. Find the output voltage when the following input voltages are present: V1 = 0.100 volt, V2 = 0.200 volt and V3 = 1 volt.

$$V_o = R4 \left(\frac{V1}{R1} + \frac{V2}{R2} + \frac{V3}{R3} \right)$$

$$V_o = (100k) \left(\frac{(0.100)}{10k} + \frac{(0.200)}{50k} + \frac{(1.00)}{100k} \right)$$

$$V_o = [(10)(0.100)] + [(2)(0.200)] + [(1)(1.00)]$$

$$V_o = (1 \text{ volt}) + (0.4 \text{ volt}) + (1 \text{ volt})$$

$$V_o = 2.4 \text{ volts}$$

Basic Design Procedure

We must consider several matters when designing inverting-follower amplifiers. First, we must obviously consider the gain required. Second, we must consider the input impedance of the circuit. That specification is needed in order to prevent the amplifier input from loading the driving circuit. In the case of the inverting follower, the input impedance is limited to the value of the input resistor (R1 in Fig. 3-1). We must follow the design rule:

MAKE THE INPUT RESISTOR (HENCE THE INPUT IMPEDANCE) NOT LESS THAN 10 TIMES THE SOURCE RESISTANCE.

The implication of this rule is that we must determine the source resistance of the driving circuit, and then make the input impedance of the operational amplifier inverting follower at least ten times larger. When the driving source is another operational amplifier we can assume that the source impedance (i.e., the output impedance of the driving op amp) is 100 ohms or less. For these cases, make the value of R1 (in Fig. 3-1) at least 1000 ohms (i.e., 10 × 100 ohms = 1000 ohms). In other cases, however, we have a slightly different problem. Some transducers, a thermistor for measuring temperature for example, have a much higher source resistance. One thermistor, for example, has a resistance that varies from 10 kilohms to 100 kilohms over the temperature range of interest, so an input impedance of 1 megohm is required. When the input impedance gets this high we might want to consider the noninverting follower amplifier (see Chapter 4).

In the inverting follower circuit the choice of input impedance drives the design, so it is part of the initial procedure:

1. Determine the minimum allowable input resistance (i.e., 10 × the source impedance.

2. If the source resistance is 100 ohms or less, try 10 kilohms as the trial input resistance (R1). This value might be lowered if the feedback resistor becomes too high for the required gain. The value of R1 or 10 kilohms whichever is higher, is the input resistance.

3. Determine the amount of gain required. In general, the gain of a single inverting follower should be less than 500. For gains higher than that figure use a multiple op amp circuit. Some low-cost op amps should not be operated at gains greater than 200.

4. Determine the frequency response (i.e., the frequency at which the gain drops to unity). From steps 3 and 4 we can calculate the minimum gain bandwidth product of the op amp required. (GBP = Gain × Frequency)

5. Select the operational amplifier. If the gain is high, e.g., over 100, then you might want to select a BiMOS or BiFET operational amplifier in order to limit the output offset voltage caused by the input bias currents. Select a 741-family device if you don't need more than a few kilohertz frequency response, and the unconditionally stable characteristics of the 741 are valuable. Also look at the package style. For most hobbyist applications the 8-pin miniDIP package is probably the easiest to handle. The 8-pin metal can is also useful because it can be made to fit 8-pin miniDIP positions by correct bending of the leads.

6. Select the value of the feedback resistor:

$$R2 = ABS(A) \times R1$$

("ABS(A)" means the absolute value of gain—i.e., without the minus sign)

7. If the value of the feedback resistor is too high, i.e., beyond the

range of standard values (about 20 megohms or so) or too high for the input bias currents, then try a lower input resistance (in the case where the value of R1 is greater than 10 times the source resistance).

8. If a high-end frequency-response limit is imposed, then calculate the value of the capacitor shunting the feedback resistor (Fig. 3-2) according to the equation:

$$C2 = \frac{1,000,000}{2\pi R2F} \qquad \text{[Eq. 3-16]}$$

where

C2 is the capacitance in microfarads (μF),

R2 is the resistance in ohms,

F is the upper −3 dB frequency response breakpoint in hertz (Hz)

Project Examples

Case No. 3-1: Gain-of-10 Preamplifier

Design an inverting amplifier that will produce an amplification of 10 for a DC potential being applied to a meter input in order to improve resolution (the meter's scale is 0–10 volts). Assume that the source impedance is 50 ohms, and that the input voltage is not greater than 1 volt.

Discussion The low source impedance means that any input resistance greater than 500 ohms is sufficient. Given the moderate gain requirement, therefore, we can set the input resistor (R1) value at 10 kilohms. Since the device operates at DC and near DC, and is relatively healthy (on the order of 1 volt), we can use any ordinary 741-family operational amplifier. The circuit for this project, including pinouts for the "industry standard" 741 operational amplifier, is shown in Fig. 3-5.

The feedback resistor, R2, is selected from the expression:

$$R2 = ABS(A) \times R1$$
$$R2 = ABS(-10) \times (10k)$$
$$R2 = (10)(10k)$$
$$R2 = 100k\Omega$$

The power supply pins for the 741 operational amplifier are as follows: V+ is pin 7, and V− is pin 4.

The values for V− and V+ are dependent on the maximum re-

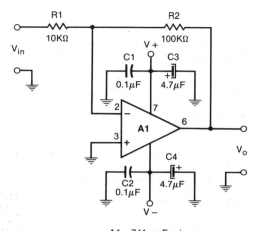

Fig. 3-5 A gain-of-10 inverting amplifier.

quired output voltage. In this case, we have a maximum V_o of 10 volts, so we know that the DC supply voltages are at least this high. There is a specification that the DC voltage be higher than the output voltage by at least 0.7 volt times the number of PN junctions between the power supply terminal and the output terminal. In the case of the 741 this value is about 2.75 volts. For the 10-volt output case, therefore, we need V— and V+ voltages of 12.75 volts or higher.

Case No. 3-2: Gain-of-100 Preamplifier

Assume that in Case No. 3-1 we find that the maximum input voltage is only 0.1 volt, and we still need to display that voltage on a 0 to 10 volt meter. The gain of this amplifier must be 10 volts/0.1 volt, or 100. How do we adjust the value of feedback resistor R2 to accommodate this change?

$$R2 = ABS(-100)(10k)$$
$$R2 = (100)(10k)$$
$$R2 = 1,000,000 \text{ ohms}$$

The circuit for this amplifier is shown in Fig. 3-6. The DC power supply connections are as shown in Fig. 3-5.

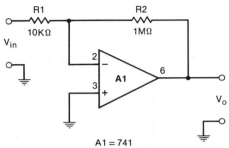

A1 = 741
(See Fig. 3-5 for Power Supply Connections)

Fig. 3-6. A gain-of-100 inverting amplifier.

Case No. 3-3: Gain-of-100, 100-Hz Inverting Amplifier With High Input Impedance

Suppose we have a source that produces 0.010 volt against a requirement of −1 volts input to an AC amplifier. This source is a temperature transducer with an output impedance of 10 kilohms, or less. Because of the rapid rise time of the transducer, we need a 100-Hz frequency response, but wish to limit the higher frequencies to reduce noise in the circuit (some temperature transducers are inherently noisy). Design an amplifier for this application.

Discussion   The 10 kilohm maximum value of the transducer impedance means that we need to set R1 at 100 kilohms. The gain required is $(-1)/(0.10) = -100$, which implies a gain-of-100 inverting amplifier. Because of the high impedances involved, one needs to consider a BiMOS or BiFET operational amplifier (Fig. 3-7). Because the RCA CA3140 device is easily available to hobbyists, we will use it. Capacitor C1 limits the higher frequencies and its value is arrived by:

$$C1 = \frac{1,000,000}{6.28 \times 10^9}$$

$$C1 = 0.000159 \ \mu F = 159 \ pF$$

Since 160 pF is the nearest standard value, we select 160 pF for C1 in Fig. 3-7.

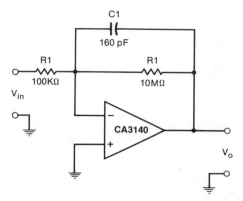

Fig. 3-7. A high-impedance, gain-of-100 inverting amplifier.

Conclusion

In this chapter we discussed the inverting-follower configuration. In the next chapter we will expand our discussion of basic op amp circuits by looking at the noninverting-follower configuration.

Chapter 4

Noninverting Followers

The second classical op amp configuration is called the noninverting follower. This type of amplifier uses the noninverting input of the operational amplifier. Because of this configuration, the output signal is in phase with the input signal. There are two basic noninverting configurations: unity gain and greater-than-unity gain.

Fig. 4-1 shows the unity gain noninverting follower circuit. The output terminal is connected directly to the inverting input, resulting in 100 percent negative feedback. Recall the voltage gain expression for all feedback amplifiers:

$$A_v = \frac{A_{vol}}{1 + A_{vol}B} \qquad \text{[Eq. 4-1]}$$

where
  A_v is the closed-loop voltage gain (i.e., gain with feedback),
  A_{vol} is the open-loop voltage gain (i.e., gain without feedback),
  B   is the feedback factor

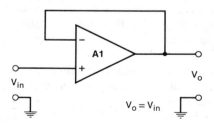

Fig. 4-1. Unity gain noninverting follower.

The feedback factor, B, represents the transfer function of the feedback network. When that network is a resistor voltage-divider network, the value of B is a decimal fraction that represents the attenuation of the op amp output voltage before it is applied to the op amp inverting input. In the unity-gain follower circuit the value of B is 1, so Eq.[4-1] reduces to:

$$A_v = \frac{A_{vol}}{1 + A_{vol}} \qquad \text{[Eq. 4-2]}$$

Consider the implications of Eq.[4-2] for a common op amp. A certain low-cost type has an open-loop gain of 50,000. For this device, the voltage gain of a circuit such as Fig. 4-1 is:

$$A_v = \frac{A_{vol}}{1 + A_{vol}}$$
$$A_v = \frac{50,000}{1 + 50,000}$$
$$A_v = 50,000/50,001 = 0.99998$$

A gain of 0.99998 is close enough to 1.0 to justify calling the circuit of Fig. 4-1 a unity-gain follower.

Applications of Unity-Gain Followers

So what use is an amplifier that does not amplify? There are two principal uses of the unity-gain noninverting follower: buffering and impedance transformation. A secondary use is boosting the drive power available (a special case of buffering).

A *buffer amplifier* is placed between a circuit and its load in order to improve the isolation of the two. A very common example is use of a buffer amplifier between an oscillator or waveform generator and its load. This use is found especially where the load exhibits a varying impedance that could result in pulling of the oscillator frequency. Such unintentional frequency modulation of the oscillator is very annoying because it makes some circuits unable to function, and others function poorly.

Another common use for buffer amplifiers is isolation of an output connection from the main circuitry of an instrument. An example might be an instrumentation circuit that uses multiple outputs, perhaps one to a controlling computer and another to an oscilloscope or strip-chart recorder. By buffering the analog output to the oscilloscope we prevent short circuits in the display wiring from affecting the signal to the computer.

A special case of buffering is represented by using the unity-gain follower as a power driver. A long cable run will attenuate low-power signals. To overcome this problem we sometimes use a low-impedance power source to drive the long cable. This application points out that a unity-gain follower does have power gain (the unity feature refers only to the voltage gain). After all, if the input impedance is typically much higher than the output impedance, yet $V_o = V_{in}$, then it stands to reason that the power output is much greater than the required input power. Thus, the circuit of Fig. 4-1 is unity gain for voltage signals and greater than unity gain for power.

The impedance transformation capability is obtained from the fact that an op amp has a very high input impedance and a very low output impedance. Let's illustrate this application by a practical example. Fig. 4-2 is a generic equivalent of a voltage source driving a load (R2). Resistance R1 represents the internal impedance of the signal source (usually called "source impedance"). The pure signal voltage, V, is reduced at the output (V_o) by whatever voltage is dropped across source resistance R1. The output voltage is found from:

$$V_o = V \left(\frac{R2}{R1 + R2} \right) \qquad \textit{[Eq. 4-3]}$$

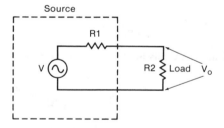

Fig. 4-2. Generic equivalent of voltage source driving a load.

In our worst case example let's assume a high impedance source is driving a low-impedance load. We will calculate the loss in a case where R1 = 10 kilohms, R2 = 1 kilohm, and V = 1 volt.

$$V_o = V \left(\frac{R2}{R1 + R2} \right)$$

$$V_o = 1 \left(\frac{(1k)}{(10k + 1k)} \right)$$

$$V_o = 1/11 = 0.091 \text{ volt}$$

We have lost more than 90 percent of the signal voltage. But if we impedance transform the circuit with a unity-gain noninverting amplifier, as in Fig. 4-3, we change the situation entirely. If the amplifier input impedance is very much larger than the source resistance (it is), and the amplifier output impedance is very much lower than the load impedance, then there is very little loss and V will closely approximate V_o.

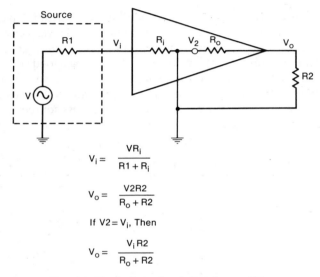

$$V_i = \frac{VR_i}{R1 + R_i}$$

$$V_o = \frac{V2R2}{R_o + R2}$$

If $V2 = V_i$, Then

$$V_o = \frac{V_i R2}{R_o + R2}$$

Fig. 4-3. Equivalent circuit for the amplifier.

Noninverting Followers with Gain

Fig. 4-4 shows the circuit for the noninverting follower with gain. In this circuit, the signal, V_{in}, is applied to the noninverting input, while the feedback network (R2/R1) is almost the same as in the inverting follower circuit.

We can evaluate this circuit using the same general method as was used in the inverting follower case (see Chapter 3). We know from Kirchhoff's current law, and the fact that the op amp input neither sinks nor sources current, that I1 and I2 are equal to each other. Thus, for these currents at the summing junction (point A):

$$I1 = I2 \qquad \qquad [Eq.\ 4\text{-}4]$$

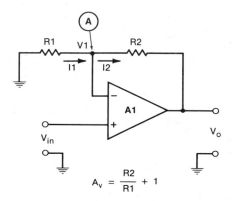

Fig. 4-4. Noninverting follower with gain.

We know from the properties of the ideal op amp that any voltage applied to the noninverting input (V_{in}) also appears at the inverting input. Therefore:

$$V1 = V_{in}$$ *[Eq. 4-5]*

From Ohm's law we know the value of current I1 is:

$$I1 = V1/R1$$ *[Eq. 4-6]*

or, because $V1 = V_{in}$,

$$I1 = V_{in}/R1$$ *[Eq. 4-7]*

Similarly, current I2 is equal to the voltage drop across resistor R2 divided by the resistance of R1. The voltage drop across resistor R1 is the difference between the output voltage (V_o) and the voltage found at the inverting input (which is equal to V_{in}). Therefore,

$$I2 = \frac{(V_o - V_{in})}{R2}$$ *[Eq. 4-8]*

We home in on the transfer equation of the noninverting follower by substituting Eqs. [4-7] and [4-8] into Eq. [4-4]:

$$\frac{V_{in}}{R1} = \frac{(V_o - V_{in})}{R2} \qquad \qquad \textit{[Eq. 4-9]}$$

We must now solve Eq.[4-9] for output voltage V_o:

$$\frac{V_{in}}{R1} = \frac{(V_o - V_{in})}{R2} \qquad \qquad \textit{[Eq. 4-10]}$$

$$V_{in}\left(\frac{R2\, V_{in}}{R1}\right) = V_o - V_{in} \qquad \qquad \textit{[Eq. 4-11]}$$

$$V_{in}\left(\frac{R2}{R1} + V_{in}\right) = V_o \qquad \qquad \textit{[Eq. 4-12]}$$

Factoring out V_{in}:

$$V_{in}\left(\frac{R2}{R1} + 1\right) = V_o \qquad \qquad \textit{[Eq. 4-13]}$$

or, reversing the order to the conventional style:

$$V_o = V_{in}\left(\frac{R2}{R1} + 1\right) \qquad \qquad \textit{[Eq. 4-14]}$$

Equation [4-14] is the transfer equation for the noninverting follower. The voltage gain portion of Eq.[4-14] should be either memorized or written down where you can easily find it.

Advantages of Noninverting Followers

The noninverting follower has several advantages. In our discussion of the unity gain configuration we mentioned that buffering and impedance transformation were advantages. Also, in the gain configuration we are able to provide voltage gain with no phase reversal—an advantage in some cases.

The input impedance of the noninverting followers shown thus far is very high, being essentially the input impedance of the op amp. In the ideal version, this impedance is infinite, while in practical devices it may range from 500 kilohms to more than 10^{12} ohms. Thus, the noninverting follower is useful for amplifying signals from any high impedance source, whether or not impedance transformation is a circuit requirement.

When the required gain is known (as it usually is), we select a trial value for R1, and then solve Eq.[4-15] to find R2. This new version of the equation is:

$$R2 = R1(A_v - 1) \qquad \textit{[Eq. 4-16]}$$

Using Eq.[4-16] we can do simple design jobs.

Example:

Design a gain-of-100 noninverting amplifier.

1. Select a trial value of resistance for R1 (typically 100 to 5000 ohms):

    R1 = 1200 ohms.

2. Use Eq.[4-16] to determine the value of R2:

    R2 = R1(A_v−1)
    R2 = (1200)(100 − 1)
    R2 = (1200)(99)
    R2 = 118,800 ohms.

3. Determine whether or not the result obtained above is acceptable to you (if it is not, work the problem again). Now is the time for a little philosophizing. What does "acceptable" mean? If the value of R2 is exactly equal to a standard, easily obtained resistor, then all is well. But, as in the case above, the value 118,800 ohms is not a standard value. What we have to determine, therefore, is whether or not the nearest standard values result in an acceptable gain error (which is determined from the application). Both 118 kilohms and 120 kilohms are standard values, with 120 kilohms being somewhat easier to obtain. Both of these standard values are within one percent of the calculated value, so this result is acceptable if the gain error with either or both standard values is within reasonable limits for the application. Fig. 4-5 shows the resultant amplifier.

AC-coupled Noninverting Amplifiers

The noninverting amplifiers discussed thus far have all been DC-coupled. In other words, they will respond to signals from DC up to the

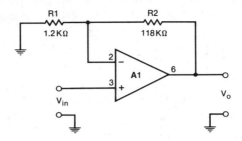

Fig. 4-5. A gain-of-100 noninverting amplifier.

limit of the amplifier selected. Sometimes, however, we do not want the amplifier to respond to DC or near-DC slowly varying signals. For these applications we select an AC-coupled noninverting follower circuit. We will examine several AC-coupled noninverting amplifiers.

Fig. 4-6A shows the simple capacitor input AC-coupled amplifier circuit. It is essentially the same as the previous circuits, except for the input coupling network, C1-R3. Capacitor C1 in Fig. 4-6A serves to block DC and very low-frequency AC signals. If the op amp has zero input bias currents, then we can delete resistor R3. Very few practical op amps even approach that ideal. As a result, input bias currents will charge capacitor C1, creating an offset voltage that is seen by the op amp as a valid DC signal, and is amplified to form an output offset voltage. In some devices, the output saturates from the C1 charge shortly after turn-on. Resistor R3 keeps C1 discharged.

Resistor R3 also sets the input impedance of the amplifier. Previous circuits had a very high input impedance because that parameter was determined only by the (extremely high) op amp input impedance. In Fig. 4-6A, however, the Z_{in} seen by the source is equal to R3.

Another effect of resistor R3 and capacitor C1 is to limit the low frequency response of the circuit. This phenomena can be either a pain in the neck or a blessing. The blessing is derived from the fact that R3C1 form a high-pass filter (see Fig. 4-6B). The −3 dB frequency, F, is found from:

$$F = \frac{1,000,000}{2\pi R1 C1} \qquad \text{[Eq. 4-17]}$$

where
    F   is the −3 dB frequency in hertz (Hz),
    R1 is the resistance in ohms,
    C1 is the capacitance in microfarads

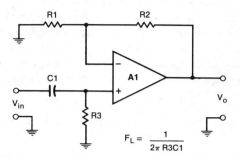

(A) Noninverting amplifier.

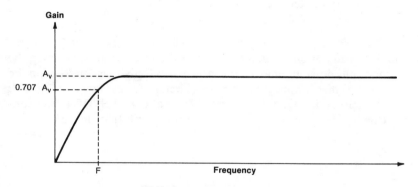

(B) Frequency response curve.

Fig. 4-6. AC-coupled amplifier and frequency response.

Example:

Find the −3 dB frequency in hertz when C1 is 0.1 μF and R1 is 10 megohms.

$$F = \frac{1,000,000}{2\pi R1C1}$$

$$F = \frac{1,000,000}{(2)(3.14)(10^7)(0.1)}$$

$$F = 0.159 \text{ Hz}$$

The form of Eq.[4-17] is backwards from what we normally need in practical design. In most cases, we know the required frequency-response limit from the application. We also know from the application what the minimum value of R3 should be (an implication from source impedance), and often set it as high as possible as a practical matter (10 megohms is popular). Thus, we want to solve Eq.[4-17] for C1:

$$C1 = \frac{1,000,000}{2\pi R1F} \qquad \textit{[Eq. 4-18]}$$

where
    F   is the -3 dB frequency in hertz (Hz),
    R1 is the resistance in ohms,
    C1 is the capacitance in microfarads

The technique of Fig. 4-6 works well for dual-polarity DC power supply circuits. In single-polarity DC power supply circuits, however, the method falls down because of the large DC offset voltage present on the output. For these applications we use a circuit such as shown in Fig. 4-7.

The circuit in Fig. 4-7 is operated from a single V+ DC power supply (the V− terminal of the op amp is grounded). In order to compen-

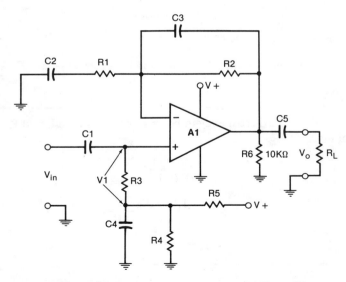

Fig. 4-7. Single power supply operation of AC amplifier.

sate for the V— supply being zeroed, the noninverting input is biased to a potential of:

$$V1 = \left(V+\right)\left(\frac{R4}{R4 + R5}\right) \qquad \text{[Eq. 4-19]}$$

If R4 = R5, then V1 will be (V+)/2. Because the noninverting input sinks no current, or very little current in the picoampere range, the voltage at both ends of R3 is the same (i.e., V1).

The circuit of Fig. 4-7 does not pass DC and some low AC frequencies because of the capacitor coupling. Also, because capacitor C3 shunts feedback resistor R2, there is a rolloff of the higher frequencies. The high frequency rolloff —3dB point is found from:

$$F = \frac{1,000,000}{2\pi R2C3} \qquad \text{[Eq. 4-20]}$$

where
  F   is the —3 dB frequency in hertz (Hz),
  R2   is in ohms,
  C3   is in microfarads

We can restate the "traditional" Eq.[4-20] into a more useful form that takes into account the fact that we usually know the value of R2 (from setting the gain), and the nature of the application sets the minimum value of frequency F. We can rewrite Eq.[4-20] in a form that yields the value of C3:

$$C3 = \frac{1,000,000}{2\pi R3F} \qquad \text{[Eq. 4-21]}$$

The lower —3 dB frequency is set by any or all of several RC combinations within the circuit:

1. R1-C2
2. R3-C1
3. R3-C4
4. R_L-C5

Resistor R1 is part of the gain-setting feedback network. Capacitor C2 is used to keep the "cold" end of R1 above ground at DC, while keeping it grounded for AC signals.

Resistor R3 is the input resistor and serves the same purpose as the similar resistor in the previous circuit. At midband the input impedance is set by resistor R3, although at the extreme low end of the frequency range the reactance of C4 becomes a significant feature. In general, X_{C4} should be less than R3/10 at the lowest frequency of operation.

Capacitor C1 is in series with the input signal path and serves to block DC and certain very low frequency signals. The value of C1 should be:

$$C1 = \frac{1,000,000}{2\pi FR3} \qquad \qquad \textit{[Eq. 4-22]}$$

where
  C1 is in microfarads,
  F   is in hertz (Hz),
  R3 is in ohms

Capacitor C5 is used to keep the DC output offset from affecting succeeding stages. The 10-kilohm output load resistor (R6) keeps C5 from being charged by the DC offset voltage. The value of C5 should be greater than:

$$C5 = \frac{1,000,000}{2\pi FR_L} \qquad \qquad \textit{[Eq. 4-23]}$$

where
  C5 is in microfarads,
  F   is the low end -3 dB frequency in hertz (Hz),
  R_L is the load resistance in ohms

Designer's Casebook Example

Design an amplifier with a gain of 200, $\pm$ 10%, with -3 dB frequencies of 300 and 3300 hertz, and an input impedance of 2.2 megohms. Assume that the stage following will have a 10-kilohm input impedance, so R_L for this design is 10,000 ohms. The V+ supply is 14.4 volts DC, and the noninverting input is biased to V+/2.

Procedure:

1. Set the value of resistor R1 to 1 kilohm as a trial value.
2. Find the value of R2:

$$R2 = R1(A_v - 1)$$

$$R2 = (1k)(200-1)$$
$$R2 = (1k)(199)$$
$$R2 = 199 \text{ kilohm}$$

The calculated value of 199 kilohms is within 0.5 percent of the standard resistor value of 200 kilohms. By specifying 5-percent tolerance resistors we ensure that the voltage gain is within tolerance. Set R1 = 1 kilohm, R2 = 200 kilohms.

3. Set the value of C2 such that X_{C2} is R1/10 or less. The minimum value of C2 is, therefore:

$$C2(min) = \frac{1,000,000}{2\pi F1R1}$$

$$C2(min) = \frac{1,000,000}{(2)(3.14)(300 \text{ Hz})(1000 \text{ ohms})}$$

$$C2(min) = \frac{1,000,000}{1,884,000}$$

$$C2(min) = 0.53 \ \mu F$$

The next higher standard value easily obtained by most hobbyists is 0.68 μF, with 1 μF being the next higher.

4. Calculate C3:

$$C3 = \frac{1,000,000}{2\pi F2R2}$$

$$C3 = \frac{1,000,000}{(2)(3.14)(3300 \text{ Hz})(200,000)}$$

$$C3 = \frac{1,000,000}{4,200,000,000}$$

$$C3 = 0.00024 \ \mu F, \text{ or } 240 \text{ pF}$$

The value 240 pF is a standard value, but is not usually stocked by local distributors. Use 220 pF if 240 pF is not easily available. Alternatively, construct a 240-pF capacitor from two smaller value capacitors (e.g., a pair of 120-pF capacitors in parallel).

5. Select R3 = 2.2 megohms to meet input impedance specification.

6. Select value for C4. The reactance of C4 should be R3/10 or less at frequency F1 (i.e., 300 Hz).

$$C4 = \frac{1,000,000}{2\pi F1X_{C4}}$$

$$C4 = \frac{1,000,000}{(2)(3.14)(300 \text{ Hz})(220,000 \text{ ohms})}$$

$$C4 = \frac{1,000,000}{420,000,000}$$

$$C4 = 0.0025 \ \mu F$$

The value of C4 should be 0.0025 μF or higher.

7. Set the value of C1:

$$C1 = \frac{1,000,000}{2\pi R3 F1}$$

$$C1 = \frac{1,000,000}{(2)(3.14)(2,200,000)(300)}$$

$$C1 = 0.00024 \ \mu F = 240 \ pF$$

8. Calculate the value of capacitor C5:

$$C5 = \frac{1,000,000}{2\pi F1 R_L}$$

$$C5 = \frac{1,000,000}{(2)(3.14)(300 \ Hz)(10,000 \ ohms)}$$

$$C5 = \frac{1,000,000}{18,840,000}$$

$$C5 = 0.053 \ \mu F \ (use \ 1 \ \mu F)$$

9. Set values of resistors R4 and R5 if the bias voltage on the noninverting input is (V+)/2. In most cases, we will set these resistors equal to each other (for that bias), at a value between 1 kilohm and 10 kilohms. Use 2.2 kilohms for R4 and R5.

Summary:

The following values apply for this amplifier:

$$R1 = 1000 \ ohms$$
$$R2 = 200,000 \ ohms$$
$$R3 = 2,200,000 \ ohms \ (2.2 \ megohms)$$
$$R4 = 2200 \ ohms$$
$$R5 = 2200 \ ohms$$
$$R6 = 10,000 \ ohms$$
$$C1 = 240 \ pF$$
$$C2 = 0.68 \ or \ 1.0 \ \mu F$$
$$C3 = 240 \ pF$$
$$C4 = 0.0025 \ \mu F$$
$$C5 = 1 \ \mu F$$

The values given will yield a gain-of-200 ($\pm$ 10%) amplifier, with a 2.2-megohm input impedance and a $-$3dB bandwidth of 300 to 3300 hertz.

Transformer-Coupled Noninverting Amplifier

Fig. 4-8 shows the circuit for a transformer-coupled noninverting follower. This type of circuit is often used in audio and broadcasting applications. For example, in those applications (see Chapter 11) where we might find audio signals passing over a 600-ohm balanced line. These circuits will be considered in greater detail later. The only point we will make here is that this circuit is an AC-only amplifier, with upper and lower $-3dB$ points determined mostly by the frequency response of the transformer (T1), the limitations of the operational amplifier, and any capacitances shunting feedback resistor R2.

The gain of the amplifier in Fig. 4-8 is given in Eq.[4-24] below:

$$A_v = (V_{in}) \left(\frac{N_s}{N_p} \right) \left(\frac{R2}{R1} + 1 \right) \qquad \textit{[Eq. 4-24]}$$

where
  A_v is the voltage gain,
  N_s is the number of turns in the secondary of T1,
  N_p is the number of turns in the primary of T1,
  R2 is the op amp feedback resistor,
  R1 is the op amp input resistor

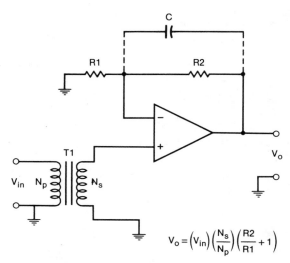

$$V_o = \left(V_{in} \right) \left(\frac{N_s}{N_p} \right) \left(\frac{R2}{R1} + 1 \right)$$

Fig. 4-8. Transformer-coupled AC amplifier.

Example:

Find the gain of an amplifier such as Fig. 4-8 if T1 has a turns ratio (N_p/N_s) of 1:4.5 (which means that $N_s/N_p = 4.5:1$), R1 = 1000 ohms, and R2 = 3900 ohms.

$$A_v = \left(\frac{N_s}{N_p}\right)\left(\frac{R2}{R1} + 1\right)$$

$$A_v = \left(\frac{4.5}{1}\right)\left(\frac{3900}{1000} + 1\right)$$

$$A_v = (4.5)(3.9 + 1) \; *$$

$$A_v = (4.5)(4.9)$$

$$A_v = 22.1$$

Chapter 5

Ideal Versus Nonideal Operational Amplifiers

The operational amplifiers that we considered in previous chapters were ideal devices. That is, they were textbook amplifiers that are "perfect" in every way. That little ploy makes our equations work out nicely, but is somewhat naive for the real world. When you go to the electronics parts store (or order by mail), the kind of operational amplifiers that you will find are somewhat short of the ideal type enshrined in textbooks. In this chapter you will find a dose of reality—and the medicine needed to correct the problems that the operational amplifiers exhibit.

There are two main problems that we will consider. First, there are DC offsets on the output that are caused by any of several defects. We will discuss these different forms of offset, and provide several means for eliminating them. Second, we will examine the problem of frequency response. There are actually two aspects to this problem. One is gain-bandwidth product, which affects the maximum frequency response of the circuit, and the other is excess frequency response. The latter problem can lead to oscillation and ringing in the output circuit.

DC Offset Problems

A DC output offset is simply a DC voltage that appears on the output terminal and is not in response to any input signal. In other words, it is an output voltage that exists when it shouldn't. There are several sources of output offset voltage in real-world operational amplifiers.

Input Offset Current

One cause of the output offset voltage is input offset currents. Fig. 5-1 shows the typical input stage used in bipolar operational amplifiers. Transistors Q1 and Q2 form an NPN differential pair. Although one of the ideal properties of the operational amplifier is that the inputs neither sinks nor sources current, real op amp inputs are transistors — and transistors need to be biased. If this were an ideal world, then the two currents would be equal and would cancel out. But real op amps use transistors that are mismatched ever so slightly. The differential input bias current forms an input offset current:

$$I_{off} = I1 - I2 \qquad \text{[Eq. 5-1]}$$

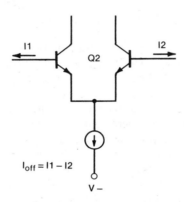

Fig. 5-1. Differential bipolar transistor amplifier.

The offset current (I_{off}) can produce an output voltage offset equal to the product of the current and the gain of the operational amplifier. While a low-gain op amp circuit may not exhibit a large output offset from the input offset current, high-gain circuits almost invariably suffer such problems.

The severity of the problem depends in part upon the design of the operational amplifier. While certain old-fashioned types (e.g., the popular 741) have rather significant offset currents, certain newer types have reduced the current to a point where it is all but negligible. Exceptionally low input-bias currents are found in those operational amplifiers that use either MOSFET transistors or JFET transistors for input transistors Q1 and Q2 (Fig. 5-1). These devices are called BiMOS and BiFET operational amplifiers, respectively.

One problem with input offset currents is seen when a feedback network is used to set the gain of the operational amplifier (including both inverting and noninverting followers). The current flows both in input resistor (R1) and feedback resistor (R2), and produces an input offset voltage equal to the product of the current and the parallel combination of R1 and R2. By Ohm's law, this voltage is equal to:

$$V = IB1 \left(\frac{R1R2}{(R1 + R2)} \right)$$ [Eq. 5-2]

Next, you will learn how to cancel this voltage in practical circuits by using a compensation resistor in series with the other (i.e., noninverting) input.

Input Offset Voltage

The ideal operational amplifier has no voltage sources in series with either input except those external sources that supply signal. Real operational amplifiers, however, have an internal voltage source in series with one or both inputs. The definition of the input offset voltage is the voltage required to force the output voltage to zero when the input signal voltages are zero. Although there are typically independent voltages in series with each input, unless they are exactly equal (in which case they cancel each other) we can model the input offset voltage as a single voltage source in series with one of the two differential inputs. The output voltage offset produced by the input offset voltage is given by:

$$V_{out} = V \left(\frac{R1 + R2}{R1} \right)$$ [Eq. 5-3]

where
V_{out} is the output offset voltage at V_o in Fig. 5-2,
V is the input offset voltage,
R1   is the input resistance,
R2   is the feedback resistance

Corrections for DC Offset Problems

Both input offset current and input offset voltage produces an output offset voltage that can adversely affect the operation of the amplifier. There are several ploys that we can use to eliminate the output offset voltage.

Fig. 5-3 shows an inverting follower circuit that uses a compensation resistor (R3) to eliminate the output offset voltage that is caused by

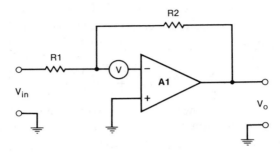

V is the voltage required to force V_o to zero
when V_{in} is, in fact, zero.

$$V_{off} = \frac{V(R1 + R2)}{R1}$$

Fig. 5-2. Input offset voltage model.

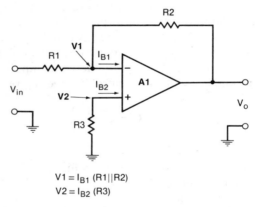

$V1 = I_{B1}(R1 \| R2)$
$V2 = I_{B2}(R3)$

Fig. 5-3. Use of a compensating resistor to null offset voltage.

the input offset current. The input bias current flowing from the inverting input (I_{B1}) will create a voltage drop (V1) across R1 and R2. This voltage was defined in Eq.[5-2]. Voltage V1 is seen by the op amp as a valid DC signal voltage. If the value of R3 is equal to the parallel combination of R1 and R2, then the voltage drop across it (V2) will be the same as the voltage applied to the inverting input. In other words, V1 = V2. This situation occurs because the two bias currents are almost equal in most operational amplifiers. The value of R3 is the parallel combination of R1 and R2, or:

$$R3 = \frac{R1R2}{R1 + R2} \qquad \text{[Eq. 5-4]}$$

Fig. 5-4 shows the use of built-in offset null terminals that are found on some operational amplifiers (typically pins 1 and 5 or 1 and 8). This circuit can eliminate output offset voltages from any source. The offset null potentiometer is connected between the offset null terminals, while the potentiometer wiper is connected to the negative DC power supply (V−). This method is preferred where the offset voltage is within the normal range of the offset null terminals.

The variant circuit shown in Fig. 5-5 is used on the LM101, LM201, and LM301 operational amplifiers. In this circuit the potentiometer is connected across the offset null terminals (as before), but the potentiometer wiper is connected to ground through a 5-megohm resistance (R4).

The potentiometer selected for any of these offset null circuits should be a ten to twenty turn trimmer potentiometer. This type of potentiometer allows maximum adjustability. The usual offset potentiometer is screwdriver operated, but if we use a shaft operated type, then we can use the same control as a position control for oscilloscopes, strip chart recorders, and other purposes where an offset is intentionally selected.

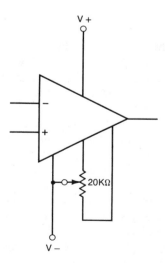

Fig. 5-4. Offset potentiometer using op-amp terminals.

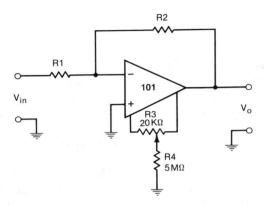

Fig. 5-5. Alternate circuit using the offset terminals.

Figs. 5-6 through 5-9 show offset null circuits that can be used with any operational amplifiers, whether or not they possess offset null terminals. The method shown in Fig. 5-6 is, perhaps, the most commonly seen. In this case we cancel the output offset voltage by inserting a counter-current (I3) into the summing junction. When V1 is the voltage at the wiper of the offset null potentiometer the output voltage due to the adjustment of R4 is:

$$V_o = V1 \left(\frac{-R2}{R3} \right) \qquad \textit{[Eq. 5-5]}$$

The idea is to adjust potentiometer R4 to obtain an output voltage that exactly cancels the output offset. For example, if the output offset potential is +1.5 volts, then we need to select a value of V1 that makes the voltage in Eq.[5-5] equal to −1.5 volts. In many cases, we make R3 = R2, so the voltage at the wiper of potentiometer R4 (i.e., V1) should be equal to the output offset voltage that it cancels.

Figs. 5-7 and 5-8 are variations on the same theme that permit better resolution adjustments of the offset voltage. These circuits are typically used in high-gain amplifier circuits with small signals. Those applications typically have very low level signal inputs. The version in Fig. 5-7 places two resistors (R4 and R5) in series with the arms of the potentiometer. Typically the value of R3 is smaller than the combined values of R4 and R5, and also R4 = R5. The version of Fig. 5-8 uses a pair of zener diodes to place the ends of the potentiometer at lower potentials than the V− and V+ voltages that operate the amplifier. In most cases the zener potentials of D1 and D2 are equal, which gives a

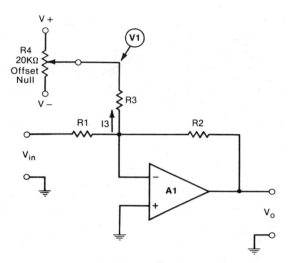

Fig. 5-6. Universal offset control.

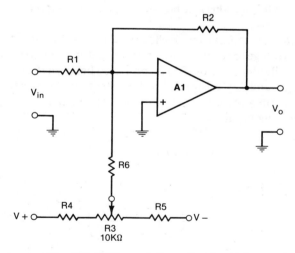

Fig. 5-7. High-resolution offset control.

symmetrical range of offset voltages that can be cancelled. There is no reason why different values can't be used if that is the situation of the specific circuit.

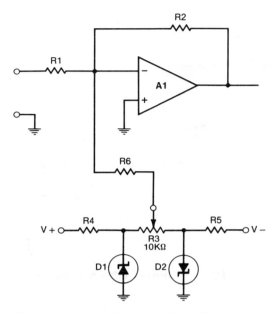

Fig. 5-8. Alternate high-resolution offset control.

One final offset null circuit is shown in Fig. 5-9. In this case we apply the countervoltage to the noninverting input rather than to the inverting input. A small value resistor (R5) is connected between the noninverting input and ground. A resistor from the potentiometer wiper (R4) acts with R5 to form a resistor voltage divider. The voltage (V2) applied to the noninverting input is:

$$V2 = V1 \left(\frac{R5}{R4 + R5} \right) \qquad \textit{[Eq. 5-6]}$$

or, given the value of R5:

$$V2 = V1 \left(\frac{100}{R4 + 100} \right) \qquad \textit{[Eq. 5-7]}$$

The output voltage produced by V2 acting on the operational amplifier's noninverting input is:

$$V_o = V2 \left(\frac{R2}{R1} + 1 \right) \qquad \textit{[Eq. 5-8]}$$

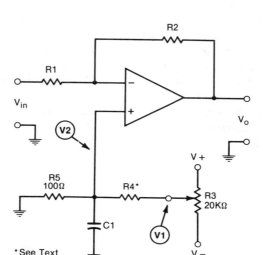

Fig. 5-9. Offset control.

Because of the gain of the circuit we typically make V2 a very small value. We can use the equations above to select values for V1 and R4 required to cancel out the offset voltage.

The capacitor used between the inverting input and ground is optional in most cases. The purpose of C1 is to set the noninverting input at ground potential for AC signals, while keeping it at a nonzero value of V2 for DC. The value of C1 is such that it has a capacitive reactance of 10 ohms at the lowest frequency of operation. This capacitor can only be used in relatively low-gain circuits, however, because one fault of op amps is that capacitors to ground from inputs increases the noise output from the circuit. In low-gain circuits, however, the benefits may outweigh the noise problems.

Frequency-Compensation Problems

The ideal amplifier of any type has an infinite bandwidth, so will amplify all signals accurately and cleanly. Real amplifiers, however, must contend with frequency-response limitations; for operational amplifiers these limitations can be quite severe. There are two problems to consider with regard to frequency response: the bandwidth of the system and the stability of the system. The frequency-response problem requires us to understand the gain bandwidth product of the amplifier.

The gain bandwidth product (GBP) is merely the product of the voltage gain and the maximum bandwidth of the device. GBP is specified as the frequency in megahertz or kilohertz at which the gain of the operational amplifier drops to unity (i.e., 1). Fig. 5-10 plots the voltage gain against the frequency response of an amplifier. The gain will remain relatively constant over a certain frequency range, but will begin to fall above a certain point. At some frequency (1,000,000 hertz in this case), the gain drops to unity.

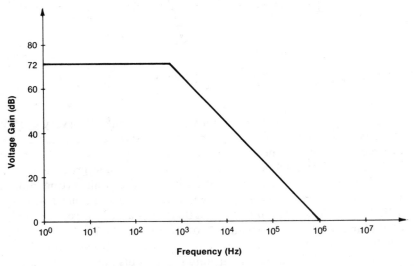

Fig. 5-10. Gain versus frequency response.

We run into GBP when we try to obtain high gain and wide frequency response in the same amplifier. A cassette tape preamplifier, a microphone preamplifier and certain instrumentation amplifiers are examples where gain and wide bandwidth frequency response go hand in hand. These examples are also where the problems of GBP show up most distinctly. Suppose we need a voltage gain of 40 dB (i.e., a gain of 100) and a frequency response of 10 kHz (i.e., 10,000 Hz). The gain bandwidth product required of the operational amplifier is:

$$GBP = (A_v) (F)$$
$$GBP = (100)(10,000 \text{ Hz})$$
$$GBP = 1,000,000 \text{ Hz} = 1 \text{ MHz}$$

[Eq. 5-9]

The stability issue pops up whenever operational amplifiers are used. Almost invariably, when breadboarding a new circuit with wideband operational amplifiers, the first attempt will result in an unwanted oscillation. One solution is to use a frequency-compensated operational amplifier such as the 741 (if the application will permit). These devices are unconditionally stable—a condition that occurs at the expense of gain bandwidth product. Such an operational amplifier will work as an AC amplifier only to frequencies of a few kilohertz.

These stability problems can be created from any of several problems. Layout, for example, can create oscillation. If the stray capacitances and inductances create a resonant situation at a frequency lower than the unity gain frequency, then the circuit will oscillate. Similarly, if the DC power supply is not properly decoupled (see Chapter 2) then problems can occur. This latter problem especially occurs in multistage circuits where one stage can affect the other. Be careful of disc ceramic capacitors, however, for some of those components have very significant stray inductances and can thus form resonant circuits that do not bypass very well at one frequency. If that resonant frequency is below the GBP frequency, then oscillation may occur.

Grounding problems in the circuit can also create a problem. One cause of oscillations in these cases is an impedance in the ground circuit that is common to both input and output circuits. Because output signal flowing in that impedance is also in series with the input circuit, feedback automatically exists.

If any combination of feedback and phase shift occurs between output and input at a frequency that is less than the unity gain GBP frequency, then oscillation can occur. There are several ploys that are used to reduce the gain at frequencies less than GBP to prevent oscillation. Some of these methods are shown in Fig. 5-11. In Fig. 5-11A we see the use of a capacitor across the frequency compensation terminals found on some op amps. The manufacturer typically specifies a capacitance in the data sheet for the device. Values in the 30 to 100 pF range are common. Standard practice is to make this capacitance the value for the noninverting unity gain follower configuration. For all other configurations with gain, the value of the capacitance required is the noninverting unity gain value multiplied by the feedback factor, B:

$$C_{req} = CB \qquad \textit{[Eq. 5-10]}$$

where
    C_{req} is the required capacitance,
    C   is the specified capacitance for noninverting unity gain,
    B   is the feedback factor

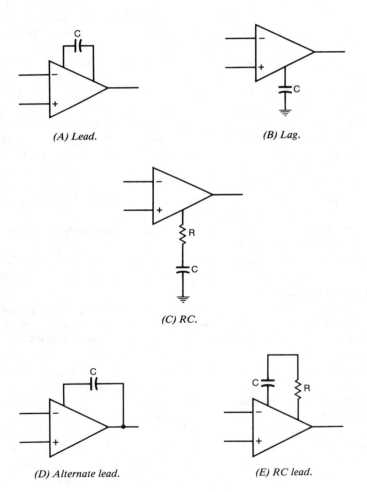

(A) Lead.   *(B) Lag.*

(C) RC.

(D) Alternate lead.   *(E) RC lead.*

Fig. 5-11. Frequency-compensation capacitor circuits.

The factor B is merely the transfer function of the feedback network. In the usual circuit with a resistor feedback network, the value of B is:

$$B = \frac{R1}{R1 + R2}$$

[Eq. 5-11]

where
   B   is the feedback factor,
   R1 is the input resistor,
   R2 is the feedback resistor

For example, let's suppose that an inverting amplifier with a gain of 10 has a rated compensation capacitance of 30 pF for the unity gain configuration. Assume the feedback resistor (R2) is 100 kilohms, and the input resistor (R1) is 10 kilohms. Using EQ.[5-11], the value of B is:

$$B = \frac{10 \text{ kilohms}}{10 \text{ kilohms} + 100 \text{ kilohms}}$$
$$B = 10/110 = 0.091$$

Using EQ.[5-10], the value of the capacitance required to stabilize this amplifier is found to be:

$$C_{req} = (C)(B)$$
$$C_{req} = (30 \text{ pF})(0.091)$$
$$C_{req} = 2.7 \text{ pF}$$

Figs. 5-11B through 5-11E show variations on the theme. The values of the components are typically taken from charts or graphs in the specifications sheet for the particular operational amplifier being used.

Input Capacitance Compensation

Fig. 5-12 shows the method for compensating for stray input capacitance. The circuit shown here is an inverting follower with a capacitance shunting the feedback resistor. From DC to a given frequency, F1, the gain of the amplifier is given by the equation:

$$A_v = -R2/R1$$

[Eq. 5-12]

At frequency F1, however, the gain begins to drop off at a rate of −6 dB per octave. The breakpoint frequency (F1) at which this happens is:

$$F1 = \frac{1,000,000}{2\pi R2 C1} \qquad \textit{[Eq. 5-13]}$$

where
　　F1　is the frequency in hertz,
　　R2　is in ohms,
　　C1　is in microfarads

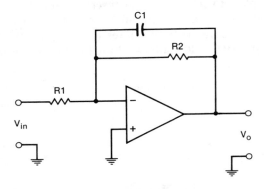

Fig. 5-12. Feedback capacitor controls frequency response.

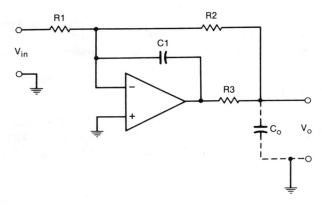

Fig. 5-13. Alternate feedback capacitor circuit.

The input resistance and the input capacitance (which consists mostly of stray capacitances) form a phase shift at certain frequencies defined by $1/2\pi R1C$, where C is the stray input capacitance. If that frequency is below the unity gain frequency, then it is possible for the phase shift that occurs at this frequency to add to the operational amplifier's ordinary phase shift (180 degrees $\pm$ error for inverting followers) to form a 360-degree phase shift, which is the criteria for oscillation. In order to compensate for this stray capacitance, select a value of C1 (Fig. 5-12) that has a capacitive reactance of approximately 1/10th the resistance of R2.

Fig. 5-13 shows the method for compensating for high output load capacitances. This situation is found when the operational amplifier drives a coaxial cable or twisted pair transmission line (and other places). Capacitor C1 is selected to have a capacitive reactance of 1/10th R2, while R3 is selected to have a value of several hundred ohms.

Chapter 6

DC Differential Operational-Amplifier Circuits

Although it is not required by the definition of operational amplifiers, most of these devices have differential inputs. That is, there are two inputs that provide the same amount of gain but have opposite sense. The inverting input of the operational amplifier provides an output that is 180 degrees out of phase with the input signal. In other words, a positive-going input signal will produce a negative-going output signal, and vice versa. The noninverting input produces an output signal that is in phase with the input signal. For this type of input, a positive-going input signal will produce a positive-going output signal.

Common-Mode Signals

The use of differential inputs is shown in Fig. 6-1. First let's consider the *common-mode* signal, V3. A common-mode signal is one which is applied to both inputs at the same time. Such a signal might be either a voltage such as V3, or, a case where voltages V1 and V2 are equal to each other (i.e., V1 = V2). The implication of the common-mode signal is that, being applied equally to inverting and noninverting inputs, the output voltage is zero. Because the two inputs have equal but opposite polarity gain for common-mode signals, the net output signal is zero.

The operational amplifier with differential inputs will cancel common-mode signals. An example is in the performance of the differential amplifier with respect to 60-Hz hum pickup. Almost all input signal cables for practical amplifiers will pick up 60-Hz energy and convert it to a voltage that is seen as a genuine input signal. In a differential amplifier, however, the 60-Hz field will affect both inverting and noninverting inputs equally, so the 60-Hz false signal will disappear in the output. Neat trick, huh?

The practical operational amplifier will not have a perfect rejection of common-mode signals. A specification called the common-mode re-

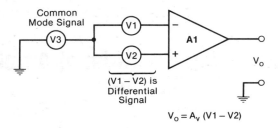

$$V_o = A_v (V1 - V2)$$

Fig. 6-1. Signal inputs to a differential amplifier.

jection ratio (CMRR) tells us something of the ability of any given op amp to reject such signals. The CMRR is usually specified in decibels (dB), and is defined as:

$$CMRR = \frac{A_v}{A_{cm}}$$ *[Eq. 6-1]*

where

CMRR is the common-mode rejection ratio,
A_v is the voltage gain to differential signals,
A_{cm} is the voltage gain to common-mode signals

In general, the higher the CMRR the better the operational amplifier. Typical low-cost devices have CMRR ratings of 60dB or more.

Differential Signals

Signals V1 and V2 in Fig. 6-1 are differential signals. The total differential signal seen by the operational amplifier is:

$$V_d = V2 - V1$$ *[Eq. 6-2]*

The output signal from the differential operational amplifier is the product of the differential voltage gain and the difference between the two input signals (hence the term *differential* amplifier). Thus, the transfer equation for the operational amplifier is:

$$V_o = A_v (V2 - V1)$$ *[Eq. 6-3]*

Differential Input Stage

Fig. 6-2 shows a hypothetical input stage for a differential input operational amplifier. Transistors Q1 and Q2 are a matched differential pair that share a common DC power supply through separate collector load resistors. The collector of transistor Q2 serves as the output terminal for the differential amplifier. Thus, collector voltage V_o is the output voltage of the stage. The exact value of the output voltage is the difference between supply voltage (V+) and the voltage drop across resistor R2 (i.e., V_{R2}).

The emitter terminals of the two transistors are connected together, and are fed from a constant current source (CCS). For purposes of analysis, we can assume that the collector and emitter currents (I1 and

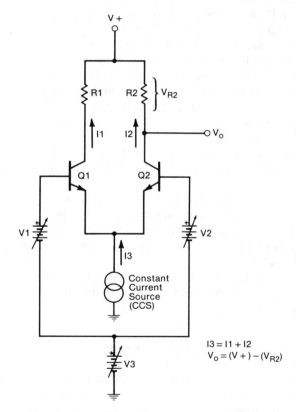

$$I3 = I1 + I2$$
$$V_o = (V+) - (V_{R2})$$

Fig. 6-2. DC differential op-amp input circuit.

I2) are equal to each other. While this convention might choke a transistor purist, it is nonetheless useful for our purposes. Because of Kirchhoff's current law, we know that:

$$I3 = I1 + I2 \qquad \text{[Eq. 6-4]}$$

Because current I3 is a constant current, a change in either I1 or I2 will change the other. For example, an increase in current I1 must force a decrease in current I2. Now let's consider how the stage works. First, the case where V1 = V2. In this case, both Q1 and Q2 are biased equally, so the collector currents (I1 and I2) are equal to each other. Under the normal situation, this case will result in V_{R2} being equal to V_o, and also equal to (V+)/2.

Next, let's consider the case where V1 is greater than V2. In this case, transistor Q1 is biased on harder than Q2, so current I1 will increase. Because I1 + I2 is always equal to I3, an increase in I1 will force a decrease in I2. A decrease of I2 will also reduce V_{R2} and increase V_o. Thus, an increase in V1 increases V_o, so the base of transistor Q1 is the noninverting input of the differential amplifier.

Now let's consider the case where V2 is greater than V1. In this case, transistor Q2 is biased on harder than Q1, so I2 will increase and I1 will decrease. An increase in I2 forces a larger voltage drop (V_{R2}) across resistor R2, so V_o will go down. Thus, an increase in V2 forces a decrease in V_o, so the base of transistor Q2 is the inverting input of the differential amplifier.

Voltage V3 is a common-mode signal, so it will affect transistors Q1 and Q2 equally. For this kind of signal the output voltage (V_o) will not change.

The base-bias currents required to keep transistors Q1 and Q2 operating become the input-bias currents that make the practical op amp nonideal. In order to make the input impedance high we need to make these currents very low. Some manufacturers offer operational amplifiers with MOSFET transistors (called BiMOS op amps) or JFET transistors (BiFET op amps). These types of transistors inherently have lower input-bias currents than bipolar NPN or PNP transistors, and in fact the bias currents approach mere leakage currents.

Practical Circuits

Fig. 6-3 shows the circuit of the simple DC differential amplifier based on the operational amplifier device. The gain of the circuit is set by the ratio of two resistors:

$$A_v = R3/R1 \qquad \textit{[Eq. 6-5]}$$

or,

$$A_v = R4/R2 \qquad \textit{[Eq. 6-6]}$$

Provided that:

$$R1 = R2$$
$$R3 = R4$$

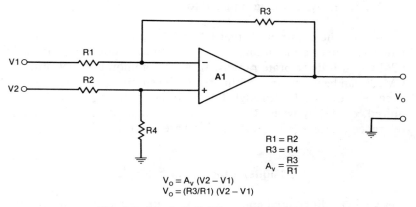

Fig. 6-3. Simple DC differential amplifier.

Example:

Find the gain of an operational amplifier connected as a DC differential circuit such as Fig. 6-3, if R1 = R2 = 1500 ohms, and R3 = R4 = 39,000 ohms.

$$A_v = R3/R1$$
$$A_v = 39000/1500$$
$$A_v = 26$$

Thus, the differential gain of the differential amplifier in the example is 26. The output voltage of the DC differential amplifier is given by:

$$V_o = (R3/R1)(V2 - V1) \qquad \textit{[Eq. 6-7]}$$

or,

$$V_o = A_v (V2 - V1) \qquad \textit{[Eq. 6-8]}$$

where
  V_o is the output voltage,
  R3 is the feedback resistor,
  R1 is the input resistor,
  A_v is the differential gain,
  V1 is the signal voltage applied to the inverting input,
  V2 is the signal voltage applied to the noninverting input

Again, the constraint is that R1 = R2, and R3 = R4. These two balances must be maintained or the common-mode rejection ratio (CMRR) will deteriorate rapidly. In most common applications, the CMRR can be maintained within reason by specifying 5-percent tolerance resistors for R1 through R4. But where superior CMRR is required, especially where the differential voltage gain is high, closer tolerance resistors (1-percent or better) are required.

Designer's Casebook Example

Design a DC differential amplifier with a gain of 100. Assume that the source impedance of the preceding stage is about 100 ohms.

1. Because the source impedance is 100 ohms, we need to make the input resistors of the DC differential amplifier ten times larger (or more). Thus, the input resistors (R1 and R2) must be 1000 ohms: R1 = R2 = 1000 ohms.

2. Set the value of the two feedback resistors (keep in mind that R3 = R4). The value of these resistors is found from rewriting Eq.[6-5]:

$$R3 = (A_v) (R1) \qquad \textit{[Eq. 6-9]}$$
$$R3 = (100)(1000)$$
$$R3 = 100,000 \text{ ohms}$$

Fig. 6-4 shows the finished circuit of this amplifier. The values of the resistors are:

R1 = 1 kilohm
R2 = 1 kilohm
R3 = 100 kilohms
R4 = 100 kilohms

For best results, make R1, R2, R3, and R4 1-percent precision resistors, or hand-match 5-percent resistors on an ohmmeter.

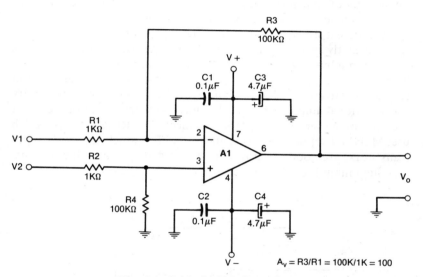

Fig. 6-4. Gain-of-100 DC amplifier.

The pin-outs shown in Fig. 6-4 are for the "industry standard" 741 family of operational amplifiers. These same pinouts are found on many different op-amp products.

The DC power supply voltages are usually either −12 or +12 volts DC, or −15 or +15 volts DC. Lower potentials can be accommodated, however, if a corresponding reduction in the output voltage swing is tolerable. A typical op amp will produce a maximum output voltage that is approximately 3 volts lower than the supply voltage. For example, when V+ is 12 volts DC, the maximum positive output voltage permitted is (12 − 3), or 9 volts. We can use −9 or +9 volts (and take advantage of 9-volt transistor radio batteries) for the DC power supplies, and that would limit the maximum signal output voltage to −6 or +6 volts.

The decoupling bypass capacitors shown in Fig. 6-4 are used to keep the circuit stable, especially in those cases where the same DC power supplies are used for several stages. The low value 0.1-μF capacitors (C1 and C2) are used to decouple high-frequency signals. These capacitors should be physically placed as close as possible to the body of the operational amplifier. The high value capacitors (C3 and C4) are needed to decouple low-frequency signals. The reason why we need two values of capacitors is that the high-value capacitors needed for low-frequency decoupling are typically electrolytics (tantalum or aluminum), which are ineffective at high frequencies. Thus, we must provide smaller value capacitors that have a low enough capacitive reactance to do the job, and are effective at high frequencies.

A different situation is shown in Fig. 6-5. Most differential amplifiers have relatively low input impedances, which is a function of factors such as input bias currents and so forth. The amplifier in Fig. 6-5 uses a high input impedance by virtue of the high values of resistors R1 and R2. In order to attain this input impedance, however, we need to specify an operational amplifier for A1 that has a very low input bias current (i.e., a natural very high input impedance). The RCA BiMOS, which uses MOSFET input transistors, and the BiFET, which uses JFET input transistors, are good selections for DC differential amplifier circuits with high input impedances.

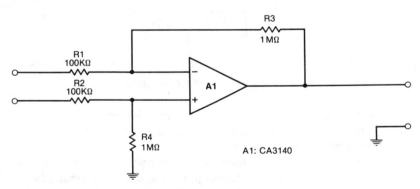

Fig. 6-5. High input impedance gain-of-10 differential amplifier

Designer's Casebook Example

Professional audio systems used in recording and broadcast applications use a 600-ohm balanced line for transmitting signals around the studio or between devices. For example, the line from the microphone to the studio console or tape recorder may have a 600-ohm balanced impedance. The transformer shown in Fig. 6-6 has a 600-ohm balanced primary. The term *balanced* means that the winding is center-tapped. The two opposite ends of the winding become the push-pull audio lines, which are balanced against ground. The secondary winding of transformer T1 can be either another 600-ohm winding, or a higher impedance. The turns ratio (N_p/N_s or N_s/N_p) of the transformer is related to the impedance ratio in the following manner:

$$N_p/N_s = \sqrt{Z_p/Z_s} \qquad \text{[Eq. 6-10]}$$

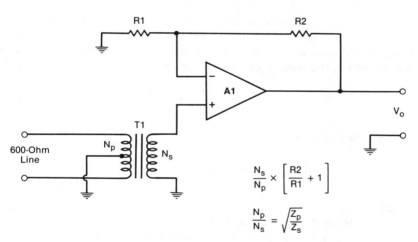

Fig. 6-6. Transformer-coupled line amplifier.

The total gain of the circuit is the product of the gain of the noninverting follower and the turns ratio of the transformer:

$$A_v = \left(\frac{N_s}{N_p}\right)\left(\frac{R2}{R1} + 1\right) \qquad \text{[Eq. 6-11]}$$

Example:

Find the gain of the circuit of Fig. 6-6 when the turns ratio of transformer T1 is $N_s/N_p = 10$, resistor R2 is 10 kilohms, and R1 is 1 kilohm.

$$A_v = \left(\frac{N_s}{N_p}\right)\left(\frac{R2}{R1} + 1\right)$$

$$A_v = (10)\left(\frac{10 \text{ kilohms}}{1 \text{ kilohms}} + 1\right)$$

$$A_v = (10)(10 + 1)$$

$$A_v = (10)(11)$$

$$A_v = 110$$

Fig. 6-7 shows a version of the 600-ohm balanced amplifier that uses no transformers. This circuit extends the concept of Fig. 6-6 into the realm of the DC differential amplifier. Here we use the two inputs of the differential amplifier to receive signals from the push-pull audio lines. The values of the input resistors should be either 270 ohms, 330 ohms, or (if possible and available) 300 ohms each in order to affect a reasonable impedance match to the 600-ohm line. Assuming R1 = R2, and R3 = R4, the voltage gain of this stage is:

$$A_v = R3/R1 \qquad \textit{[Eq. 6-12]}$$

or, with the values shown in Fig. 6-7,

$$A_v = R3/330 \qquad \textit{[Eq. 6-13]}$$

where
A_v is the voltage gain (differential) of the circuit,
R3 is the resistance of R3 and R4 in ohms

We can rewrite Eq.[6-13] to make it more useful. After all, we will usually know voltage gain A_v, and need to find R3. This rewritten equation is:

$$R3 = 330\, A_v \qquad \textit{[Eq. 6-14]}$$

Capacitor C1 is optional for those cases where the gain bandwidth product of the device used for A1 is much higher than required. The value of this capacitor is derived from a published value given by the operational amplifier manufacturer (typically 30 pF) multiplied by the feedback factor of the R2/R1 network:

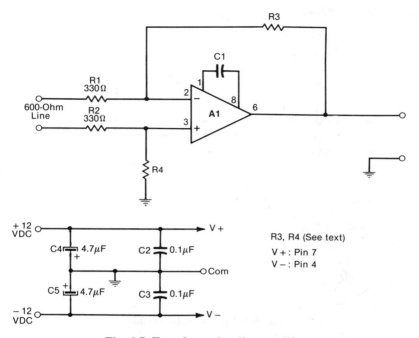

Fig. 6-7. Transformerless line amplifier.

$$C1 = C \left(\frac{R1}{R1 + R2} \right)$$

[Eq. 6-15]

where

   C   is the specified capacitance (typically 30 pF),

   C1 is the actual value required

CMRR Adjustment

The common-mode rejection ratio (CMRR) of the operational amplifier DC differential circuit is dependent upon two main factors. First, the natural CMRR of the operational amplifier used as the active device. Second, the balance of the resistors, R1 = R2 and R3 = R4. Unfortunately, the balance is typically difficult to obtain with fixed resistors. We can use a circuit such as seen in Fig. 6-8. In this circuit, R1 through R3 are exactly the same as in previous circuits. The fourth resistor (R4), however, is a potentiometer. The potentiometer will "adjust out" the CMRR errors caused by resistor and related mismatches.

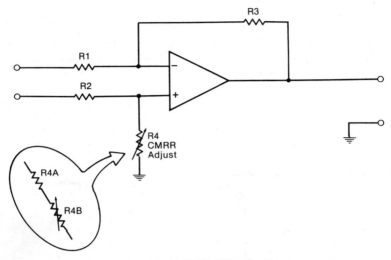

Fig. 6-8. CMMR adjustment.

A version of the circuit with greater resolution is shown in the inset to Fig. 6-8. In this version the single potentiometer is replaced by a fixed resistor and a potentiometer in series; the sum resistance (R4A + R4B) is approximately 20 percent greater than the normal value of R3. Ordinarily, the maximum value of the potentiometer is ten to twenty percent of the overall resistance.

The adjustment procedure for either version of Fig. 6-8 is the same (see Fig. 6-9):

1. Connect a zero-center DC voltmeter (M1) between the output terminal and ground as (shown in Fig. 6-9).

2. Short together inputs A and B, and then connect them to either a moderate voltage source, or ground.

3. Adjust potentiometer R4 (CMRR Adj) for zero volts output on M1.

4. If the output indicator (meter M1) has several ranges, then switch to a lower range and repeat stages 1–3 above until no further decrease in output reading is noted.

Alternatively, connect the output to an audio voltmeter or oscilloscope, and connect the input to a 1-volt peak-to-peak AC signal that is within the frequency range of the particular amplifier. For audio amplifiers, a 400 to 1000 hertz 1-volt signal is typically used.

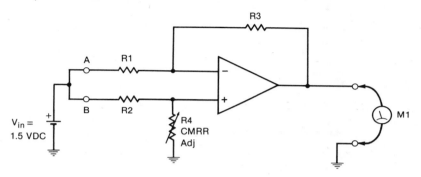

Fig. 6-9. Adjustment test circuit.

Additional Differential Amplifiers

The simple DC differential amplifier circuit shown in this chapter is useful for low-gain applications, and for those applications where a low to moderate input impedance is permissible (e.g., 300 to 200,000 ohms). Where a higher gain is required, then we must resort to a more complex circuit called the operational amplifier instrumentation amplifier, or "IA." In the next chapter we will examine the classical three-op amp IA circuit, as well as several integrated circuit instrumentation amplifiers (ICIA) that offer the advantages of the IA in a single small IC package. Some of those devices are now among the most commonly used in many instrumentation applications.

Chapter 7

Instrumentation Amplifier (IA)

The simple DC differential amplifier discussed in Chapter 6 suffers from several drawbacks. First, there is a limit to the input impedance. Both inputs look (impedancewise) like an inverting follower, so the input impedance is essentially twice the value of the two equal input resistors. Second, there is also a practical limitation on the available gain to the simple DC differential amplifier. If we attempt to obtain high gain, the input bias currents tend to cause output offset voltages to a great extent. In this chapter we will demonstrate a solution to these problems in the form of the instrumentation amplifier (IA). All of these amplifiers are differential amplifiers, but they offer superior performance over the simple DC differential amplifiers discussed in Chapter 6.

Simple IA Circuit

The simplest form of instrumentation amplifier circuit is shown in Fig. 7-1. In this circuit we bootstrap the input impedance by interfacing the "outside world" to the inputs of a simple DC differential amplifier (A3). The two input amplifiers (A1 and A2) are each in the unity gain, noninverting-follower configuration. They are used here as buffer amplifiers. They offer an extremely large input impedance (a result of the noninverting configuration) while driving the input resistors of the actual amplifying stage (A3). The overall gain of this circuit is the same as for any simple DC differential amplifier:

$$A_v = R3/R1 \qquad \text{[Eq. 7-1]}$$

where

A_v is the voltage gain, assuming: $R1 = R2$, and $R3 = R4$.

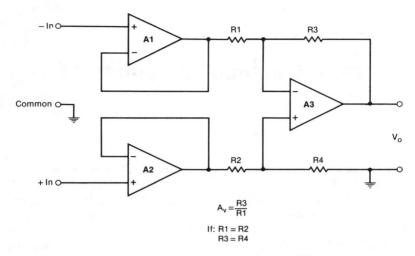

Fig. 7-1. A simple instrumentation amplifier.

Example:

Find the gain of an amplifier, such as that in Fig. 7-1, if the input resistors (R1 and R2) are 3.3 kilohms, and the feedback resistors (R3 and R4) are 220 kilohms.

$$A_v = R3/R1$$
$$A_v = 220 \text{ kilohms}/3.3 \text{ kilohms}$$
$$A_v = 67$$

For best performance, it is best that A1 and A2 be identical operational amplifiers. In fact, it is advisable to use a dual operational amplifier for both A1 and A2. The common thermal environment of the dual amplifier will reduce thermal drift problems. The very high input impedance of Superbeta, BiMOS and BiFET operational amplifiers make them ideal for use as the input amplifiers.

Perhaps one of the biggest problems with the circuit of Fig. 7-1 is that it wastes two good operational amplifiers. The most common form of instrumentation amplifier circuit uses the input amplifiers to provide additional voltage gain. Such amplifier circuits are discussed in the next section.

Standard Instrumentation Amplifier

The standard instrumentation amplifier is shown in Fig. 7-2. Like the simple circuit discussed above, this circuit uses three operational amplifiers. The biggest difference is that the input amplifiers (A1 and A2) are used in the noninverting follower with gain configuration. Like the circuit of Fig. 7-1, the input amplifiers are ideally BiMOS, BiFET, or superbeta input types. For best thermal performance use a dual, triple, or quad operational amplifier for this application.

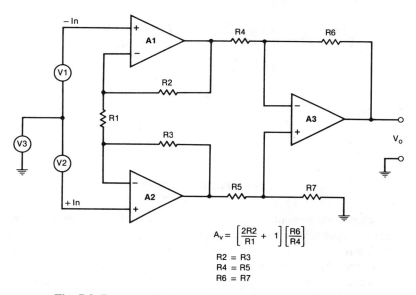

$$A_v = \left[\frac{2R2}{R1} + 1\right]\left[\frac{R6}{R4}\right]$$

R2 = R3
R4 = R5
R6 = R7

Fig. 7-2. Instrumentation amplifier with more flexible gain.

The signal voltages shown in Fig. 7-2 follow the standard pattern. Voltages V1 and V2 form the differential input signal (V2−V1). Voltage V3 represents the common-mode signal (it affects both inputs equally).

The voltage gain of the instrumentation amplifier is the product of the DC differential stage (A3) and the input amplifier stage:

$$A_v = \left(\frac{2R2}{R1} + 1\right)\left(\frac{R6}{R4}\right) \qquad \text{[Eq. 7-2]}$$

Provided:

$$R2 = R3$$

$$R4 = R5$$
$$R6 = R7$$

Example:

Find the gain of the instrumentation amplifier of Fig. 7-2 if the following values of resistors are used: $R1 = 220$ ohms, $R2 = R3 = 2200$ ohms, $R4 = R5 = 10$ kilohms, and $R6 = R7 = 82$ kilohms

$$A_v = \left(\frac{2R2}{R1} + 1\right)\left(\frac{R6}{R4}\right)$$

$$A_v = \left(\frac{(2)(2200)}{(220)} + 1\right)\left(\frac{(82,000)}{(10,000)}\right)$$

$$A_v = \left(\frac{(4400)}{(220)} + 1\right)(8.2)$$

$$A_v = (20 + 1)(8.2)$$

$$A_v = (21)(8.2)$$

$$A_v = 172$$

Gain Control for the IA

It is notoriously difficult to provide a gain control for a differential amplifier without adding either an extra amplifier stage (for example an inverting follower with a gain of 0 to −1) or something even more onerous: a dual potentiometer. For the instrumentation amplifier, however, we can use resistor R1 as a gain control provided we do not let the resistance go to a value near zero ohms. Fig. 7-3 shows a revised circuit with resistor R1 replaced by a series circuit consisting of fixed resistor R1A and potentiometer R1B.

We don't use a potentiometer alone in this circuit because it can have a disastrous effect on the gain. Note in Eq. [7-2] that the term "R1" appears in the denominator of the formula. If the value of R1 gets close to zero, then the gain goes sky high (in fact, theoretically to infinity if $R1 = 0$). By using a fixed resistor in series with the potentiometer we limit the maximum gain of the circuit. The gain of the circuit in Fig. 7-3 varies from a minimum of 167 (when R1B is set to 2000 ohms) to a maximum of 1025 (when R1A is zero). The gain expression for Fig. 7-3 is:

$$A_v = \left(\frac{2R2}{R1A + R1B} + 1\right)\left(\frac{R6}{R4}\right) \qquad \textit{[Eq. 7-3]}$$

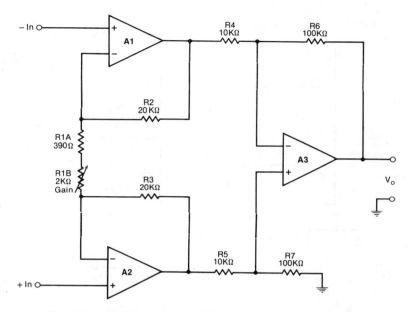

Fig. 7-3. Instrumentation amplifier with variable gain control.

or, rewriting Eq.[7-3] to take into account that R1A is fixed,

$$A_v = \left(\frac{2R2}{390 + R1B} + 1 \right) \left(\frac{R6}{R4} \right)$$

[Eq. 7-4]

where

R1B varies from 0 to 2000 ohms

Common-Mode Rejection Ratio Adjustment

The instrumentation amplifier is no different from any practical differential amplifier in that there will be imperfect balance between the two inputs. The operational amplifiers are not ideally matched, so there will be a gain imbalance. This gain imbalance is further aggravated by the mismatch of the resistors. The result is that the instrumentation amplifier will respond to some extent to common-mode signals (bad, bad, bad). As in the simple DC differential amplifier we can provide a common-mode rejection ratio adjustment by making resistor R7 variable (see Fig. 7-4).

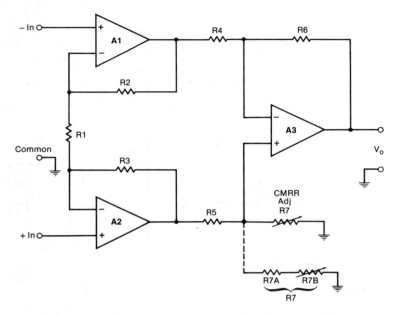

Fig. 7-4. CMRR adjustment for instrumentation amplifier.

One configuration of Fig. 7-4 uses a single potentiometer (R7) that has a value ten to twenty percent larger than the required resistance of R6. For example, if R6 is 100 kilohms, then R7 should be 110 to 120 kilohms. Unfortunately, these values are somewhat difficult to obtain, so we would pick a standard value for R7 (e.g., 100 kilohms), and then select a value for R6 that is somewhat lower (e.g., 82 kilohms or 91 kilohms).

The second configuration in Fig. 7-4 uses a fixed resistor in series with a potentiometer. The general rule is to make R7A approximately 80 percent of the total required value, and R7B 20 percent of the required value. As was true in the other configuration, the sum of R7A and R7B is approximately 110 to 120 percent of the value of resistor R6. The adjustment of the CMRR Adj control follows exactly the same procedure as is given in Chapter 6 for all differential amplifiers.

AC Instrumentation Amplifiers

What is the difference between DC amplifiers and AC amplifiers? A DC amplifier amplifies both AC and DC signals up to the frequency limit of the particular circuit being used. The AC amplifier, on the other hand, will not pass or amplify DC signals. In fact, it will not pass AC signals from close to DC to some lower bandpass limit. The gain in the region between near-DC and the full-gain frequencies rises at a rate determined by the design usually +6 dB per octave (an octave is a 2:1 frequency change). The official low-end point in the frequency-response curve is the frequency at which the gain drops off −3 dB from the full gain.

Fig. 7-5 shows a modified version of the instrumentation amplifier that is designed as an AC amplifier. The input circuitry of A1 and A2 is modified by placing a capacitor in series with the noninverting input of each op amp. Resistors R8 and R9 are used to keep the input bias currents of A1 and A2 from charging capacitors C1 and C2. In some modern, superlow input-current operational amplifiers, these resistors are optional because of the extremely low levels of current.

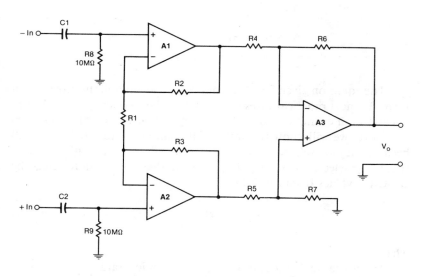

Fig. 7-5. AC-coupled instrumentation amplifier.

The −3 dB frequency of the amplifier in Fig. 7-5 is a function of the input capacitors and resistors:

Assumption: C1 = C2, and R9 = R10

$$F = \frac{1,000,000}{2\pi R9 C1} \qquad \textit{[Eq. 7-5]}$$

where
  F   is the −3 dB frequency in hertz,
  R9 is in ohms,
  C1 is in microfarads

Example:

Find the lower −3 dB breakpoint frequency if R9 = R10 = 10 megohms, and C1 = C2 = 0.1 μF.

$$A_v = \frac{1,000,000}{2\pi R9C1}$$

$$A_v = \frac{1,000,000}{(2)(3.14)(10,000,000)(0.1)}$$

$$A_v = \frac{1,000,000}{6,280,000}$$

$$A_v = 0.16 \text{ Hz}$$

The equation given for frequency response is not in the most useful form. In most practical cases we will know the frequency from the application (an example is given below: an animal ECG amplifier). Furthermore, we will know the value of the input resistors (R9 and R10) because they are selected for high input impedance. Typically, these resistors are selected as 10 megohms. We will therefore want to select the capacitor values from Eq.[7-6] below:

$$C_{\mu F} = \frac{1,000,000}{2\pi R9F} \qquad \text{[Eq. 7-6]}$$

where
  $C_{\mu F}$ is the capacitance of C1 and C2, in microfarads,
  R9 is the resistance of R9 and R10 in ohms,
  F   is the −3 dB frequency in hertz (Hz)

The AC instrumentation amplifier can be adapted to all the other modifications of the basic circuit discussed earlier in this chapter. We may, for example, use a gain control (replace R1 with a fixed resistor and a potentiometer), or add a CMRR Adj control. In fact, these are probably necessary in practical AC instrumentation-amplifier circuits.

Designer's Casebook Project: Animal ECG Amplifier

The heart in man and animals produces an electrical signal that can be recorded with surface electrodes and displayed on an oscilloscope or paper strip-chart recorder. This signal is called the *electrocardiograph* or *ECG* signal. The peak values of the ECG signal are on the order of one millivolt (1 mV). In order to produce a 1-volt signal from the one-millivolt ECG signal to apply to a recorder or oscilloscope, we need a gain-of-1000 amplifier. Our ECG amplifier, therefore, must provide a gain of 1000 or so.

Another requirement for the ECG amplifier is that it be an AC amplifier. The reason for this requirement is that metallic electrodes applied to the electrolytic skin produces a small *halfcell potential*. This potential tends to be on the order of 1 to 2 volts, so is more than 1000 times higher than the signal voltage. By making the amplifier respond only to AC, we eliminate the signal voltage caused by the DC halfcell potential.

The frequency selected for the −3 dB point of the ECG amplifier must be very low, close to DC, because the standard ECG waveform contains very low frequency components. The typical ECG signal has significant frequency components in the range 0.05 to 100 hertz.

The typical ECG amplifier has differential inputs. In most simple cases, the right arm (RA) and left arm (LA) electrodes form the inputs to the amplifier, with right leg (RL) being the common (see Fig. 7-6). The basic configuration of the amplifier in Fig. 7-6 is the AC-coupled instrumentation amplifier discussed earlier. The gain for this amplifier is set to a little over ×1000, so a 1-millivolt ECG peak signal will produce a 1-volt output from this amplifier. Because of the high gain it is essential that the amplifier be well balanced. This requirement all but forces us to use a dual amplifier for A1 and A2. A choice might be the RCA CA3240 device, which is a dual BiMOS device that is essentially two CA3140's in a single eight-pin miniDIP package. Also in the interest of balance we should either use 1-percent or better tolerance resistors for the equal pairs, or match them ourselves with an ohmmeter from a selection of 5-percent tolerance but otherwise ordinary metal film resistors.

The lower end −3 dB frequency response point is set by the input resistors and capacitors. In this case, the combination forms a response of:

$$F(\text{Hz}) = \frac{1,000,000}{2\pi RC}$$

$$F(\text{Hz}) = \frac{1,000,000}{(2)(3.14)(10,000,000 \text{ ohms})(0.33\mu F)}$$

$$F(Hz) = \frac{1,000,000}{20,724,000}$$

$$F(Hz) = 0.048 \text{ Hz}$$

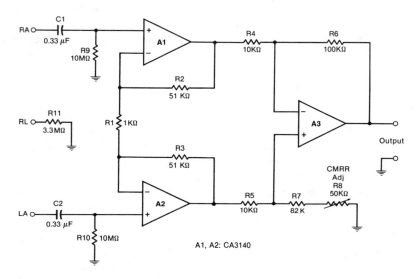

Fig. 7-6. Animal ECG amplifier based on the IA circuit.

The CMRR Adj control is a 10–20 turn trimmer potentiometer. It is adjusted in the following manner:

1. Short together the RA, LA, and RL inputs.
2. Connect a DC voltmeter to the output (either a digital voltmeter or an analog meter with a 1.5 volt DC scale). (Alternatively, a DC-coupled oscilloscope can be used, but be sure to identify the zero baseline.)
3. Adjust CMRR Adj control (R7) for zero volts output.
4. Disconnect the RL input, and connect a signal generator between RL and the still-connected RA-LA terminal. Adjust the output of the signal generator for a sine-wave frequency of 10 to 100 Hz, and a peak-to-peak potential of 1 volt.
5. Using an AC scale on the voltmeter (or better, if you own one, the oscilloscope), again adjust CMRR Adj (R7) for the smallest possible output signal. It may be necessary to readjust the voltmeter or oscilloscope input range for best null.
6. Remove the RA-LA short. The ECG amplifier is ready to use.

Note: The output of the amplifier will probably saturate if the leads are left open, so either use the device or turn it off. No damage will result from leaving the leads open, however, but the output indicator will read full scale.

A suitable post amplifier for the ECG preamplifier is shown in Fig. 7-7. This amplifier is placed in the signal line between the output of the circuit in Fig. 7-6, and the input of the oscilloscope or paper chart recorder used to display the waveform. The gain of the post amplifier is 0 to +2, so it will produce a 2-volt output when a 1-millivolt ECG signal provides a 1-volt output from the preamplifier. Because of the high level signals used, this amplifier can use ordinary 741 operational amplifiers.

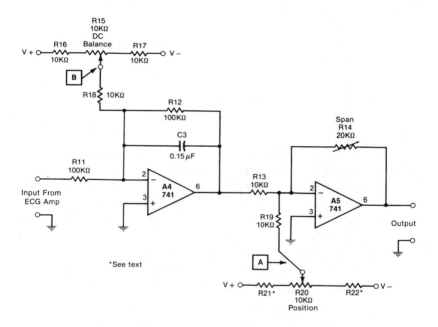

Fig. 7-7. Post amplifier for the ECG preamplifier.

The frequency response of the amplifier is set to an upper −3 dB point of 100 Hz, with the response dropping off at a −6 dB per octave rate above that frequency. This frequency-response point is determined by capacitor C3 operating with resistor R12:

$$F(Hz) = \frac{1,000,000}{2\pi RC}$$

$$F(Hz) = \frac{1,000,000}{(2)(3.14)(100,000)(0.015\mu F)}$$

$$F(Hz) = \frac{1,000,000}{9420}$$

$$F(Hz) = 106 \text{ Hz}$$

There are three controls in the post-amplifier circuit: Span, Position, and DC Balance. The Span control is the 0–2 gain control, and the label "span" reflects instrumentation language rather than electronics. The Position control sets the position of the output waveform on the display device. Resistors R21 and R22 are selected to limit the travel of the beam or pen. A good starter trial value for these resistors is 10 kilohms, but a better selection is made when the input sensitivity of the display device is known.

The DC Balance control is used to cancel the effects of collective offset potentials created by the various stages of amplification. This control is adjusted as follows:

1. Follow the CMRR Adj procedure, and then reconnect the short-circuit from RA, LA and RL. The voltmeter is moved to the output in Fig. 7-7.

2. Adjust the Position control for zero volts at point "A".

3. Adjust the DC Balance control for zero volts at point "B".

4. Adjust the Span control (R14) through its entire range from zero to maximum while monitoring the output voltage. If the output voltage does not shift, then no further adjustment is needed.

5. If the output voltage in the previous step varied as the Span control is varied, then adjust DC Balance until varying the span control over its full range does not produce an output voltage shift. Repeat this step several times until no further improvement is possible.

6. Remove the RA, LA, RL short. The amplifier is ready for use.

Ordinarily, the DC Balance control need only be adjusted once, and is then glued in place. Additional adjustment might not be required for years.

The animal ECG amplifier is a "science fair" type of project, and is intended only to illustrate an instrumentation amplifier application. This amplifier is not usable on humans because it is not an isolation amplifier (which is required for safety). Any good book on medical electronics can give further details on that type of equipment, or consult either a Certified Clinical Engineer, or a Biomedical Engineer.

Chapter 8

Isolation Amplifiers

There are a number of situations where ordinary amplifiers are either in danger themselves, or present a danger to the users (e.g., in medical equipment). An example of the former might be an amplifier in a high voltage experiment such as an electrophoresis system, while the latter is represented by cardiac monitors and other devices used in the hospital.

An *isolation amplifier* is one in which there is an extremely high impedance between the signal inputs and those power supply terminals that are connected to a DC power supply that is, in turn, connected to the AC power mains. In the case of the medical equipment, we are trying to prevent minute leakage currents from the AC power lines from being applied to the patient. Current levels that are normally negligible to people can be fatal to a hospitalized patient in some cases. In other cases, the high impedance is used to prevent high voltages at the signal inputs from adversely affecting the rest of the circuitry. Modern isolation amplifiers can provide up to 10^{12} ohms of isolation between the power lines and the signal inputs.

There are several different popular circuit symbols for the isolation amplifier, but the one that seems to be most common is shown in Fig. 8-1. It consists of the regular triangular amplifier symbol, but broken in the middle to indicate isolation between the "A" and "B" portions. In most cases, there will be the following connections to the isolation amplifier:

Nonisolated "A" Side: V+ and V− DC power supply lines (to be connected to a DC supply powered by the AC lines), output to the rest of the (nonisolated) circuitry, and (in some designs) a nonisolated ground or common. This ground is connected to the chassis or main system ground also served by the main DC power supplies.

Isolated "B" Side: Isolated V+ and V−, isolated ground or common, and the signal inputs. The isolated power supply and ground are not connected to the main power supply or ground systems. In some cases, batteries are used for the isolated side, while in others special DC power supplies derived from the main supplies are used.

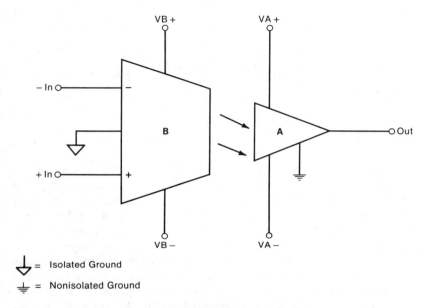

Fig. 8-1. Symbol for an isolation amplifier.

Different manufacturers use different approaches to the design of isolation amplifiers—battery power, carrier operated, optically coupled, and current loading.

Battery-Powered Designs

This approach is perhaps the simplest to implement, but it is not always most suitable for your convenience due to problems inherent in battery upkeep. A few products exist, however, that use a battery-powered front-end amplifier, even though the remainder of the product is AC powered.

Carrier Operated

Fig. 8-2 shows an isolation amplifier that uses the carrier technique. The circuitry inside of the dashed line is isolated from the AC power lines (in other words, the "B" side of Fig. 8-1). In most cases, the voltage gain of the isolated section is in the medium gain range of ×10 to ×500.

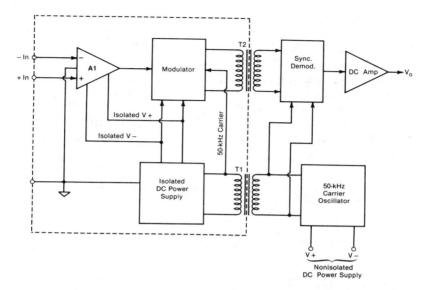

Fig. 8-2. Transformer-coupled carrier-type isolation amplifier.

The isolation is provided by separation of the ground, power supply, and signal paths into two mutually exclusive sections by ultrasonic transformers T1 and T2. These transformers have a design and core material that works very well in the ultrasonic (20 kHz to 500 kHz) region, but is terribly inefficient at the 60-Hz frequency of the AC power lines. This design feature allows the transformers to easily pass the high-frequency carrier signal, while attenuating severely all 60-Hz energy that might be present.

Although most models use a carrier frequency in the 50 to 60 kHz range, it is possible to find examples of carrier frequencies in the entire 20 to 500 kHz spectrum.

The carrier oscillator signal is coupled through transformer T1 to the isolated stages. Part of the energy from the secondary of T1 is directed to the modulator stage; the remainder of the energy is rectified and filtered, and then used as an isolated DC power supply. The DC output of this power supply is used to power the input "B" amplifiers and the modulator stage.

An analog signal applied to the input is amplified by A1, and is then applied to one input of the modulator stage. This stage amplitude modulates the signal onto the carrier.

Transformer T2 couples the signal to the input of the demodulator stage on the nonisolated side of the circuit. Either envelope or synchronous demodulation may be used, although the latter is more popular. Part of the demodulator stage is a low-pass filter that removes any residual carrier signal from the output signal. Ordinary DC amplifiers following the demodulator complete the signal processing chain.

An example of a synchronous demodulator circuit is shown in Fig. 8-3. These types of circuit are based on switching action. Although the example shown uses bipolar PNP transistors as the electronic switches, other circuits use NPN transistors, FETs or CMOS electronic switches (e.g., 4066 device).

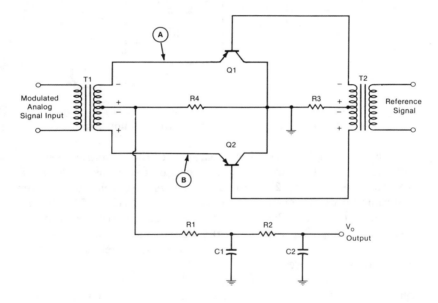

Fig. 8-3. Synchronous demodulator circuit.

The signal from the modulator has a fixed frequency between 20 kHz and 500 kHz, and is amplitude modulated with the input signal from the isolated amplifier. This signal is applied to the emitters of transistors Q1 and Q2 (via T1) in push-pull. On one-half of the cycle, therefore, the emitter of Q1 will be positive with respect to the emitter of Q2. On alternate half-cycles, the opposite situation occurs—Q2 is positive with respect to Q1.

The bases of Q1 and Q2 are also driven in push-pull, but by the carrier signal (called here the "reference signal"). This action causes transistors Q1 and Q2 to switch on and off, but out of phase with each other.

On one-half of the cycle, we will have the polarities shown in Fig. 8-3. Transistor Q1 is turned on. In this condition point "A" on T1 is grounded. The voltage developed across load resistor R4 is positive with respect to ground.

On the alternate half-cycle, Q2 is turned on, so point "B" is grounded. But the polarities have reversed, so the polarity of the voltage developed across R4 is still positive. This causes a full-wave output waveform across R4, which when filtered becomes a DC voltage level proportional to the amplitude of the input signal. This same description of synchronous demodulators also applies to the circuits used in some carrier amplifiers (a specialized laboratory amplifier used for low-level signals).

A variation on this circuit replaces the modulator with a voltage-controlled oscillator (VCO) that allows the analog signal to frequency modulate a carrier signal generated by the VCO. The power supply carrier signal is still required, however. A phase detector, phase-locked loop (PLL), or pulse-counting FM detector on the nonisolated side recovers the signal.

Optically Coupled Circuits

Electronic optocouplers (also called optoisolators) are sometimes used to provide the desired isolation. In early designs of this class a light-emitting diode (LED) was sandwiched with a photoresistor or phototransistor. Modern designs, however, use integrated circuit (IC) optoisolators that contain a LED and a phototransistor in a single DIP IC package.

There are actually several approaches to optical coupling. Two very popular methods are the *carrier* and *direct* methods. The carrier method is the same as discussed previously, except that an optoisolator replaces transformer T2.

The carrier method is not the most widespread in optically coupled isolation amplifiers because of the frequency-response limitations of some IC optoisolators. Only recently have these problems been resolved.

A more common approach is shown in Fig. 8-4. This circuit uses the same DC to DC converter to power the isolated stages as was used in other designs. This will keep A1 isolated from the AC power mains but it is not used in the signal-coupling process. In some designs, the high frequency "carrier" power supply is actually a separate block from the isolation amplifier.

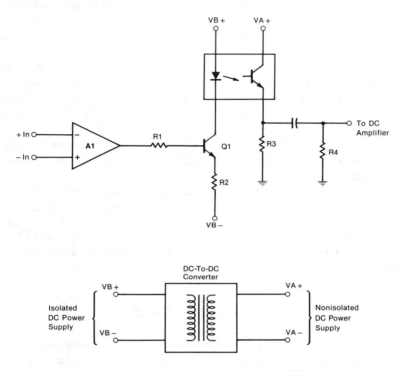

Fig. 8-4. Optoisolator type isolation amplifier.

The LED in the optoisolator is driven by the output of isolated amplifier A1. Transistor Q1 serves as a series switch to vary the light output of the LED proportional to the analog signal from A1. Transistor Q1 normally passes sufficient collector current to bias the LED into a linear portion of its operating curve. The output of the phototransistor is AC-coupled to the remaining amplifiers on the nonisolated side of the circuit, so that the offset condition created by the LED bias is eliminated.

Current-Loading Methods

A current-loading isolation amplifier was once featured in a popular medical monitoring device. Although not practical for most electronic hobbyists, the method is interesting enough to include it here. A simplified schematic is shown in Fig. 8-5. Notice that there is no *obvious* coupling path for the signal between the isolated and nonisolated sides of the circuit!

The gain-of-24 isolated input preamplifier (A1) in Fig. 8-5 uses a JFET input operational amplifier to provide a very high input impedance. The output of A1 is connected to the isolated − 10 volt DC power supply through load resistor R1. This power supply is a DC to DC converter operating at 250 kHz. Transformer T1 provides isolation between the floating power supplies on the isolated "B" side of the circuit and the nonisolated "A" side of the circuit (which are AC powered).

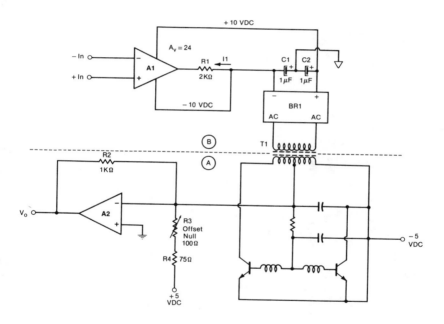

Fig. 8-5. Current-starved isolation amplifier.

An input signal causes the output of A1 to vary the current loading of the floating − 10 volt DC power supply. Changing the loading proportional to the analog input signal causes a variation of the T1 primary current that is also proportional to the analog signal. This current variation is converted to a voltage variation by amplifier A2. An offset null control (R3) is provided in the A1 circuit to eliminate the offset at the output due to the quiescent current flowing when the analog input signal is zero. In that case, the current loading of T1 is constant—but still provides an offset to the A2 amplifier.

Conclusion

Isolation amplifiers are an interesting, even though somewhat special-ized, form of IC amplifier. Although several products exist on the mar-ket, they tend to be costly ($25 and up-up-up). Most readers with a genuine need for an isolation amplifier will either have to pony-up the bucks, or design and build one of their own.

Chapter 9

Operational Transconductance IC Amplifiers

The operational amplifier is a simple voltage amplifier with a transfer function of V_o/V_{in}. While that type of device is typically the most commonly used form, there are cases where we need a transconductance amplifier. This form of amplifier is based on a transfer function that relates an output current to a an input voltage. In other words:

$$g_m = \frac{I_o}{V_{in}} \qquad \textit{[Eq. 9-1]}$$

where
  g_m is the transconductance in mhos or micromhos,
  I_o is the output current,
  V_{in} is the input voltage

The operational transconductance amplifier equivalent circuit is shown in Fig. 9-1. The differential input circuit is much like the input circuit of the operational amplifier because both have differential voltage inputs. The output side of the circuit, however, is a current source that produces an output current, I_o. This current is proportional to the gain and the input voltage. The current gain (A_i) of this circuit is a function of the transconductance (I_o/V_{in}) and the load resistance, R:

$$A_i = g_m \times R \qquad \textit{[Eq. 9-2]}$$

where
  A_i is the current gain (dimensionless),
  g_m is the transconductance (I_o/V_{in}),
  R   is the load resistance (one-half the output resistance R_o).

Note: g_m and R must be expressed in equivalent reciprocal units. In other words, when g_m is in mhos then R is in ohms.

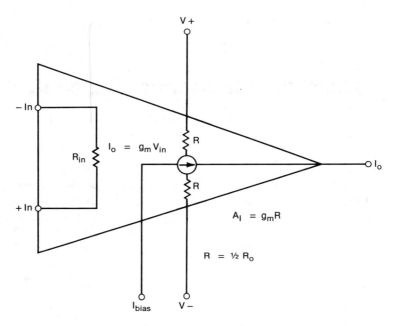

Fig. 9-1. Equivalent circuit for operational transconductance amplifier.

Likewise, millimhos/milliohms and micromhos/microohms are also paired.

Perhaps the most common version of the operational transconductance amplifier (OTA) are the RCA CA3080 and CA3080A devices. These popular devices are available in the eight-pin metal IC package using the pinouts shown in Fig. 9-2. The CA3080 devices will operate over DC power supply voltages from minus and plus 2 volts to minus and plus 15 volts, with adjustable power consumption of 10 microwatts to 30 milliwatts. The gain is 0 to g_mR. The input voltage spread is from −5 volts to +5 volts. The bias current can be set to as high as 2 mA.

Note that the pinouts for the CA3080 device are "industry standard" operational amplifier pinouts, except for the bias current applied to pin number 5: V− on pin 4; V+ on pin 7; inverting input on pin 2; noninverting input on pin 3; output on pin 6.

The parameters of the operational transconductance amplifier are set by the bias current (I_{bias}). For example, the transconductance is 19.2 times higher than the bias current:

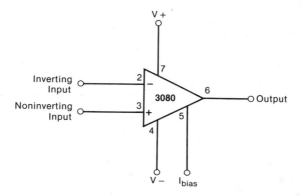

Fig. 9-2. Pinouts for the RCA CA3080 OTA.

$$g_m = 19.2 \times I_{bias} \qquad \textit{[Eq. 9-3]}$$

where

g_m is in millimhos,
I_{bias} is in milliamperes

In many actual design cases we will know the required value of g_m from our knowledge of I_o/V_{in}, so can set the g_m required by adjusting the bias current. In those cases, the I_{bias} is found by rewriting the above expression:

$$I_{bias} = \frac{g_m}{19.2} \qquad \textit{[Eq. 9-4]}$$

The output resistance of the device is also a function of the bias current:

$$R_o = \frac{7.5}{I_{bias}} \qquad \textit{[Eq. 9-5]}$$

where

R_o is the output resistance in megohms,
I_{bias} is the bias current in milliamperes (mA)

Example:

What is the output resistance (R_o) when the bias current is 500 μA (i.e., 0.5 mA)?

$$R_o = 7.5/I_{bias}$$
$$R_o = 7.5/0.5$$
$$R_o = 15 \text{ megohms}$$

Voltage Amplifier from the OTA

The OTA is a current-output device, but it can be used as a voltage amplifier by using various circuit strategies. The simplest method is the resistor load shown in Fig. 9-3. Because the output of the OTA is a current (I_o), we can pass this current through a resistor (R1) to create a voltage drop. The value of the voltage drop (and the output voltage, V_o) is found from Ohm's law:

$$V_o = I_o \times R1 \qquad \textit{[Eq. 9-6]}$$

A problem with this circuit is that the source impedance is very high, being equal to the value of R1. In the example shown in Fig. 9-3,

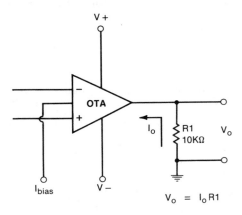

Fig. 9-3. Converting OTA output current to a voltage signal.

the output impedance is 10 kilohms. We can overcome this problem by adding a unity gain noninverting operational amplifier, such as A2 in Fig. 9-4. The output voltage in this case is the same as for the nonamplifier version: $I_o \times R1$.

Another form of low-impedance output circuit is shown in Fig. 9-5. This form uses the inverting follower configuration of the operational amplifier (A2). The output voltage is the product of the OTA output current (I_o) and the op-amp feedback resistor (R1):

$$V_o = I_o \times R1 \qquad \textit{[Eq. 9-7]}$$

Both Figs. 9-4 and 9-5 have an output impedance equal to the operational amplifier output impedance, or something less than 100 ohms.

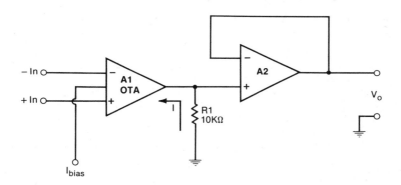

Fig. 9-4. Low output impedance current-to-voltage converter.

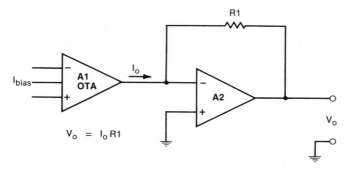

Fig. 9-5. Alternate low output impedance converter.

Chapter 10

Current Difference Amplifier

The current difference amplifier (CDA), also called the Norton amplifier, is a nonoperational amplifier that performs in much the same way as the op amp, but not quite exactly the same. The CDA has certain features that make it uniquely useful for certain applications. One place where the CDA is more useful than the operational amplifier is in circuits that process AC signals, but are limited to a single-polarity DC power supply. For example, in automotive equipment we are limited to a single 12 to 14.4 volt DC battery power supply that uses the car chassis for negative common return.

There are other cases where the linear IC amplifier is but a minor feature of the circuit, most of which operates from a single DC power supply. It would wasteful in such circuits to use the operational amplifier. We would either have to bias the operational amplifier with an external resistor network, or provide a second DC power supply.

The normal circuit symbol for the CDA is shown in Fig. 10-1. This symbol looks much like the regular op amp symbol, except that a *current source* is placed along the side opposite the apex (the circle with an arrow enclosed). This symbol is typically used for several products such as the National Semiconductor LM3900 device, which is a quad Norton amplifier. You may sometimes find schematics where the op amp symbol is used for the CDA, but that is technically incorrect usage.

CDA Configuration

The input circuit of the CDA differs radically from the operational amplifier. Recall that the op amp used a differential amplifier driven with a constant current source supplying the collector-emitter current. The CDA is quite different, however, as can be seen in Fig. 10-2.

The overall circuit of a typical CDA is shown in Fig. 10-2A, while an alternate form of the input circuit is shown in Fig. 10-2B. Transistor Q7

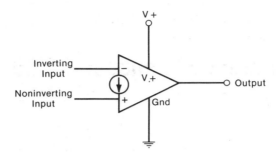

Fig. 10-1. Normal circuit symbol for current difference amplifier.

in Fig. 10-2A forms the output transistor, while Q5 is the driver. Both the NPN output transistor and the PNP driver transistor operate in the emitter-follower configuration. Transistors Q4, Q5, Q6, and Q8 are designed as current sources. The input transistor is Q3, and it operates in the common-emitter configuration. The base of Q3 forms the inverting (−In) input for the CDA.

The noninverting input of the CDA is formed with a *current mirror* transistor, Q1 (transistor Q1 in Fig. 10-2A is "diode connected" and serves exactly the same function as diode D1 in Fig. 10-2B). The dynamic resistance offered by the current mirror transistor (Q2) is given by:

$$r = 26/I_b \qquad\qquad \textit{[Eq. 10-1]}$$

where

    r   is the dynamic resistance of Q2 in ohms,
    I_b is the base-bias current of Q3 in milliamperes

Equation [10-1] holds true only at normal room temperature, and will vary with wide temperature excursions. For most readers, however, the room temperature version of the equation will suffice. Data sheets for specific current difference amplifiers give additional details for amplifiers that must operate outside of the relatively narrow temperature range specified by the equation.

Inverting-Follower Circuits

Like its operational amplifier cousins, the CDA can be configured in either inverting- or noninverting-follower configurations. The inverting

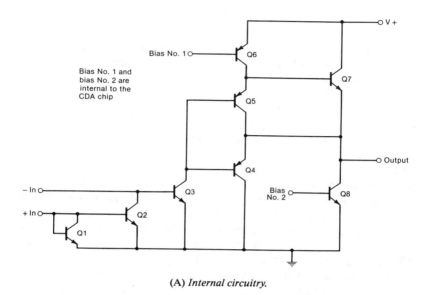

(A) *Internal circuitry.*

(B) *Current mirror input circuit.*

Fig. 10-2. Overall circuit of a typical current difference amplifier.

follower is shown in Fig. 10-3. In many respects this circuit is very similar to its operational amplifier cousins. The voltage gain of the circuit is set approximately by the ratio of the feedback to the input resistor:

$$A_v = -R2/R1 \qquad \text{[Eq. 10-2]}$$

where
    A_v is the voltage gain,

R2 is the feedback resistance,
R1 is the input resistance

Note: R1 and R2 are in the same units. The minus sign indicates that a 180-degree phase reversal occurs between input and output signals.

We must provide a bias to the current mirror transistor (i.e., Q2 in Fig. 10-2A), so resistor R_{ref} is connected in series with the noninverting input of the CDA and a reference voltage source, V_{ref}. In many practical circuits the reference voltage source is merely the V+ supply used for the CDA. In other cases, however, some other potential might be required, or alternatively the reference current is required to be regulated more tightly (or with less noise) than the supply voltage. Ordinarily we set the reference current to some convenient value between 5 μA and 100 μA. For V+ power supply values of +12 VDC, for example, it is common to find a 1-megohm resistor used for R_{ref}. In that case, the input reference current is: $I_{ref} = 12/1,000,000 = 12 \mu$A.

A constraint placed on CDAs is that the input resistor (R1) used to set gain must be high compared with the value of the current mirror dynamic resistance (Eq.[10-1]). The CDA becomes nonlinear (i.e., distorts the input signal) if the input resistor value approaches the current

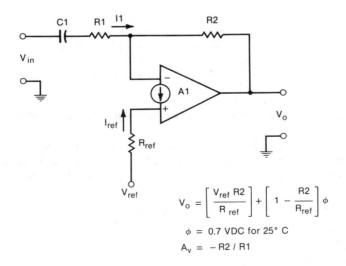

$$V_o = \left[\frac{V_{ref}\ R2}{R_{ref}} \right] + \left[1 - \frac{R2}{R_{ref}} \right] \phi$$

$$\phi = 0.7 \text{ VDC for } 25° \text{ C}$$

$$A_v = -R2\ /\ R1$$

Fig. 10-3. Inverting follower CDA circuit.

mirror resistance, r. In that case, the voltage gain is not $-R2/R1$, but rather:

$$A_v = \frac{R2}{R1 + r} \qquad \qquad \textit{[Eq. 10-3]}$$

where

    A_v is the voltage gain,
    R2 is the feedback resistance,
    R1 is the input resistance,
    r   is the current mirror resistance

Equation [10-3] essentially reduces to Eq.[10-2] when we can force R1 to be very much larger than r. This goal is easily achieved in most circuits because r is tiny (work a few examples with normal bias currents in Eq.[10-1]).

The output voltage of the CDA will exhibit an offset potential even when the AC input signal is zero. This potential is given by:

$$V_o = \left(\frac{V_{ref} R2}{R_{ref}} + 1 \right) - \left(\frac{R2}{R_{ref}} \right) \phi \qquad \qquad \textit{[Eq. 10-4]}$$

where

    V_o is the output potential in volts,
    V_{ref} is the reference potential in volts (usually $V+$),
    R2 is the feedback resistance in ohms,
    R_{ref} is the current mirror bias resistance in ohms,
    ϕ is a temperature dependent factor (0.70 volt for room temperature

The capacitor in series with the input circuitry has the effect of limiting the low end frequency response. The -3 dB cutoff frequency is a function of the value of this capacitor and the input resistance, R1. This frequency, F, is given by:

$$F = \frac{1,000,000}{2\pi R1 C1} \qquad \qquad \textit{[Eq. 10-5]}$$

where

    F is the lower end -3 dB frequency in hertz (Hz),
    R1 is in ohms,
    C1 is in microfarads

In some CDA circuits there is also a capacitor in series with the output terminal. The purpose of that capacitor is to prevent the DC offset that is inherent in this type of circuit from affecting following circuits. The output capacitor also limits the low-end frequency response. The same form of equation (i.e., Eq.[10-5]) is used to determine this frequency, but using the input resistance of the load as the "R" term.

As is often the case with equations presented in electronics books, Eq.[10-5] is not in the most useful format. In most cases, we will know the input resistance (R1) from the application. It is typically not less than 10 times the source impedance, and forms part of the gain equation. Consideration of driving source impedance and voltage gain tends to determine the value of R1. The required low-end frequency response is usually determined from the application. We generally know (or can find out) that frequency spectrum of input signals. From the lower limit of the frequency spectrum we can determine F. Thus, we will determine F and R1 from considerations other than the circuit. We therefore need a version of Eq.[10-5] that will allow us to calculate capacitor C1:

$$C1 = \frac{1,000,000}{2\pi R1F} \qquad \textit{[Eq. 10-6]}$$

where

    F   is the lower end -3 dB frequency in hertz (Hz),
    R1 is in ohms,
    C1 is in microfarads

Designer's Casebook Example

Design a gain-of-100 AC amplifier based on a CDA in which the input impedance is at least 10 kilohms and the -3 dB frequency response is 3 Hz or lower. Assume DC power supplies of $+15$ volts and -15 volts DC (see Fig. 10-4 for final circuit).

1. Set the reference current to the noninverting input to a value between 5 and 100 μA. Select 15 μA.

        R3 $= V/I_{ref}$
        R3 $= (15 \text{ VDC})/(0.000015)$
        R3 $= 1$ megohm

2. Set the gain resistors. R1 can be 10,000 ohms in order to meet the input impedance requirement.

    (From $A_v = R2/R1$, we know that R2 $= (A_v)(R1)$

        R2 $= (A_v)(R1)$

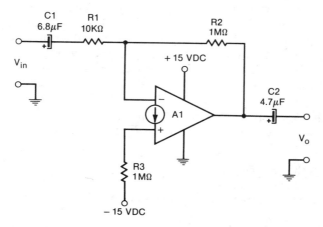

Fig. 10-4. Gain-of 100 CDA amplifier.

$$R2 = (100) (10,000)$$
$$R2 = 1,000,000 \text{ ohms} = 1 \text{ megohm}$$

3. Find the value of input capacitor C1 when F(−3 dB) is 3 hertz.

$$C1 = \frac{1,000,000}{2\pi R1F}$$

$$C1 = \frac{1,000,000}{(2)(3.14)(10,000)(3)}$$

$$C1 = \frac{1,000,000}{188,400}$$

$$C1 = 5.3 \ \mu F$$

Because 5.3 μF is a nonstandard value, we select the next higher standard value (which is 6.8 μF).

The value of output capacitor C2 can be arbitrarily set to 6.8 μF if the load impedance is 10,000 ohms. If the load impedance is higher than that value, then use 4.7 μF or 6.8 μF. If the load impedance is very much higher than 10,000 ohms or is lower than 10,000 ohms, then calculate the value using the same equation as for C1 but with the load resistance substituted for the input impedance.

Noninverting Amplifier Circuits

The noninverting amplifier CDA configuration is shown in Fig. 10-5. This circuit retains the reference-current bias applied to the noninverting input, but rearranges some of the other components. As in the case of the inverting amplifier configuration, the noninverting amplifier uses R2 to provide negative feedback between the output terminal and the inverting input. Unlike the inverting CDA circuit, however, input resistor R1 is connected in series with the noninverting input. The gain of the noninverting CDA amplifier is given by:

$$+A_v = \frac{R2}{\left(\dfrac{26\,R1}{I_{ref}\,(mA)}\right)} \qquad\qquad [Eq.\ 10\text{-}7]$$

where
  $+A_v$ is the voltage gain,
  R1 and R2 are in ohms,
  I_{ref} is the bias current in milliamperes (mA)

The reference current, I_{ref}, is set to a value between 5 μA and 100 μA (i.e., 0.005 to 0.1 mA). Unlike the situation in the inverting amplifier, the value of this current is partially responsible for setting the gain of the circuit. Some clever designers have even used this current as a limited gain control for some CDA stages. The value of the resistor that provides the reference current (R_{ref}) is set by Ohms law, taking into consideration the required value of reference current and the reference

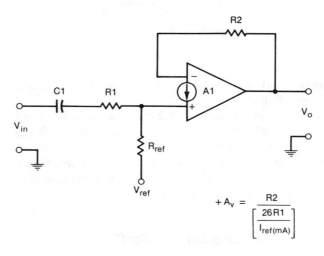

Fig. 10-5. Noninverting follower CDA circuit.

voltage, V_{ref}. In most common applications, the reference voltage is merely one of the supply voltages. The value of R_{ref} is determined from:

$$R_{ref} = \frac{V_{ref}}{I_{ref}} \qquad \textit{[Eq. 10-8]}$$

where

R_{ref} is the reference resistor in ohms,
V_{ref} is the reference potential in volts,
I_{ref} is the reference current in amperes (note: 1 μA = 0.000001 ampere)

The value of input impedance is approximately equal to R1, if R1 is much higher than the dynamic resistance of the current mirror inside the CDA (which is typically the case).

As was true in the inverting follower case, the input capacitor (C1) sets the low-end frequency response of the amplifier. The -3 dB frequency is given by exactly the same equation as for the inverting case (see Eqs.[10-5] and [10-6]).

Fig. 10-6 shows a modification of the noninverting follower circuit that allows for a noisy reference source. This type of amplifier circuit might be used where the DC power supplies that are used for the reference voltage are electrically noisy. Such noise could come from other stages in the circuit, or from outside sources.

The purpose of the circuit in Fig. 10-6 is to form a reference voltage from a resistor voltage divider circuit consisting of R3 and R4. The value of V_{ref} will be:

$$V_{ref} = V+ \left(\frac{R3}{R3 + R4} \right) \qquad \textit{[Eq. 10-9]}$$

where

V_{ref} is the reference potential in volts,
$V+$ is the supply potential in volts,
R3, R4 are in ohms

Inspection of Eq.[10-9] reveals that $V_{ref} = (V+)/2$ when R3 = R4, which is the usual case in practical circuits. The reference current is:

$$I_{ref} = \frac{V_{ref}}{R1} \qquad \textit{[Eq. 10-10]}$$

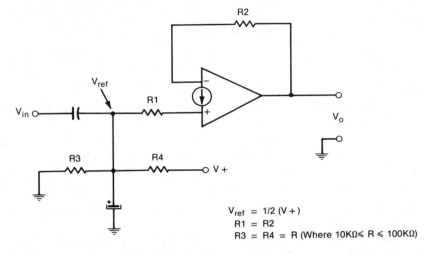

$$V_{ref} = 1/2 \, (V+)$$
$$R1 = R2$$
$$R3 = R4 = R \ (Where \ 10K\Omega \leqslant R \leqslant 100K\Omega)$$

Fig. 10-6. Single-supply operation.

Supergain Amplifier

There is a practical limit to voltage gain using standard resistor values and standard circuit configurations. (A similar problem also exists for operational amplifiers.) In Fig. 10-7 we see a circuit intended for overcoming this limitation. This supergain amplifier forms a noninverting follower in a manner similar to an earlier circuit, except that feedback resistor R2 is driven from an output-voltage divider network rather than directly from the output terminal of the CDA. The voltage gain of the circuit of Fig. 10-7 is given by:

$$A_v = \left(\frac{R2}{R1}\right)\left(\frac{R3 + R4}{R3}\right) \qquad \text{[Eq. 10-11]}$$

Example:

Find the gain of the circuit shown in Fig. 10-7 if R1 = 10 kilohms, R2 = 100 kilohms, R3 = 10 kilohms and R4 = 100 kilohms.

$$A_v = \left(\frac{R2}{R1}\right)\left(\frac{R3 + R4}{R3}\right)$$
$$A_v = \left(\frac{100k}{10k}\right)\left(\frac{100k + 10k}{10k}\right)$$

$$A_v = (10)(110/10)$$
$$A_v = (10)(11) = 110$$

Capacitor C1 is set using the same Eq.[10-5] that was used previously, while C2 is set to have a capacitive reactance of R4/10 at the lowest frequency of operation (in other words, the low end −3 dB point).

$$\frac{V_o}{V_{in}} = A_v = \left[\frac{R2}{R1}\right]\left[\frac{R3 + R4}{R3}\right]$$

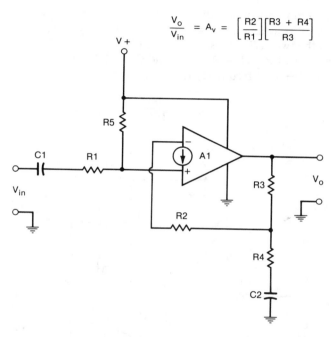

Fig. 10-7. Single-supply AC amplifier.

Differential Amplifier

A differential amplifier is one that will produce an output that is proportional to the gain and the difference between potentials applied to the inverting and noninverting inputs. Fig. 10-8 shows the circuit of a CDA differential amplifier. It is similar to the operational amplifier version of this simple circuit in several respects. For example, the two input resistors are equal and the differential voltage gain is the ratio of the negative feedback resistor (R3) and the input resistor:

$$A_v = \frac{R3}{R2}$$ *[Eq. 10-12]*

If:

$$R1 = R2$$
$$R3 = R4 = R5$$

The input impedance (differential) of this circuit is twice the value of the input resistances: $R_{in} = R1 + R2$. The bias current is provided through the two series resistors, R4 and R5.

Assuming that $R1 = R2 = R$, and $C1 = C2 = C$, we can calculate the low end -3 dB frequency from the equation:

$$F = \frac{1,000,000}{2\pi RC}$$ *[Eq. 10-13]*

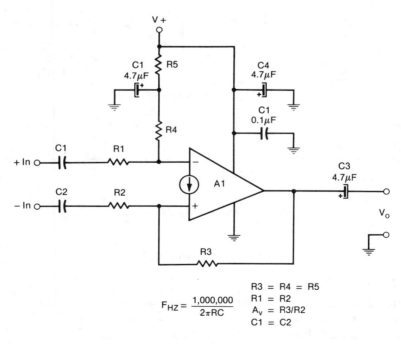

$$F_{HZ} = \frac{1,000,000}{2\pi RC}$$

$$R3 = R4 = R5$$
$$R1 = R2$$
$$A_v = R3/R2$$
$$C1 = C2$$

Fig. 10-8. A CDA differential amplifier.

where
F is the −3 dB frequency in hertz (Hz),
R is in ohms,
C is in microfarads (μF)

When this circuit is used as a 600-ohm line receiver, we can make the two input resistors 330 ohms each (or 270 ohms), if a small mismatch can be tolerated. Ideally, the input resistors will be 300 ohms each (which may require two resistors for each input resistor).

AC Mixer/Summer Circuits

The CDA mixer or summer circuit is shown in Fig. 10-9. This circuit is used to combine two or more inputs into one channel. The basic circuit is an inverting follower. Each input sees a gain that is the quotient of the feedback resistor to its input resistor:

$$A_v(1) = -R2/R3$$

[Eq. 10-14]

$$A_v(2) = -R2/R4$$

[Eq. 10-15]

$$A_v(3) = -R2/R5$$

[Eq. 10-16]

From Eqs.[10-14] through [10-16] we can deduce that the output voltage is found from:

$$V_o = R2 \left(\frac{V1}{R3} + \frac{V2}{R4} + \frac{V3}{R5} \right)$$

[Eq. 10-17]

The frequency response of each channel is found from the usual equation for −3 dB frequency:

$$F = \frac{1,000,000}{2\pi RC}$$

[Eq. 10-18]

where
F is the −3 dB frequency in hertz (Hz),

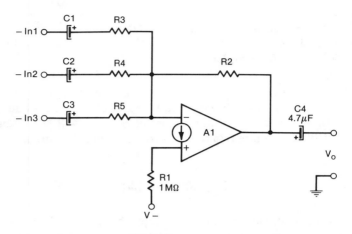

Fig. 10-9.

R is the input resistance (R3, R4. or R5),
C is the input capacitance (C1, C2, or C3)

More about audio mixers, a special case of Fig. 10-9 where the frequency response is in the audio range, will be given in Chapter 11.

Differential Output 600-Ohm Line Driver Amplifier

The 600-ohm line used in audio requires either a center-tapped output transformer, or a linear amplifier with a push-pull output to drive the line. Fig. 10-10 shows the circuit of a CDA 600-ohm line driver amplifier. This circuit basically consists of two separate amplifiers, one an inverting follower and the other a noninverting follower.

The bias resistors (R5 and R6) are set to provide a small bias current of 5–100 μA. This current is found from Ohm's law, $I_{ref} = (V+)/R$. In the example shown in Fig. 10-10 the resistors are set to 2 megohms for a supply voltage of +15 volts DC.

The capacitors in the circuit set the low end −3 dB point in the frequency-response curve. These capacitor values are set from the following:

Assuming that R1 = R2 = R3 = R4, and R5 = R6:

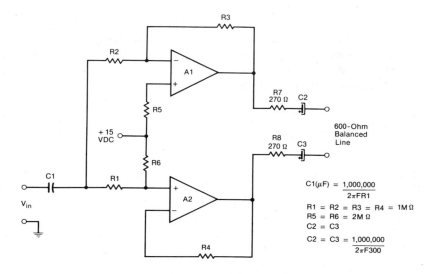

Fig. 10-10. Line driver amplifier.

$$C1 = \frac{1,000,000}{2\pi FR1}$$

[Eq. 10-19]

Assuming C2 = C3:

$$C2 = \frac{1,000,000}{2\pi F300}$$

[Eq. 10-20]

where
C1 and C2 are in microfarads,
F is in hertz (Hz),
R1 is in ohms

For best results use a multiple CDA integrated circuit, such as the LM3900, for this application. Such a circuit would allow the drift to be controlled because the two halves would both drift at the same rate (they share a common thermal environment).

Using Bipolar DC Power Supplies

The current difference amplifier (CDA) is designed primarily for single-polarity power supply circuits. In most cases, the CDA will operate with a V+ DC power supply in which one side is grounded. We can, however, operate the CDA in a circuit with a bipolar DC power supply using a circuit such as that in Fig. 10-11. Reference resistor R_{ref} is connected from the noninverting input to ground. The V− and V+ power supplies are each ground referenced and of equal potential. Thus, the 5–100 μA bias current is found from $(V+)/R_{ref}$.

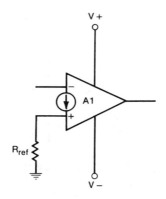

Fig. 10-11. Use of a ground-referenced noninverting input.

Chapter 11

Solid-State Audio Circuits: Transistor and IC

Audio circuits are among the most popular week-end and one-evening projects for electronic hobbyists. Part of the reason for this situation is that audio circuits are so useful to so many. Another reason is that the circuits are generally well behaved, so they can be easily built with low-cost components. In this chapter we will discuss the basic circuits in both discrete transistor and integrated circuit form.

Transistor Biasing Methods

One of the most important factors in understanding solid-state audio circuits is to understand the methods used to achieve the proper biasing of transistors. Fig. 11-1 shows several of the most common methods for biasing transistors. These circuits, or variations of them, are used in most solid-state audio circuits, both discrete and IC.

Fixed Base-Current Bias

Fig. 11-1A shows the simplest method of all bias arrangements—and the most impractical. Bias is established by current flow from the emitter-base junction of the transistor, through R1, to the supply voltage. The amount of bias is dependent on the value of R1 and the value of the supply voltage. The primary disadvantage of this bias arrangement is that it provides no means of automatically limiting collector current (i.e., stabilization).

Collector-Feedback

Another simple form of self-bias is shown in Fig. 11-1B. Because R1 is connected to the transistor side of the load resistor R2, any change in collector current will cause a proportional, but opposite, change in transistor bias. For example, if collector current increases because of a temperature increase, the voltage at the collector decreases (becomes less positive) which, in turn, reduces the current through the circuit comprised of the emitter-base junction and R1. Although this bias system does provide a degree of stabilization, it also introduces degeneration, caused by feedback of any AC signal voltage developed across the load resistor.

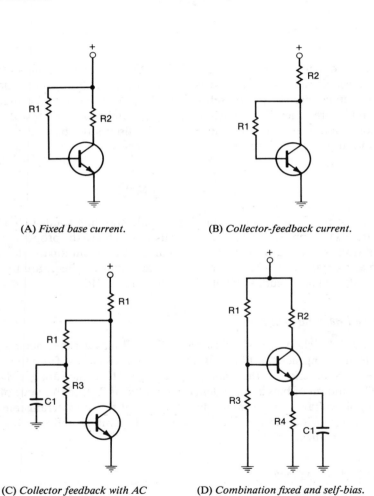

(A) *Fixed base current.*

(B) *Collector-feedback current.*

(C) *Collector feedback with AC bypassing.*

(D) *Combination fixed and self-bias.*

Fig. 11-1. Various methods for biasing transistors.

Collector-Feedback with AC Bypassing

This method, shown in Fig. 11-1C, is the same as described for Fig. 11-1B except that an electrolytic capacitor has been added to filter out, or bypass, AC variations.

Combination Fixed and Self-Bias

This configuration (shown in Fig. 11-1D) provides both good stabilization and minimum degeneration. The fixed emitter-base bias is developed by the voltage divider consisting of resistors R1 and R3. Usually, the value of resistor R3 is substantially less than that of R1. Resistor R4 performs the function of stabilizing the transistor. For example, if the emitter-to-collector current increases because of an increase in temperature, the voltage drop across R4 increases, thus placing a more positive voltage on the emitter, which reduces the forward bias on this NPN transistor. Capacitor C1 bypasses AC variations around the emitter resistor to prevent degeneration. The value of R4 usually is five to ten times less than that of R3.

Dual-Supply Method

A biasing circuit that is not so universally recognized as some of the others, but is being used more and more, is the dual-supply circuit of Fig. 11-2A. It can be identified by the fact that the ground (or common) is not returned to the positive or negative side of the DC power supply. The circuit in Fig. 11-2B represents the kind of DC power supply that should be used: two voltages, one positive to ground and the other negative to ground. Instead, in most applications, the ground, which is usually the chassis or a printed wiring board ground bus, "floats" at the electrical midpoint of the two supplies. In most cases, the two voltages are equal, but in others V− and V+ are different values.

Increased output voltage swing is one of the advantages of the dual supply circuit, regardless of whether discrete transistors or integrated circuits are used. Another advantage is improved thermal stability. This can mean a lot in an amplifier that has marginal heat sinking or that is used inside of a closed cabinet. A third advantage is that these circuits tend to be less sensitive to hum pickup caused by power-supply ripple.

Darlington Amplifiers

Another type of circuit that is being used more often in solid-state audio applications is the Darlington amplifier, also called the Darlington pair,

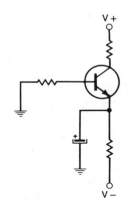

(A) *Bias circuit.*

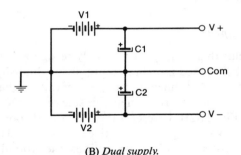

(B) *Dual supply.*

Fig. 11-2. Dual-supply biasing method.

or the "super beta transistor" (when both transistors are inside the same package). An example of this configuration is shown in Fig. 11-3A. Notice that the collectors of the two transistors are tied together. Also note that the emitter of the input transistor is tied directly to the base of the output transistor. This arrangement produces higher current gain and a much higher range of input impedance than is possible with single bipolar (NPN or PNP) transistors. The beta gain is the product of the gains of Q1 and Q2:

$$H_{fe} = (H_{fe(Q1)}) (H_{fe(Q2)})$$

[Eq. 11-1]

If the transistors are identical, then the overall beta gain is the square of the beta gain of any one transistor. You can see why they call this configuration super beta by a simple example. Suppose two moderate beta transistors (e.g. B = 100) are connected in a Darlington configuration such as Fig. 11-3A. The overall beta of the combination is (100) (100), or 10,000.

Although discrete transistors can be connected in the Darlington circuit, several manufacturers offer "Darlington transistors" in one package, or integrated circuit Darlington amplifiers. Fig. 11-3A shows the internal circuit of a Darlington transistor. Most often, the device is a power amplifier in which Q1 is a driver transistor and Q2 is a power output transistor. One device commonly used in hi-fi amplifiers used a 2N3053 for Q1 and a 2N3055 for Q2. Fig. 11-3C shows an IC dual Darlington amplifier. This particular device is the RCA CA3036. There are also operational amplifiers and special purpose ICs on the market that use a Darlington amplifier as the input circuit.

Audio Power Amplifiers

There are several basic designs for audio power amplifiers. For purposes of discussion let's introduce only one for the present. The circuit of Fig. 11-4A is the basic audio amplifier chain that has been used in a lot of equipment over the years. There are three stages shown: preamplifier, driver, and power amplifier. The preamplifier builds up the voltage level of the input signal, while the driver raises the power level to the point where it will drive the output power amplifier stage. The output power amplifier develops the power to drive the loudspeaker.

Fig. 11-4B shows a simple circuit used in many car and home radios, but rarely in high-fidelity applications. This circuit is a single-ended class-A amplifier that uses a choke or autotransformer for output impedance matching. There are several disadvantages to this circuit. For one thing, as a class-A amplifier the output collector current flows 100 percent of the time, even when there is no input signal. As a result, much heat is generated. In some cases, a 3- to 5-watt fusible resistor is placed in series with the transistor to protect the circuit if the excess heat causes Q1 to short. The other disadvantage is that fidelity is not too good unless feedback is provided. The fusible resistor contributes a small amount of beneficial degenerative feedback, but in most cases additional feedback must be provided.

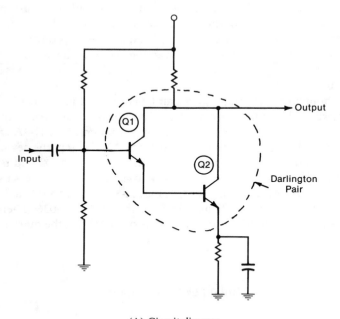

(A) *Circuit diagram.*

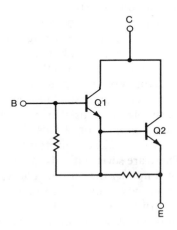

(B) *Single-device Darlington.*

Fig. 11-3. Darlington amplifiers.

Feedback

There are two basic kinds of feedback circuits normally used in audio circuits. One, shown in Fig. 11-5A, is called the "second collector-to-first emitter" system. With correct values of components, this circuit can make a relatively mediocre amplifier sound like a more expensive one. Fig. 11-5B shows the second widely used feedback system. This one has been dubbed the "second emitter-to-first base" system. This circuit often employs only one resistor to supply feedback signals.

Push-Pull Amplifiers

The push-pull circuit is widely preferred over other types, for both power handling ability and overall fidelity. Fig. 11-6 shows the standard transistor push-pull circuit which has been used in almost every audio application, from $5 portable radios to relatively high-priced, medium-grade radios and stereos. It is, however, a lot less cost efficient when compared with other circuits of more recent design.

The circuit in Fig. 11-7 is another breed of push-pull amplifier. This circuit is often called the "split-secondary, totem-pole" circuit, and is used in many domestic and (especially) imported radios. The series connection of the output transistors and the split-secondary interstage transformer (T1) are the two identifying features of this circuit.

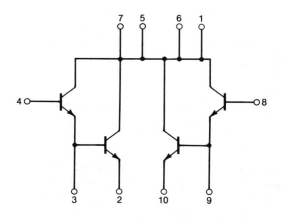

(C) *IC Darlington.*

Fig. 11-3—cont. Darlington amplifiers.

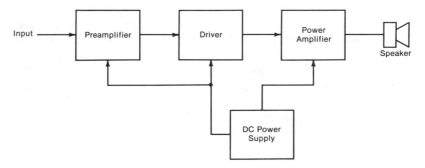

(A) *Basic block diagram.*

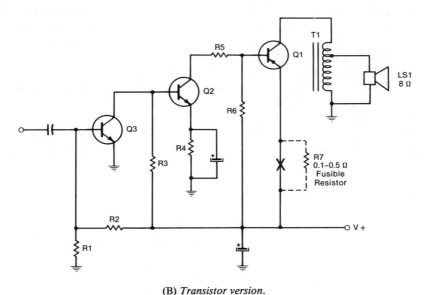

(B) *Transistor version.*

Fig. 11-4. Audio power amplifier.

One thing that all push-pull amplifiers have in common is the necessity of phase-splitting the input signal to provide two new signals 180 degrees out of phase to drive the two halves of the push-pull circuit. In older designs, this job was accomplished by either a center-tapped transformer (Fig. 11-6) or a split-secondary interstage transformer (Fig. 11-7). In many modern circuits, however, the interstage transformer is deleted and another means is used to split the input signal.

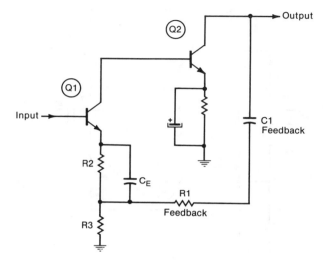

(A) *Collector to emitter.*

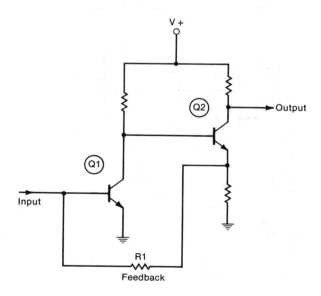

(B) *Emitter to base.*

Fig. 11-5. Feedback schemes.

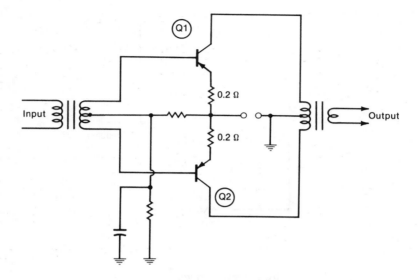

Fig. 11-6. Classical push-pull amplifier.

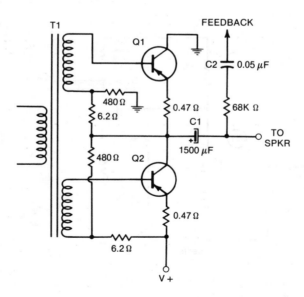

Fig. 11.7. Split-secondary, totem-pole push-pull amplifier.

The transistor phase inverter is one possible replacement for the interstage transformer. This circuit (Fig. 11-8) has one driving signal taken from the collector and the other taken from the emitter of the transistor.

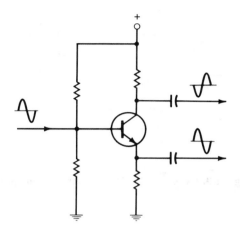

Fig. 11-8. A phase-inverter circuit.

Another method of providing drive signals of opposite polarity is to use an integrated circuit preamplifier that has both inverted and noninverted output terminals. Such units provide wideband, push-pull outputs from a common input signal. An example is shown in Fig. 11-9. This particular circuit is based on the RCA CA3020 IC device.

Designers have other methods of accomplishing phase inversion that is often more economical than the methods just mentioned. These methods used in IC and hybrid audio power amplifiers, are effected using *complementary-symmetry* and *quasi-complementary* amplifiers. The complementary symmetry method is shown in simplified form in Fig. 11-10, and takes advantage of the fact that PNP and NPN bipolar transistors require signals of opposite polarity to perform the same basic function. Notice that the speaker, minus an output transformer, is connected to the midpoint of the two series-connected power transistors. Versions of this circuit which use a single asymmetrical DC power supply usually employ a capacitor to block DC from the speaker circuit (the voltage at point "A" is usually V+/2). Dual-polarity power supply circuits do not require the capacitor.

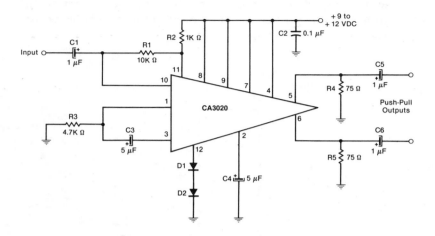

Fig. 11-9. RCA CA3020 IC wideband audio amplifier.

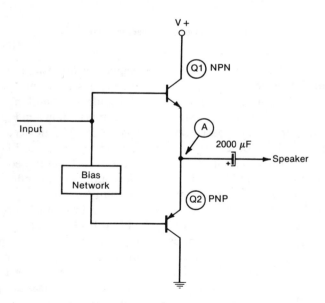

Fig. 11-10. Complementary-symmetry push-pull amplifier.

Complementary-symmetry amplifier circuits do have at least one major disadvantage. It is difficult to locate matching PNP and NPN transistors. Manufacturer "spec" sheets reveal that there are only a few types that can be paired up for complementary service at any given output power level. As the amplifier's power level increases, the number of available types decreases dramatically. The problem becomes even more acute when selecting service replacements for these transistors.

It is relatively easy to find matched pairs of transistors for low- and medium-power complementary circuits. It is even relatively easy to find matched pairs for medium-power applications (i.e., a few watts). But at high power, the problem is greater. This situation has led to an interesting modification of the complementary-symmetry circuit called the quasi-complementary circuit (Fig. 11-11). The quasi-complementary circuit uses a "totem-pole" output (i.e., the same type of NPN or PNP transistors in series with each other), and a complementary driver stage (Q1/Q2). It is relatively easy to find the medium-power complementary drivers and matched (identical) output transistors.

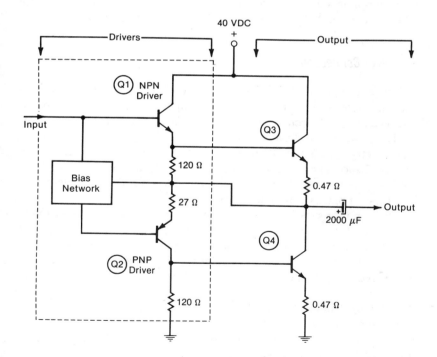

Fig. 11-11. Quasi-complementary push-pull amplifier.

Audio Preamplifiers

The purpose of a preamplifier is to boost the tiny voltage output from sources such as microphones, tape heads, phonograph cartridges, and so forth. In audio amplifiers the preamplifier might have a gain as little as 2 or 3, and as high as 5000. The gain required of the preamplifier is a function of the input signal required by the power amplifier (or other load) and the voltage available from the source. For example, suppose a microphone outputs a voltage of 5 millivolts at normal speaking levels. Further, suppose that the public address power amplifier wants to see a 250-millivolt input signal for maximum output power. We would thus have the V_{in} and V_o potentials of the preamplifier, and could calculate the voltage gain required: $A = V_o/V_{in} = 250 \text{ mV}/5 \text{ mV} = 50$.

There are several options in designing preamplifiers for audio use. One popular approach is to use a special purpose integrated circuit (IC) such as the LM381 device. Others prefer ordinary operational amplifiers, such as the 741 or LM301 devices. Still others prefer special operational amplifiers designed for audio and stereo applications, such as the LM1303 device. All of these devices are easily obtained by hobbyists.

DC Power Connections

The IC audio preamplifier may have quite a bit of gain and could thus oscillate under some conditions. It also might easily influence, or be influenced by, other circuits because of signals passed between stages over the DC power lines. Because of these potential problems it is necessary to correctly bypass the DC power lines of the IC preamplifier device. Fig. 11-12 shows an operational amplifier device, although the same decoupling methods apply to other audio IC devices whether single-polarity or dual-polarity power supplies are used.

Each power supply line must be bypassed with at least one capacitor, and preferably two (as in Fig. 11-12). Capacitors C1 and C2 are 0.1 μF each, and are used to decouple high-frequency signals. Capacitors C3 and C4 have larger values (typically 4.7 μF) and are used to decouple lower-frequency signals. These latter two capacitors are usually tantalum electrolytics.

So why would we want to use two capacitors? Would just one low value capacitor work just as well? The problem is caused by the fact that electrolytic capacitors don't work well at higher frequencies, so we are forced to parallel a lower value capacitor (of a type that is competent at high frequencies) with the higher value electrolytic unit. In many cases,

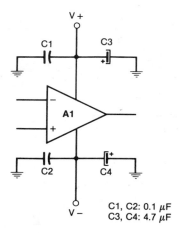

Fig. 11-12. Power supply decoupling.

however, we find that the single 0.1 μF capacitor on each DC power supply line is sufficient, so this "overkill" is not needed.

Special Purpose IC Amplifiers

Several companies make IC preamplifiers especially for audio applications. Typical of these are the LM381 and LM382 devices. (See the National Semiconductor *Linear Data Book* for details.) Fig. 11-13 shows two circuits based on the LM381 device.

The LM381 is similar to a dual operational amplifier except for the single-polarity DC power supply used. The circuit in Fig. 11-13A is a wideband, low-distortion audio preamplifier. With the values shown it will yield a voltage gain of 10 at a total harmonic distortion (THD) of less than 0.05 percent. The frequency response of this circuit is essentially flat throughout the audio spectrum (up to the limit of the amplifier).

The circuit shown in Fig. 11-13B is a tape preamplifier. A large number of cassette tape players use the LM381 device as the preamplifier, and I suspect that was the intended market. The tape head is coupled to the noninverting input of the LM-381 device through a 0.1 μF capacitor. Because of the low input bias of the preamplifier no resistor is needed from the noninverting input to ground. On many versions of this circuit a resistor is needed in order to prevent charging of the capacitor by input bias currents.

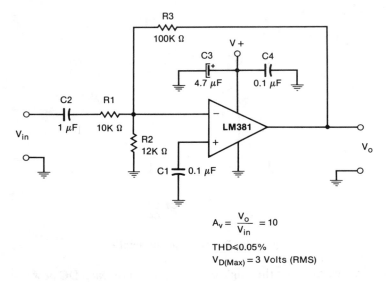

$$A_v = \frac{V_o}{V_{in}} = 10$$

THD≤0.05%
$V_{D(Max)} = 3$ Volts (RMS)

(A) *Low-distortion audio preamplifier.*

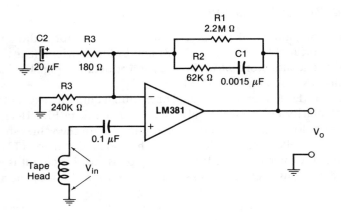

(B) *Tape preamplifier.*

Fig. 11-13. Dual operational amplifiers.

The low-frequency response of the circuit is set by the combined action of resistor R3 and capacitor C2 according to the expression:

$$F = \frac{1,000,000}{6.28R3C2} \qquad \text{[Eq. 11-2]}$$

where

F   is the low end -3 dB frequency in hertz (Hz),
C2 is expressed in microfarads,
R3 is expressed in ohms

The values shown for R3 and C2 in Fig. 11-13B yield a low end -3dB frequency of about 45 Hz. The shape of the frequency response of this preamplifier is set to correspond to that required for the cassette tape equalization curve.

Operational Amplifier Preamps

The classical operational amplifier is one of the most useful ICs in the electronics catalog. It is easy to apply, is usually well behaved, and is low in cost. Designing circuits with the operational amplifier is generally so easy that one wag was tempted to correctly claim that it makes " . . . the contriving of contrivances a game for all." Circuits that only very advanced hobbyists could tackle are now open to even the newcomer.

Fig. 11-14 shows the basic operational amplifier configurations used in audio circuits; Fig. 11-14A is the inverting follower, and Fig. 11-14B is the noninverting follower. In the inverting circuit, the output signal will be 180 degrees out of phase with the input signal (i.e., reversed). In the noninverting signal, on the other hand, the output signal is in phase with the input signal. In both cases, the gain is set by the combined action of the input resistor (R1) and a feedback network. The expressions for the special cases where the feedback network is a single resistor (see Fig. 11-15A) are shown with each circuit.

Several popular variations of the feedback network that find application in audio preamplifiers are shown in Fig. 11-15. The version in Fig. 11-15A is for a wideband amplifier that has a frequency response with no tailoring, except by the natural bandwidth of the amplifier. We can calculate the approximate available bandwidth from the gain-bandwidth product (F_t) of the device, which is the frequency at which gain drops to unity (1). The expression is:

$$F_t = \text{Gain} \times \text{Bandwidth} \qquad \text{[Eq. 11-3]}$$

One use of this expression is to determine which op amp is needed.

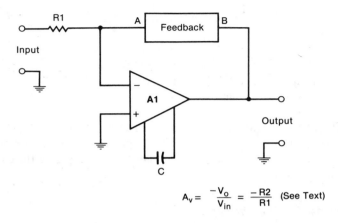

$$A_v = \frac{-V_o}{V_{in}} = \frac{-R2}{R1} \quad \text{(See Text)}$$

(A) *Inverting feedback amplifier.*

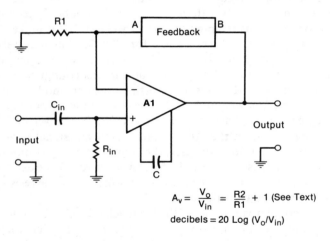

$$A_v = \frac{V_o}{V_{in}} = \frac{R2}{R1} + 1 \text{ (See Text)}$$

$$\text{decibels} = 20 \text{ Log } (V_o/V_{in})$$

(B) *Noninverting feedback amplifier.*

Fig. 11-14. Basic op amp configurations used in audio circuits.

For example, suppose we need a frequency response of 20,000 Hz in an amplifier with a gain of 150. The required F_t is $150 \times 20,000 = 3$ Mhz.

Alternatively, we could also rearrange the expression to calculate the maximum frequency response of any given circuit (if we know F_t). For example, suppose we have a 1-MHz op amp in a circuit with a gain

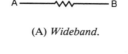

(A) *Wideband.*

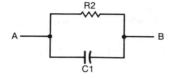

(B) *Frequency compensated.*

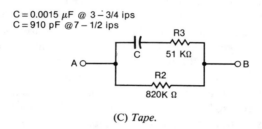

(C) *Tape.*

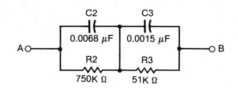

(D) *RIAA phono.*

**Fig. 11-15. Variations of feedback networks
used in audio preamplifiers.**

of 100. The maximum frequency response of the amplifier will be F_t/
Gain = 3 MHz/100 = 30 kHz.

At low frequencies, the feedback network shown in Fig. 11-15B produces a flat gain equal to that of the resistor alone. At frequencies above
a certain point, however, the gain of the amplifier will roll off at −6 dB
per octave. The "breakpoint" between the low-frequency gain and the
rolled off segment (i.e., the high end −3 dB point) is:

$$F = \frac{1,000,000}{6.28R2C1}$$

[Eq. 11-4]

where
F   is in hertz (Hz),
R2 is in ohms,
C1 is in microfarads

The remaining feedback networks are used in special preamplifiers. The network in Fig. 11-15C is used for NAB-compensated tape preamplifiers, while that of Fig. 11-15D is used for RIAA-compensated phonograph preamplifiers.

Operational amplifiers are normally used in dual-polarity power supply circuits. In cases where the device must be used in single-supply circuits we can use a configuration such as that in Fig. 11-16. In this type of circuit the V− power supply terminal is grounded, and the V+ terminal is connected to the single power supply. The noninverting input is biased to a point midway between V+ and ground by a voltage divider consisting of R3 and R4. The value of R3/R4 can be any resistance between 2 kilohms and 100 kilohms, with the value 3.3 kilohms being common.

A problem with this circuit is that the inverting input and the output terminals are also biased to a high DC potential. In order to prevent these voltages from affecting other circuits we need to use capacitive coupling in this circuit. Capacitor C1 couples the input signal to the amplifier while preventing the DC bias at point "A" from affecting the

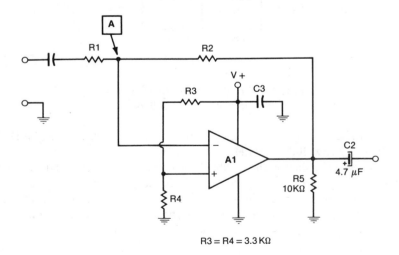

R3 = R4 = 3.3 KΩ

Fig. 11-16. Single-supply audio preamplifier.

input source. Similarly, capacitor C2 will pass the audio output signal while blocking the DC offset bias.

Fig. 11-17 shows an example of a stereo audio preamplifier based on the op amp. Once called the MC1303 when Motorola was the source of the chip, others now make it so it is now available from many sources under the type number LM1303. The chip contains two operational amplifiers that are completely independent except for the V— and V+ DC power supply connections.

Tone-Control Circuits

Tone controls allow the user to custom tailor the frequency response of an audio preamplifier. The *bass* control emphasizes the low frequencies, while the *treble* control emphasizes the high frequencies. In some circuits a single control serves both ends of the spectrum, while in others

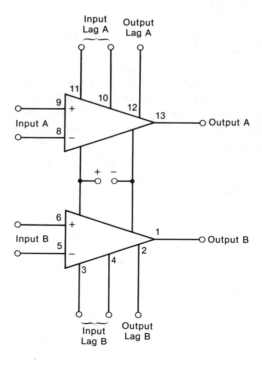

Fig. 11-17. MC 1303P stereo preamplifier.

separate bass and treble controls are provided. Fig. 11-18 shows several varieties of tone control circuits.

The circuit in Fig. 11-18A is a simple rolloff tone control found in low-cost equipment. This is the simplest and least desirable variety, and consists of two components connected in series across the audio line. These components form a treble rolloff circuit that mimmicks the effect of "bass boost" (poorly) by rolling off the high frequencies. Unfortunately, while simple, this type of tone control reduces the signal amplitude.

Another variety of tone control is shown in Fig. 11-18B. In this version a pair of frequency-sensitive RC or RLC networks is placed in the negative feedback circuit of the amplifier. These circuits selectively amplify different bands of frequencies. An example of the RLC version is shown in the inset in Fig. 11-18B. This circuit is popular in graphic equalizers.

The Baxandall tone control circuit shown in Fig. 11-18C is used in almost all decent audio amplifiers. The Baxandall circuit consists of two cascade frequency-selective RC networks, one each for bass and treble ranges. Each control will boost its design frequencies at one end of the control's range, and will cut it at the other end of the range.

Fig. 11-19 shows the circuit for a tone-control preamplifier stage based on the Baxandall circuit. The basic circuit is a CA3140 operational amplifier connected in a basic inverting-follower configuration, with a single power supply. Resistors R1 and R2 bias the noninverting input to $V+/2$. These resistors are higher in value than in certain other op amps because of the very large input impedance of the BiMOS CA3140 op amp. The three-terminal Baxandall tone circuit of Fig. 11-19B is essentially the same as Fig. 11-18C, and is used as shown in the circuit of Fig. 11-19A. This circuit will provide a boost or cut of about 20 decibels in either the bass or treble ranges.

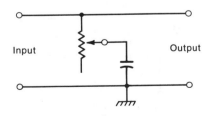

(A) *Simple shunt rolloff.*

Fig. 11-18. Tone-control circuits.

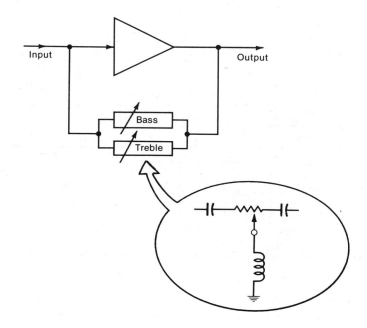

(B) *Feedback.*

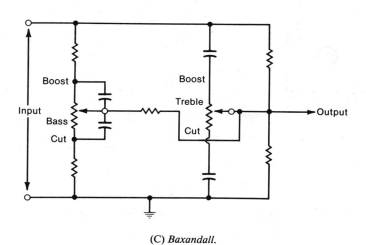

(C) *Baxandall.*

Fig. 11-18—cont. Tone-control circuits.

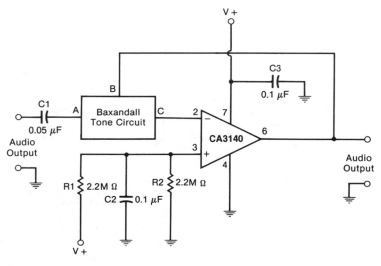

(A) *Preamplifier circuit*

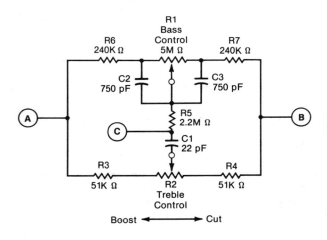

(B) *Baxandall tone circuit.*

Fig. 11-19. Tone-control preamplifier stage.

Some Additional Projects

Most readers of this book are probably activists in that they prefer to go
to the workbench and try some of the things that they learned in the

text. In this section we serve that constituency and present several practical circuits that can be used in audio and wideband amplifier applications.

Audio Mixers

An audio mixer is a circuit that combines audio signals from two or more inputs into a single channel. Application examples include multiple microphone public-address systems, multiple guitar systems (music), or radio station audio console service where inputs from tape players, record players, and two or more microphones are combined into a single line that goes to the transmitter modulation input.

Audio Mixer I The first audio mixer is an operational amplifier version shown in Fig. 11-20. This circuit is basically nothing more than a unity gain inverting follower with multiple inputs. Three audio lines are identified here: AF1, AF2 and AF3. Each of these sources is applied to the input of the operational amplifier, and gains of R4/R1, R4/R2 and R4/R3, respectively, are realized. Because all resistors are 100 kilohms, the gain for each channel is unity.

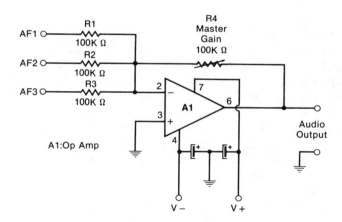

Fig. 11-20. Three-input audio mixer with master gain control.

Gain can be customized on a channel by channel basis by varying the input resistance value. The gain of any given channel will be 100 kilohm/R, where R is the input resistance (R1, R2, or R3) in kilohms. Be careful not to reduce the input resistance so far that the source is loaded. If the source is another operational amplifier preamplifier (or other voltage amplifier), then the input resistance can be reduced to several kilohms without a problem. But if the source is a high impedance phono cartridge or some similar device, then 50 kilohms is probably the minimum acceptable value.

In some cases, it might be beneficial to increase the value of the feedback resistance to 1 megohm or so, in order to make the corresponding input resistances higher for any given gain. Remember, the input impedance seen by any single channel is the value of the input resistor.

A master gain control is provided by making the feedback resistor variable from 0 to 100 kilohms. If no gain control is needed, then make this resistor fixed. An audio taper potentiometer is used for most applications. If the application calls for a one-time set and forget gain control adjustment (as might be true in radio station applications), then make R4 a trimmer-type potentiomer, otherwise it should be a panel type, with a shaft appropriate for a knob (quarter inch half or full round).

The operational amplifier selected can be almost any good op amp with a gain bandwidth product sufficient for audio applications. Because the gain is unity, any GBW over 20 Hz will suffice (which means almost all devices except the 741 family— which will work in communications applications).

Audio Mixer II The circuit in Fig. 11-21 is an improved audio mixer based on the RCA CA3048 amplifier array. This circuit provides approximately 20 dB of gain at each channel. The CA3048 device is a 16-pin DIP integrated circuit that contains four independent AC amplifiers. Offering a gain of 53 dB with a GBW of 300 kHz (typical), the CA-3048 has a 90 kilohm input impedance, and an output impedance less than 1 kilohm. It will produce a maximum low-distortion output signal of 2 volts RMS, and can accept input signals up to 0.5 volt RMS.

Each DC power supply can output up to +16 volts DC. There are two V+ and two ground connections. These multiple connections are used to reduce the internal coupling between amplifiers. The two V+ terminals are tied together externally, and the two ground terminals are tied together also. The V+ terminals are bypassed with a dual capacitor. C5 in Fig. 11-21 is a 0.1 μF unit, and is used for bypassing the high frequencies, while C6 is a 4.7 μF tantalum electrolytic for bypassing the low frequencies. Both capacitors must be mounted as close as possible to the CA3048 body, with C5 taking precedence for closeness over C6 (high frequencies are more critical).

An RC network from the amplifier output to ground (R3-C2) is

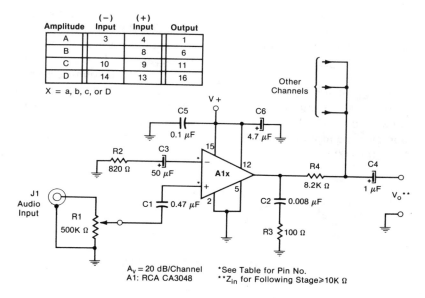

Amplitude	(−) Input	(+) Input	Output
A	3	4	1
B		8	6
C	10	9	11
D	14	13	16

X = a, b, c, or D

A_v = 20 dB/Channel
A1: RCA CA3048

*See Table for Pin No.
**Z_{in} for Following Stage ≥10K Ω

Fig. 11-21. RCA CA3048 four-channel mixer circuit.

used to stabilize the amplifier, thus preventing oscillation. Like the power supply bypass/decoupling capacitors, these components need to be mounted as close as possible to the body of the amplifier.

Only one channel is shown in detail in Fig. 11-21 because of space limitations. Each of the other three channels is identical, and are joined with the circuitry shown at the output capacitor (C4) as shown. Each of the four channels has its own level control (R1), which also provides a high input impedance for the mixer.

600-Ohm Audio Circuits

Professional audio and broadcast applications generally use a 600-ohm balanced line between devices in the system. For example, a remote preamplifier will have a 600-ohm balanced output and will connect to the next stage through a three-wire line. Such a system uses two "hot" lines and a ground as the stage to stage interconnection. An amplifier with a 600-ohm balanced output is called a line driver amplifier, while an amplifier with a 600-ohm balanced input is a line receiver. Some amplifiers, of course, are both line drivers and line receivers.

Fig. 11-22 shows a line receiver amplifier based on the 301 operational amplifier used in the unity gain, noninverting configuration. The input circuit is a line transformer. If the turns ratio of transformer T1 is 1:1, then the overall gain of the circuit is unity. But if the transformer has a turns ratio other than 1:1, then the gain is essentially the turns ratio of the transformer. For example, suppose a transformer is selected with a 600-ohm balanced input winding, and a 10,000 ohm secondary winding. Such a transformer will have a sec/pri impedance ratio of 10,000/600, or about 17:1, so the turns ratio is on the order of the squareroot of 17, or about 4.1. Thus, the voltage actually applied to the noninverting input will be 4.1 times higher than the input signal voltage from the 600-ohm line.

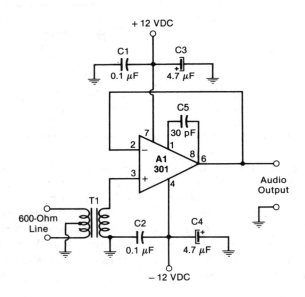

Fig. 11-22. Transformer-coupled line amplifier.

Like most other op-amp circuits, Fig. 11-22 requires two DC power supplies (V− and V+). Typically, these power supplies can be anywhere from −6 and +6 volts to −15 and +15 volts. As in other circuits, each DC power supply is decoupled with a pair of capacitors, a 0.1 μF unit for higher frequencies and a 4.7 μF unit for lower frequencies.

The output of this circuit is an ordinary single-ended voltage amplifier (as in other op-amp circuits), so will typically have a very low impedance. Some designers use a transformer-coupled output circuit. It is possible to get away with a 600-ohm 1:1 transformer if the natural output impedance of the op amp is on the order of 50 ohms or so. The general rule of thumb is that for best voltage transformation, the primary impedance of any transformer selected should be 10× the natural output impedance of the device.

Another way to make a 600-ohm line input amplifier is to use the simple DC differential circuit of Chapter 6, and make sure the input resistors are 300-ohms each. (Note: 330 ohms is the closest easily obtained standard value of simple resistor, and will work fine in most cases.)

Fig. 11-23 shows a line driver amplifier based on a pair of operational amplifiers (the DC power supply connections are deleted, but all pinouts are as in Fig. 11-22). The output circuitry is balanced because it is made from two single-ended op amps driven out of phase with each other. The low output impedance of the operational amplifier, plus the 270-ohm series resistance, makes the balanced output impedance a total of approximately 600 ohms.

The circuit of Fig. 11-23 is a good example of the clever use of one of the properties of the ideal op amp. Recall from Chapter 2 that one of

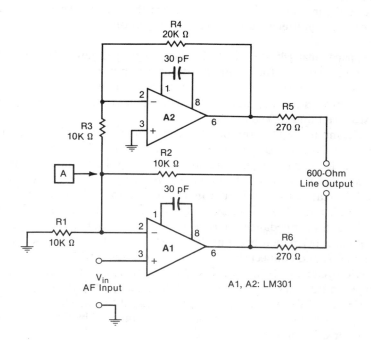

Fig. 11-23. Transformerless line driver amplifier.

the ideal properties is that inputs "stick together." In other words, applying a voltage to one input causes the same voltage to appear at the other input. In this case, for example, the AF input signal voltage applied to the noninverting input of amplifier A1 also appears on the inverting input of that same amplifier. Thus, we will see V_{in} both on the noninverting input and at point "A" in Fig. 11-23. We can therefore use point "A" to feed the other half of the balanced circuit, amplifier A2. Because A1 is a noninverting gain-of-two circuit, and A2 is a gain-of-two inverting circuit, the two sides are out of phase with each other—which is the condition required of the two "balanced" output lines.

Preamplifier Circuits

A preamplifier circuit is an audio amplifier that gives some initial amplification to the signal before passing it to another circuit for additional amplification or other processing. For example, a microphone has a low-level output (several millivolts to 0.2 volt). A preamplifier typically boosts the microphone signal to 100 to 1000 millivolts before it is applied to the input of a power amplifier (for the loudspeaker), or the input of a transmitter modulator (depending upon use).

Microphone Preamplifier Fig. 11-24 shows a simple gain-of-100 microphone preamplifier for communications and non-hi fi public address uses. This circuit uses an LM301 operational amplifier in the noninverting-follower gain configuration. With the values of feedback and input resistors (R1 and R2) shown, the gain is 101.

The input circuit of this preamplifier is capacitor coupled to the microphone. In order to keep the input bias currents of the op amp from charging the capacitor (and thereby latching up the op amp), we use a 2.2-megohm resistor (R3) from the noninverting input to ground. This circuit is relatively general, but can be modified toward the less complex if we use a dynamic microphone only. Dynamic microphones use either a high- or low-impedance coil (like a loudspeaker, but reversed in function) that is permanently connected into the circuit. In that case, delete R3 and C7, and connect the microphone between ground and pin 3. If the microphone is to be disconnected from time to time, however, we must keep R3 in the circuit to prevent the op amp output from saturating at or near V+ when the noninverting input "goes open."

The frequency response of this circuit is tailored by C5 and also by capacitor C6 shunting the feedback resistor. With the values of capacitance shown, the upper −3 dB point in the response curve is a little over

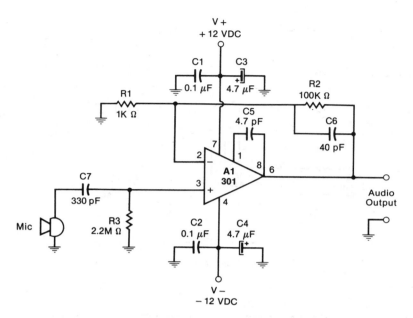

Fig. 11-24. Microphone preamplifier.

3000 hertz, and falls off at a rate of approximately −6 dB/octave above that frequency.

General Preamplifier   Fig. 11-25 shows two general purpose preamplifiers based on the RCA CA3600E device. This IC is a complimentary COS/MOS transistor array. A single-stage design is shown in Fig. 11-25A, while a multistage design is shown in Fig. 11-25B. The internal transistor array equivalent circuit for one transistor pair is shown in the inset to Fig. 11-25A. The single-stage design is capable of up to 30 dB of gain at a V+ of 15 volts DC, and slightly more at lower potentials (but only at a sacrifice of the 1-MHz −3-dB point).

The multistage design shown in Fig. 11-25B is capable of voltage gains to 100 dB at frequencies up to 1 MHz, assuming a 10 volt DC supply; the gain drops to 80 dB for +15 volt supplies). This gain and frequency response is quite useful in audio and other applications, but must be approached with caution when actually built. Be sure to keep the input and output sides of the amplifier separated as much as possible. Also, make sure that the power supply decoupling capacitors are mounted as close as possible to the body of the IC.

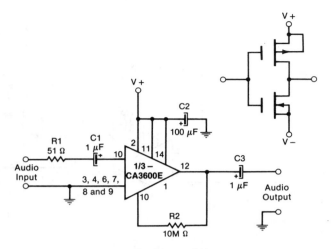

(A) *Single-stage design.*

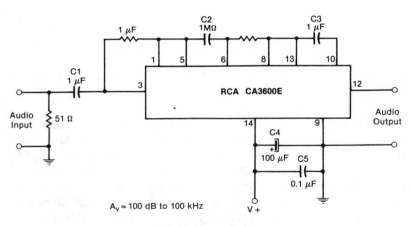

$A_v \approx 100$ dB to 100 kHz

(B) *Multistage design.*

Fig. 11-25. General purpose preamplifiers using the RCA CA3600E IC.

The 50-ohm input impedance of this amplifier removes it from the audio-amplifier category (which usually wants to see higher imped-ances), unless a preamplifier stage is provided that will have a higher impedance. A good candidate is the circuit of Fig. 11-25A.

Compression Amplifier

A compression amplifier is one that reduces its gain on input signal peaks, and increases the gain in the input signal valleys. These circuits are used by electronic music fans and by broadcasters to raise the average power in the signal without appreciable distortion (Fig. 11-26).

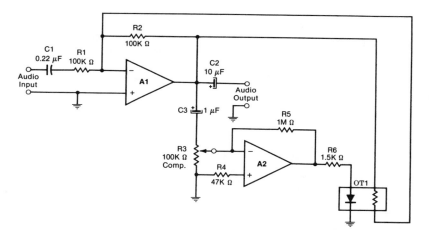

Fig. 11-26. Audio compression amplifier.

The amplifier (A1) is any good audio operational amplifier, such as the LM301. (Power supply and compensation circuits are not shown, but see earlier circuits in this chapter.) The gain of the circuit is set by input resistor R1, and a feedback resistance that consists of the parallel combination of R2 and the resistance of the optocoupler (OT1) output element. The OT1 resistance is set by the intensity of the light emitting diode (LED) brightness, which is, in turn, set by the signal amplitude produced by A2. Because the A2 output signal is proportional to the A1 output signal, overall gain "reduces itself" (i.e., compresses). Optoisolator OT1 can be any resistance output device such as the Clairex, or a modern type (e.g., H11) that uses a JFET for the resistance element.

Chapter 12

Instrumentation and Other Circuits

Electronic instrumentation circuits represent a very large class, depending upon how you define "instrumentation." In this chapter, therefore, we will take a look at several miscellaneous circuits that are generally useful in constructing electronic instruments. We will also take a look at the general class of circuits called proximity detectors. The reason for this is to demonstrate the concept of transduction by using a nonstandard example.

Keeping the Circuits Stable

Although we discussed op-amp stability problems in an earlier chapter, I want to reopen the issue briefly in order to drive the point home. In preparing this chapter I had to breadboard several circuits (integrators and differentiators) to check out the principles presented. Ordinarily, common 741 operational amplifiers are used for casual projects because those devices are both low-cost and well-behaved. Unfortunately, the well-behaved point is due to their being unconditionally stable. In other words, the frequency response is rolled off so much that there is little chance of oscillation. That fact makes it easy to become slack in such matters as power-supply bypassing. The 741 will frequently operate normally with the power supply leads unbypassed, but op amps with higher frequency responses (like the CA3140 BiMOS device) will become unstable and oscillate if the power supply is unbypassed.

Fig. 12-1A shows the first circuit that I connected. Because the differentiator and integrator circuits being checked are based on the inverting follower, I first connected an inverting follower with a gain of one (R1 = R2 = 470 kilohms) to test the op amp from my junk box and the connections. The idea was to then replace the appropriate resistors with the correct integrator or differentiator components. When a 400-Hz sine-wave signal was applied to the input, the oscilloscope showed

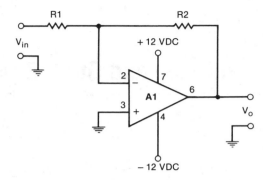

Test Circuit: R1 = R2 = 470KΩ
A = CA3140E

$$A_v = \frac{-V_o}{V_{in}} = \frac{-R2}{R1}$$

(A) *First version—test circuit.*

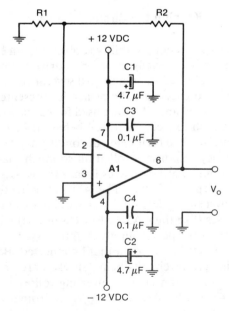

(B) *Second version—corrected circuit.*

Fig. 12-1. Inverting-follower circuits.

the waveform of Fig. 12-2A. Note the thickening of the trace: the fuzziness indicates oscillation at high frequency. Expanding the trace (shown in Fig. 12-2B) demonstrated that the oscillation was at a frequency somewhat higher than 20 kilohertz.

The CA3140 operational amplifier has a higher gain bandwidth product than the old-fashioned 741, and required the addition of bypass capacitors shown in Fig. 12-1B. When I connected those capacitors into the circuit, the oscilloscope showed the trace in Fig. 12-2C, which is the correct trace.

Integrators and Differentiators

Integration and differentiation are mathematical processes that are used frequently in electronic instrumentation circuits. Although the details of these processes are from calculus and are thus beyond the scope of this book, you need to know a few details about them on at least a descriptive level. Fig. 12-3 demonstrates some of these principles. Keep in mind two facts: the integral is the area under a mathematical curve. For a time varying voltage signal, the integral is the time average of the signal. The derivative is the instantaneous rate of change of the curve at a point.

Consider Fig. 12-3A. In this case, we have a DC voltage that is turned on at time T1 and turned off at time T2. Between T1 and T2 the voltage remains at a constant level, V1. The mathematical "curve" represented by voltage V is rather simple because V = V1 at all times. The integral of this curve is the area under the curve, which for this simple case is merely the product of the base and the height of the rectangle: V1 × (T2-T1). Because the curve is constant, the rate of change is zero, so the derivative of the curve is zero. If the signal of Fig. 12-3A is applied to an integrator, the output of the integrator will initially be zero, and will rise at a constant rate from T1 until T2, reaching a value dependent upon the values of V1 and (T2-T1).

A second case is shown in Fig. 12-3B. In this case, the voltage signal is a constantly rising voltage. Because the rate of change is constant, we can measure the voltage change between any two time points and find the rate of change. For the situation shown in Fig. 12-3B:

$$\frac{\Delta V}{\Delta T} = \frac{(V2-V1)}{(T2-T1)}$$

[Eq. 12-1]

where

ΔV represents the change in voltage V,

ΔT represents the change in time

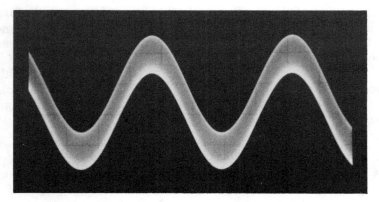

(A) *400-Hz sine wave with superimposed oscillation.*

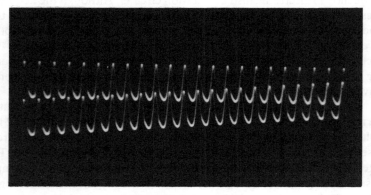

(B) *Oscillation waveform.*

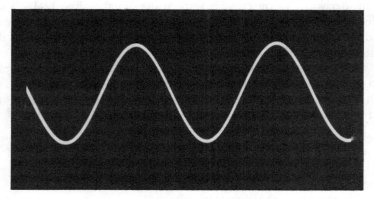

(C) *Corrected waveform of Fig. 12-1B.*

Fig. 12-2. Waveforms from circuit of Fig. 12-1.

In many cases, when the interval is small enough, the Greek letter "delta" (Δ) is replaced with a lower case "d." That convention makes the expression above read:

$$\frac{dV}{dT} = \frac{(V2-V1)}{(T2-T1)} \qquad \textit{[Eq. 12-2]}$$

Some purists would find the above distinction between "delta" and "d" somewhat lacking, but that fact does not harm our discussion here.

The integral of the curve in Fig. 12-3B is a little harder to calculate because we have a figure other than a square or rectangle. It is still merely the area under the curve, however.

Fig. 12-3C shows a practical example from medical electronics. Arterial blood pressure monitors represent blood pressure with a voltage. In modern devices, the voltage analog of pressure is usually 10 millivolts per millimeter of mercury (i.e., Torr) of pressure (10 mV/mmHg). Thus, for the case shown (which is where this overweight author wishes his blood pressure was), a systolic pressure of 120 mmHg is represented by 1200 mV, while the 80 mmHg diastolic pressure is represented by 800 mV.

Doctors, especially in intensive care cases, sometimes want the mean arterial pressure, or MAP. The MAP is the time average of the blood pressure waveform (P) over one cardiac cycle (i.e., between two beats of the heart, as represented by points T1 and T2). If we apply the pressure voltage waveform to an integrator, the output of the integrator will be the MAP.

Researchers sometimes want to know the derivative of blood pressure, or dP/dT. Because the waveform is constantly varying, its rate of change, hence its derivative, is also constantly changing. Thus, we can only talk about the derivative at a particular point, such as P1 in Fig. 12-3C. We calculate that on paper by taking the slope of a line that is tangent to P at point P1. A differentiator will yield a continually varying voltage that represents the rate of change. Some medical blood pressure monitors are equipped to output voltages representing diastolic pressure, systolic pressure, mean arterial pressure (MAP) and pressure derivative (dP/dT). Later in this chapter we will develop the block diagram of the monitor using some of the circuits discussed.

Integrators

Electronic integrators must find the time average of the input waveform. The simplest form of integrator is the resistor-capacitor (RC) network shown in Fig. 12-4. In this circuit, the output voltage changes as the charge I1 accumulates in the capacitor. The rate of increase in V_o

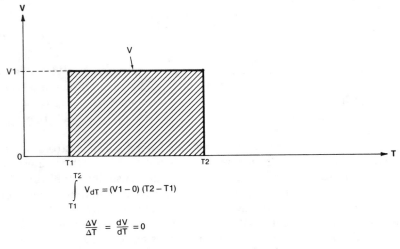

$$\int_{T1}^{T2} V_{dT} = (V1 - 0)(T2 - T1)$$

$$\frac{\Delta V}{\Delta T} = \frac{dV}{dT} = 0$$

(A) *Integration of rectangular function.*

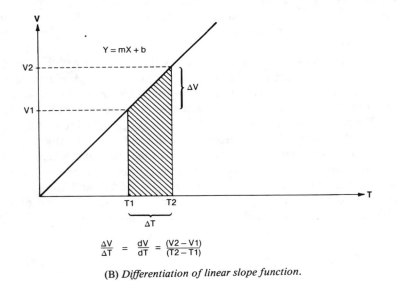

$$\frac{\Delta V}{\Delta T} = \frac{dV}{dT} = \frac{(V2 - V1)}{(T2 - T1)}$$

(B) *Differentiation of linear slope function.*

Fig. 12-3. Integration and differentiation.

is dependent upon the input voltage and the values of R and C. If you recognize the circuit as a low-pass filter, you are correct. The integrator also functions as a low-pass filter with a rolloff of −6 dB/octave above the −3 dB knee frequency (1/6.28 RC).

The electronic integrator is shown in Fig. 12-5. The active element is an operational amplifier, and it has a capacitor in the feedback network. This circuit is basically the inverting follower with the feedback resistor (R2) replaced by a capacitor. The transfer equation of this circuit is:

$$\frac{-1}{RC} = V_{in}\ dT$$

[Eq. 12-3]

where

    R   is the resistance in ohms,
    C   is the capacitance in farads,
    V_{in} is the input voltage,
    dT indicates that we are integrating with respect to time

The constant factor −1 indicates that the circuit is inverting, so a

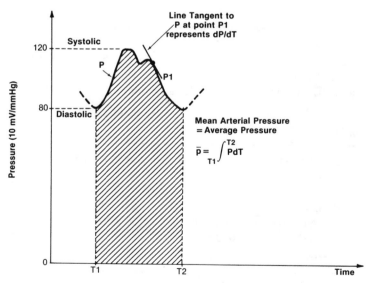

(C) *Integration and differentiation of varying waveform.*

Fig. 12-3—cont. Integration and differentiation.

positive-going input voltage produces a negative-going output voltage, and vice versa.

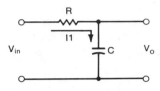

Fig. 12-4. RC integrator.

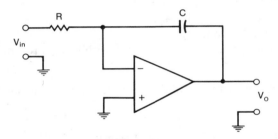

Fig. 12-5. Active integrator, textbook version.

The gain of this circuit is $-1/RC$. Keep in mind that with small values of R and C, this gain can be very, very high— with resulting problems for the designer. Consider an example.

Example:

What is the gain of an inverting integrator in which R = 10 kilohms and C = 100 picofarads?

$$\text{GAIN} = -1/RC$$
$$\text{GAIN} = -1/((10,000 \text{ ohms}) \times (100 \times 10^{-12} \text{ farads}))$$
$$\text{GAIN} = -1/0.000001$$
$$\text{GAIN} = -1,000,000$$

With a gain of 1,000,000, a small error or DC offset in the input signal will cause a tremendous change in the output. For example, suppose we have a 1-volt peak-to-peak sine wave that has a 10-mV DC offset (not very much). This DC offset will be integrated with a gain of 1,000,000 so the 10 mV now becomes 10,000 volts (10 mV) × (1,000,000). Of course, the output of the op amp is limited to about 10 or 12 volts, so the output will saturate really quick. The normal offset of a 741 will saturate the output of such an integrator so fast you'll think it's shorted! In general, the rule of thumb is to make the time constant of the RC network long (i.e., 5×) relative to the period of the input signal.

Fig. 12-6 shows some common electronic signals at the input and output of an electronic integrator. In each case, the upper trace is the input and the lower trace is the output. For the case of the sine wave shown in Fig. 12-6A, the output is phase shifted 90 degrees to become a cosine wave. Thus, the output is in quadrature with respect to the input signal.

The integrator action on square waves is shown in Fig. 12-6B. Because the amplitude of a square wave is constant, the integrator output will rise at a constant rate until the square wave drops low again. At that time, the slope of the output waveform changes and starts decreasing. Thus, the integrator makes a triangle waveform out of a square wave. Incidentally, this technique is used by function generators to form triangle waveforms.

A Practical Integrator

Almost all textbooks on linear integrated circuits or operational amplifiers show the circuit of Fig. 12-5. There is only one problem with the circuit—with real operational amplifiers it doesn't work! Unfortunately, some articles and books don't tell you what the problem is, and how to deal with it. When I first started building integrators I discovered the problem the hard way.

The principal problem in practical integrators is that the DC offset voltage normally present at the output of real operational amplifiers will charge capacitor C1, and thereby soon saturates the op amp. The output voltage will start rising immediately after turn on, and will soon be off the scale. If you have a signal applied to V_{in}, then the output will show that signal with a constantly increasing DC offset potential.

One tactic used to cancel the effects of offset is to use an operational amplifier that has a very low offset potential, and no input bias current (or very little). For low-cost applications, the CA3140 BiMOS op amp (which uses MOSFET input transistors) is a good selection (see Fig. 12-7). Devices of the 741 family are almost useless for integrator service.

Another tactic is to connect a resistor across the integrator capaci-

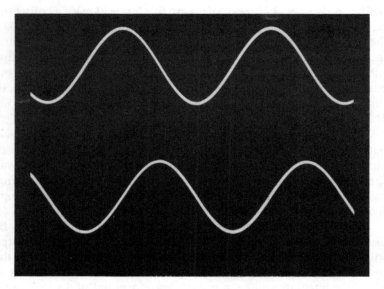

(A) *Action of integrator on a sine wave.*

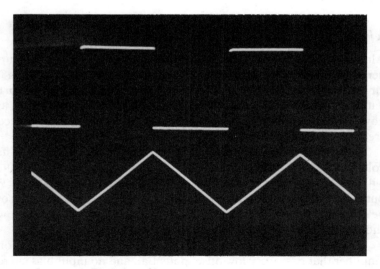

(B) *Action of integrator on a square wave.*

Fig. 12-6. Signals at input and output of an electronic integrator.

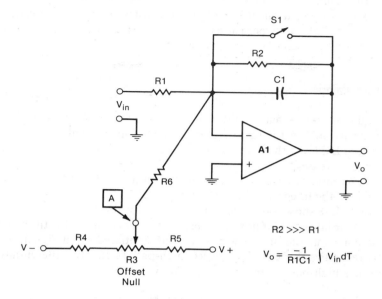

Fig. 12-7. A practical active integrator.

tor in order to keep the DC from building up. This tactic is especially useful for integrators that see periodic input signals. The rule of thumb is to make the shunt resistor (R2) very much larger than R1. In the test case, I used a 470-kilohm input resistor, and an 18-megohm shunt resistor, which worked quite nicely.

Finally, we may also have to use an offset null potentiometer in some circuits. In my test case, with 400-hertz sine, square, and triangle wave input signals, the potentiometer was not needed. Other cases, however, may require a counter offset provided by R3. Although the values of the resistors in this network are dependent upon the application, most of the time a 5-kilohm value for R3, and 10 to 27 kilohms for R4 and R5 will suffice. Make R6 equal to R1 for starters; it can be increased or decreased as needed after the circuit is tested.

To adjust the potentiometer, short the input of the integrator (making $V_{in} = 0$). Adjust R3 for a potential of zero volts at point "A." Momentarily close S1 to force the output voltage to zero. If the output voltage rises to either positive or negative values after S1 is opened, adjust R3 to cause the rate of increase to slow down to zero. Again close S1 and see if the output voltage changes. Repeat the procedure until the output voltage remains at zero following every closing of S1.

In normal operation, switch S1 is used to reset the integrator after it performs an operation. It is used in some instruments where a value is calculated, but is only occasionally needed in cases where an integrator sees a periodic signal with no DC offset component.

Differentiators

Recall from above that the differentiator is used to produce a signal that is proportional to the rate of change of the input signal. Thus, for a constant DC level, the output of the differentiator is zero. As the rate of change increases, the output potential also increases. For sine waves, the differentiator circuit will output a quadrature signal (in a manner similar to the integrator, but of opposite phase shift).

Fig. 12-8 shows the basic resistor-capacitor (RC) differentiator circuit. As long as the input signal period is short compared with the RC time constant, the output will be the differentiated input signal. You may recognize this circuit as an RC high-pass filter. The differentiator acts as a high-pass filter with a knee frequency of

$$F = \frac{1,000,000}{2\pi RC} \qquad \textit{[Eq. 12-4]}$$

where
  F is in hertz,
  R is in ohms,
  C is in microfarads

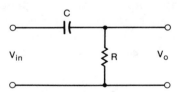

Fig. 12-8. RC differentiator.

At frequencies above the knee frequency the response of the circuit rolls off at a rate of −6 dB/octave.

Fig. 12-9 shows the effects of an RC integrator on square-wave signals. The square wave was selected because its leading and trailing edges have about the fastest rise times producible from our signal generator.

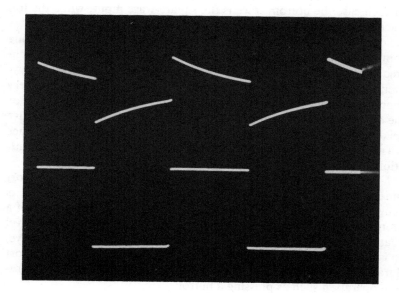

(A) *Long time constant.*

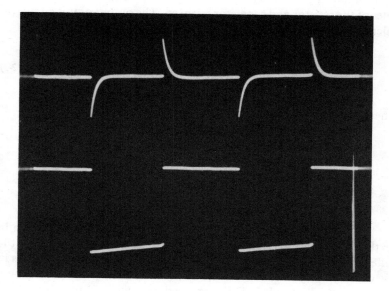

(B) *Short time constant.*

Fig. 12-9. Action of a differentiator on square waves.

In each case,the bottom trace is the square-wave input, while the top trace is the differentiated waveform.

In Fig. 12-9A we see the case for an RC time constant that is long compared with the period of the signal. The top trace shows some high-frequency rolloff. As the frequency is increased (RC = constant), however, we get the situation shown in Fig. 12-9B. Here the period is very short compared with the time constant. Notice the pronounced effect of the differentiator—the output signals are almost positive and negative spikes. The distortion of the input square-wave "flatness" on this trace is a measurement problem with my probe, and was not due to differentiation.

You will see differentiator circuits such as Fig. 12-8, with a short time constant, in certain applications where the differentiation is sought, but only by implication. For example, in the trigger input of a monostable multivibrator, the "input" to the RC network is a level change caused by a switch. Such a level change resembles a square wave, so is treated something like that shown in Fig. 12-9B. Thus, the short duration pulse needed to trigger a one-shot is derived from a long duration operation such as pressing a button.

An example of an active differentiator is shown in Fig. 12-10A. This operational amplifier circuit is similar to the integrator case, but has the roles of the resistor and capacitor reversed. The output of this circuit (in calculus notation) is:

$$V_o = -RC \frac{dV_{in}}{dt} \qquad \text{[Eq. 12-5]}$$

where
  R is in ohms,
  C is in farads,
  the product RC is in seconds,
  dt is in seconds,
  V_o and V_{in} are in the same units (i.e., volts, mV, μV)

Like the operational amplifier, the differentiator circuit shown in textbooks is not quite right for real operational amplifiers. Because the differentiator is a high pass filter, and because of certain instabilities in the circuit, we need to roll off high frequencies above the point where they are actually needed. Thus, we need capacitor C2 to roll off high frequencies (Fig. 12-10B). We also need a 50- to 250-ohm resistor (R2) in series with the input.

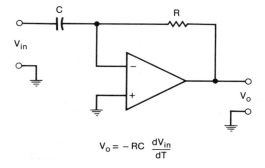

$$V_o = -RC \frac{dV_{in}}{dT}$$

(A) *Textbook circuit.*

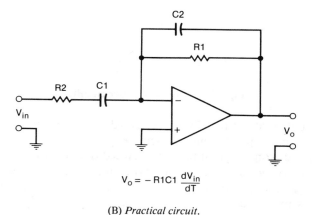

$$V_o = -R1C1 \frac{dV_{in}}{dT}$$

(B) *Practical circuit.*

Fig. 12-10. Active differentiator.

Precise Rectifiers

A rectifier is a device that passes current in only one direction. Thus, it can convert bidirectional alternating current (AC) signals to unidirectional pulsating DC (see waveforms in Fig. 12-11). Normally, ordinary silicon diodes are used for rectifier service both in power supplies and in signal applications. Although the type of diodes used in both applications are different, the principles are the same.

At low signal levels, however, there is a slight problem. The ordinary diode has a nonlinear "knee" region between 0 volts and a certain

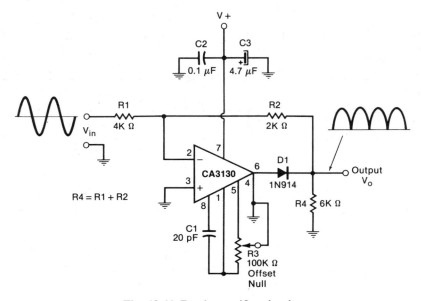

Fig. 12-11. Precise rectifier circuit.

junction potential (0.6 to 0.7 volt in silicon diodes). This potential is low in power supply applications, but can be quite significant in low-level signal applications (and, in fact, may exceed the signal voltage).

Fig. 12-11 shows a method for serving out the junction potential of the diode by using an operational amplifier. The gain of this inverting follower is approximately one-half. Diode D1 is connected so that it will pass only positive output signals from the operational amplifier; negative signals appearing at pin 6 reverse-bias the diode, so they are blocked. When the input signal is negative, the output voltage will be positive, with an amplitude of one-half the input signal. But on positive input signals, the signal at the op amp output is negative, so it is blocked. In this case, however, the circuit resistors form a voltage divider with a transfer function of:

$$V_o = \frac{V_{in}\,R4}{R1 + R2 + R4} \qquad \text{[Eq. 12-6]}$$

Thus, if $R1 + R2 = R4$, the transfer function is $1/2$. The output voltage V_o is the same $V_{in}/2$ as seen in the negative input case.

With the values shown in Fig. 12-11, we can expect to process signals up to about 200 Hz. I have successfully built CA3130-based precise rectifiers for 2-MHz using smaller resistor values. It should be possible to make a 10.7-MHz AM detector using this method—a project that I am working on for a homebrew spectrum analyzer.

Peak-Detector Circuits

A peak detector is a circuit that will hold the highest amplitude voltage applied to the input. Fig. 12-12 shows a simple example of such a circuit. The operational amplifier can be almost any form of high input impedance device.

The holding device is capacitor C1. The charge voltage across this capacitor will be the high potential applied. A low-leakage (i.e., very high reverse resistance) diode (D1) prevents the low output impedance of the op amp from discharging C1.

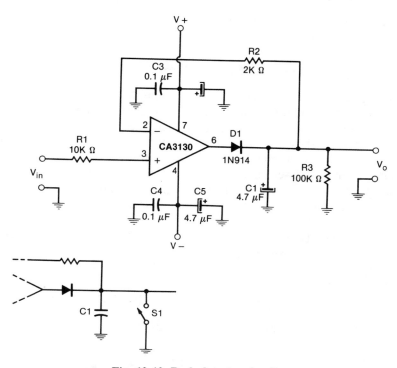

Fig. 12-12. Peak-detector circuit.

When the input voltage drops below the previous peak, the charge on C1 leaks off through resistor R3, so the capacitor voltage takes on the new "peak" after a period of time. Generally speaking, the RC time constant of R3C1 is very, very long compared with the period of the input signal. If R3 is too low a value, there will be a "droop" error, i.e., a decrease in V_o too soon. Some peak-detector circuits use no bleed resistor (R3), but reset the capacitor to zero volts with a switch (see S1 in inset to Fig. 12-12).

Three factors affect the usefulness of a peak holder. First, the blocking diode must have a very high reverse resistance. Second, capacitor C1 must be a low leakage type (for fast signals, use a mica, polycarbonate, or polystyrene capacitor for C1). Third, the circuit used to detect V_o (not shown) must have a very high input impedance. Normally, an operational amplifier unity gain noninverting follower is used for output buffering. The BiMOS or BiFET op amps are best suited to this application.

A negative-output peak detector can be made using either of two strategies. First, we can always place a unity gain inverter ahead of the circuit. Second, we can reverse the polarities of diode D1 and capacitor C1.

Quadrature Detector

A quadrature phase detector is used to demodulate AM signals in instrumentation circuits. Shortly, we will consider a practical instrumentation application that uses this type of circuit.

Fig. 12-13 shows the phase detector circuit. The active element is a unity gain DC differential amplifier with common-mode rejection ratio adjustment (R4). Each input is controlled by a CMOS electronic switch. In early circuits, a vibrator switch was used for this purpose, but today CMOS switches are preferred. The input signal voltage is amplitude modulated, and has a "carrier" frequency of F_{in}. The reference signal at the same frequency is used to drive the switch. An improved version of the circuit is shown in Fig. 12-14. In this case, four CMOS switches are used for the same purpose. A single CMOS 4066 device can be used for this circuit.

An Instrumentation Example

Now let's consider a practical example of a real instrument that uses some of the circuits discussed in this chapter. Earlier (Fig. 12-3C) we used the human blood pressure waveform as an example, so let's make

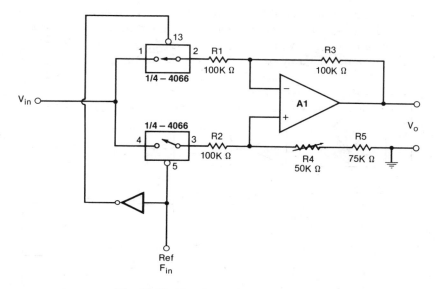

Fig. 12-13. Simple quadrature detector.

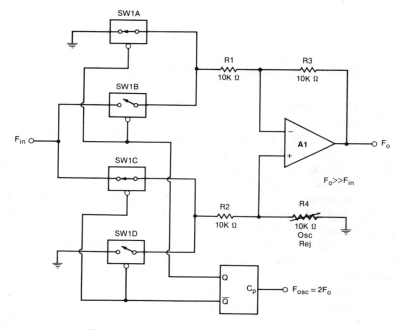

Fig. 12-14. Improved quadrature detector.

our instrument an arterial blood pressure meter. The curve shown in Fig. 12-3C graphs a voltage that represents blood pressure; the waveform is more or less typical of human arterial waveforms. Fig. 12-15 shows the block diagram of a blood pressure meter.

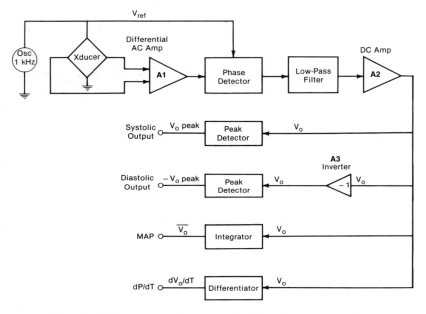

Fig. 12-15. Instrumentation example—blood pressure monitor.

The transducer (XDUCER) is either a piezoresistive Wheatstone bridge, or a linear variable differential transformer (LVDT). In either case, it is excited by a 1000-Hz reference voltage (V_{ref}). The differential outputs of the transducer are applied to an AC differential amplifier, which builds them up to about 1 volt or so. A DC representation of the waveform (which actually looks like Fig. 12-3C) is produced at the output of a quadrature phase detector, and is fed to a low-pass filter that removes the residual carrier frequency. A DC amplifier is used for scaling of the output voltage, V_o.

Our sample instrument is a supergrade research instrument instead of a mere clinical device, so we need the following signal processing stages: systolic, diastolic, mean arterial pressure (MAP), and dP/dt.

The systolic output voltage is a DC level that represents the peak voltage attained by the pressure waveform. Thus, a positive-peak detector is used. For diastolic output, on the other hand, we need to invert the waveform and detect the peak that had once been the valley—that is, the diastolic value.

The MAP is merely the time average of the pressure waveform. That waveform is typically derived from a simple op-amp integrator in medical instruments. Similarly, the dP/dt signal (the pressure waveform derivative) is derived from an op-amp differentiator.

All of the signals except the dP/dt are DC levels proportional to the value being measured. For these, any analog or digital DC voltage reading instrument can be used. For the dP/dt, however, only an oscilloscope or oscillographic paper recorder is permitted.

Proximity Detectors

The director of plant operations in a building where I once worked was a veteran practical joker. He loved gadgets that could be used in setting traps for coworkers and any other poor soul who got lost wandering around the bowels of the building. One such toy was a lamp that turned on and off simply by touching the shade, or the body, or the potted plant that formed its base. What it wouldn't do, however, was turn on and off by the switch. He challenged me to tell him how it worked. At first mystified, I soon found out that the gag lamp worked on the basis of a capacitive proximity detector.

In addition to toys for gagsters, proximity detector circuits are widely used in electronic security systems and other For example, one automatic door design uses a capacitive proximity detector to sense the approach of a pedestrian who wants to pass through the door.

Capacitance is an electrical property that exists between any two conductors. The classic "textbook" capacitor is a pair of parallel metallic plates separated by a "dielectric" consisting of a tiny air gap or other insulating material. The capacitance (specified in farads, or the subunits microfarads, nanofarads, or picofarads) is a function of the area of the plates, the spacing between them and the nature of the insulating material. Fig. 12-16A shows the expressions for several different geometries of capacitor plates, including those most useful in proximity detectors. Because most of our proximity detector sensors will be single wires to ground, take a look at that expression in Fig. 12-16A. The two factors that seem most important (and controllable to the designer) are the diameter of the wire used, and its height above the ground. Also affecting the capacitance (but not accounted for in the simplified equation) are the humidity and temperature of the air dielectric between the wire and ground.

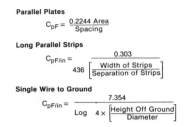

(A) *Capacitance equations.*

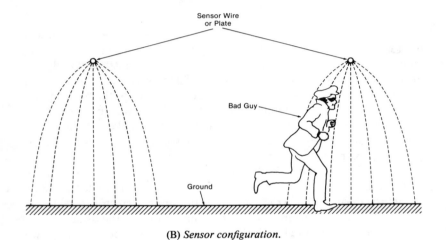

(B) *Sensor configuration.*

Fig. 12-16. Capacitor proximity detector.

How Do Proximity Detectors Work

All sensors rely on what the experts call a "transducible property;" in other words, some physical parameter that can be converted into a voltage or current. In capacitive proximity detectors we rely on the fact that the capacitance is dependent upon the dielectic of the capacitor. Dry air is said to have a "dielectic constant" of 1, while the human body has a dielectric constant of about 80. Thus, when a human enters the field of a capacitor (see Fig. 12-16B), the capacitance will increase by up to 80 times the former value. The electrical flux between the sensor wire and ground increases dramatically by this effect. There are several methods for using the capacitance: oscillator, electrometer, and bridge circuits.

Oscillator Circuits

An LC oscillator (see Fig. 12-17) produces an output that is determined by the inductance and capacitance of the resonant tank circuit. In Fig. 12-17, the inductance is L1, while the capacitance is made up from variable capacitor C1A, and the sensor capacitance (C1B). There are also stray capacitances and inductances in the circuit, but they are not shown as discrete components. The circuit shown here will oscillate at frequencies from about 20 kHz to 10 MHz, depending upon the LC tank circuit components, and the particular values of feedback capacitors, C2 and C3, that are selected.

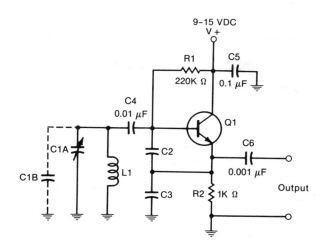

Fig. 12-17. Oscillator for ultrasonic signals.

Fig. 12-18 shows a method by which the oscillator can be used in a proximity detector circuit. The reason for this is that changes in temperature and humidity will easily change the oscillation frequency because they change the capacitance. Two sense wires are used in this circuit (Fig. 12-18A). Each sense wire is a length of #12 or #14 insulated wire mounted on insulated supports such as fence posts.

Fig. 12-18B shows the scheme for using the capacitances in a heterodyned "beat-frequency" circuit. There are two oscillators selected so that the third harmonic of oscillator 1 will be close to the fourth harmonic of oscillator 2. For example, a common scheme sets oscillator 1 to a frequency of 100 kHz, while oscillator 2 is set to 74.875 kHz. The third harmonic of oscillator 1 is therefore 300 kHz, while that of oscillator 2 is 299.5 kHz. Therefore, the beat note at the output of the mixer stage will be the difference frequency, or 500 Hz. By using this seemingly complicated method we obtain a very large percentage change of beat note for relatively small changes in operating frequency. For example, causing oscillator 1 to shift to 100.010 kHz causes the beat note frequency to shift to 530 Hz. The difference between the "same-frequency" method and the harmonics method is that a 10-Hz change represents a 0.01 percent change in operating frequency, and a 6-percent change in harmonic beat note.

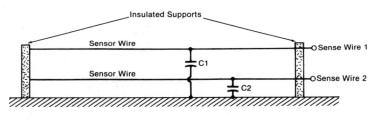

C1, C2 are wire capacitance with respect to ground

(A) *Sensors.*

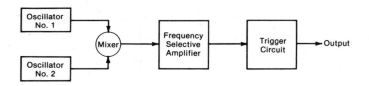

(B) *Block diagram.*

Fig. 12-18. Two-wire proximity detector.

The filter circuit in Fig. 12-18B is a sharply tuned operational amplifier passband filter centered on the normal beat note (500 Hz in our example). As long as the output of the filter sees a signal the trigger circuit will not be alarmed. But if the operating frequencies of the oscillators changes, the beat note is no longer within the filter passband, so the trigger circuit sounds the alarm.

Electrometer Circuits

An electrometer is an amplifier with an extremely high input imped-ance. Traditionally, electrometers have been used to measure the out-puts of devices such as very high impedance transducers and capacitor charges. The high input impedance does not bleed the charge off the capacitor as it measures the capacitor charge voltage.

Fig. 12-19A shows the basic circuit for an electrometer proximity detector. The sensor wire produces a capacitance (C1) at the input of the electrometer amplifier (A1). The capacitor is charged from a DC power supply through a high value resistor. The value of the voltage across the charged capacitor is given by the expression:

$$V_{C1} = \frac{Q}{C1} \qquad\qquad \textit{[Eq. 12-6]}$$

where

V_{C1} is the voltage across the charged capacitor,
Q   is the charge in coulombs,
C   is the capacitance in farads

When a human enters the field of the protected area, the capaci-tance increases tremendously, so the voltage across the capacitor will take a dip. That change of voltage is amplified by the electrometer and is used to indicate intrusion.

Examples of electrometers are shown in Figs. 12-19B and 12-19C. The circuit shown in Fig. 12-19B uses a single MOSFET transistor as the electrometer amplifier. For most cases, we can also use a CMOS inverter, or one of the transistors in the CMOS 4017 complementary transistor ar-ray device. The protection diode shown in Fig. 12-19B is inherent in B-series CMOS devices, but for other MOSFETs it must be provided. The purpose of the diode is to shunt the harmful high voltage from electro-static potentials harmlessly around the delicate gate structure.

Another variant electrometer is shown in Fig. 12-19C. This circuit is based on a special class of operational amplifiers that have MOSFET transistors at the input. The device shown here is part of the RCA BiMOS line of devices. The CA3140 device is an ordinary operational amplifier with "industry standard" pinouts, and an input impedance of 1.5×10^{12} ohms. The DC power connections are not shown.

Bridge Methods

The basic bridge circuit is shown in Fig. 12-20. Similar to a Wheatstone bridge, this circuit is basically two voltage dividers in parallel; resistors

R1-R2 form one voltage divider, while capacitors C1-C2 form the other. An oscillator in the 100-kHz region drives the bridge, and is its voltage source. As long as the ratio of the resistors R2/R1 is equal to the ratio C1/C2, the output voltage (V_o) across terminals A-B is zero. But if either ratio changes, then V_o is nonzero. In a proximity detector, the capacitances will be sense wires, and the capacitance changes when a person comes close to them.

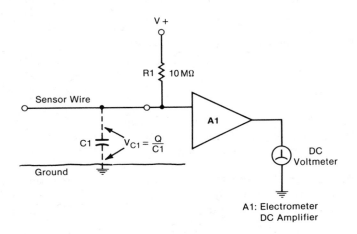

(A) *Basic circuit using an op amp.*

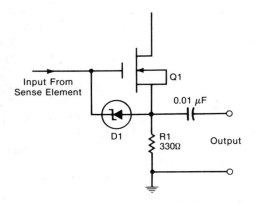

(B) *Using a MOSFET transistor.*

Fig. 12-19. Electrometer proximity detector.

Fig. 12-21 shows a method for using a single sensor wire in a bridge circuit. Resistors R1 and R2 will be fixed (although in some circuits adjustment is possible for balance sake), as will capacitor C1. A sensor wire is plugged into jack J1 to complete the bridge. The output voltage (A-B) is applied to a differential rectifier circuit, and then to a trigger circuit. Alternatively, we can apply the output of the bridge to a differential tuned amplifier before being applied to the rectifier. The purpose of this neat little trick is to be selective as to the signals accepted. A long sensor wire will act as an antenna, so it will pick up signals that can pass though the untuned rectifier with ease. A tuned amplifier will pass only those from the bridge circuit.

The variant circuit shown in Fig. 12-22 uses two sense wires in the same manner as the system shown earlier, and for exactly the same reasons (temperature and humidity). In this case, however, we have an unbalanced bridge circuit in which one end of the output is grounded. The output terminal can be a coaxial connector that conveys the signal to the electronics package.

Single-Object Protection

The protection of specific objects in a space is a problem that proximity detectors can solve. Fig. 12-23 shows a method that is similar to the lamp my clowning friend at the beginning of this article used to spoof the rest of us. It can also be used to spoof the criminal who would try to break into the protected cabinet or safe.

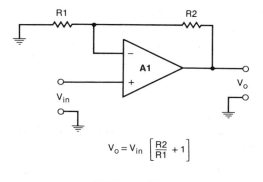

$$V_o = V_{in} \left[\frac{R2}{R1} + 1 \right]$$

(C) *Preamplifier.*

Fig. 12-19—cont. Electrometer proximity detector.

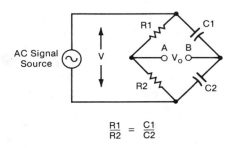

$$\frac{R1}{R2} = \frac{C1}{C2}$$

Fig. 12-20. Bridge sensor.

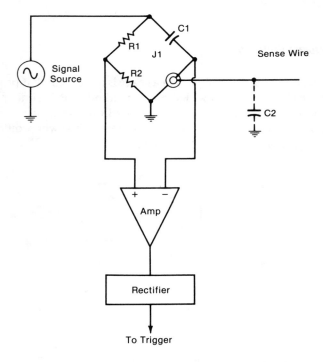

Fig. 12-21. Block diagram of bridge sensor circuit.

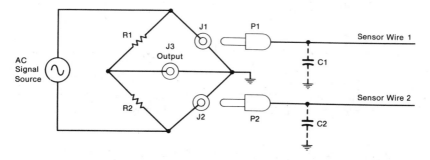

Fig. 12-22. Two-wire bridge sensor.

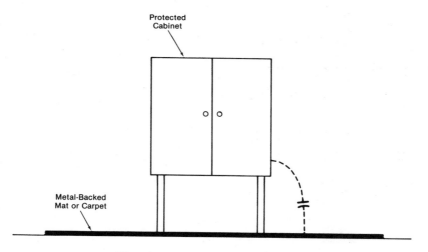

Fig. 12-23. Single-object protection.

In the system of Fig. 12-23, if the protected object is conductive (i.e., metallic), it can form one plate of the capacitor in lieu of the sensor wire. The ground forms the other plate in some systems, in which case the circuit is the same as other proximity detectors. But in many cases, especially indoors, the floor is nonconductive so it will not act as a ground. However, we can place either a metal-backed mat on the floor, or a large area of either metal screen or foil underneath a carpet, dustmat, or masonite walk board. The idea is to place a large metallic surface underneath, and insulated from, the protected cabinet. The capacitance can be used in any of the circuits discussed earlier.

Conclusion

Proximity detectors can be used for both entertaining and serious security systems. They represent a class of circuits that are easily constructed at low cost, but work well even for hobbyist constructors.

Chapter 13

Active Filters

A frequency-selective filter is a circuit that will discriminate against certain frequencies or bands of frequencies. In other words, a filter circuit will pass some frequencies and reject others. Passive filters are made of combinations of passive components such as resistors (R), capacitors (C), and inductors (L). An active filter is one based on an active device such as an operational amplifier along with passive components. In most cases, the passive components are resistors and capacitors (although a few with inductors are known).

The topic of active filters is too complex for comprehensive coverage in a single chapter, so we will just make a few observations that allow you to build practical circuits. If you want a more comprehensive treatment, then see the references given at the end of the chapter.

Filter Characteristics

Filters of all types can be divided into categories based on the passbands. Fig. 13-1 shows several popular combinations. In Fig. 13-1A we see the low-pass filter. This type of filter passes all frequencies below a certain critical frequency (F_c). The breakpoint between the passband and the stopband is the point at which the gain of the circuit has dropped off -3 dB from its lower frequency value. Above the critical frequency the gain falls off at a certain slope. The steepness of the slope is usually given in terms of dB of gain per octave of frequency (an octave is a 2:1 change in frequency); alternatively, dB/decade (a decade is a 10:1 change in frequency) is sometimes used.

The high-pass filter frequency response is shown in Fig. 13-1B. In this case, the filter circuit will pass all frequencies above the critical frequency (F_c) and reject frequencies below that point. The high-pass filter is the inverse of the low-pass filter.

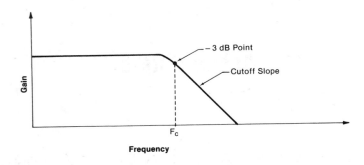

(A) *Low-pass filter.*

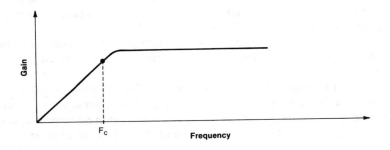

(B) *High-pass filter.*

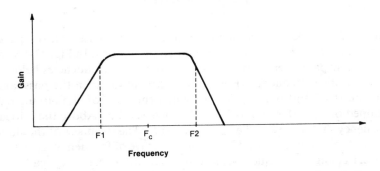

(C) *Bandpass filter.*

Fig. 13-1. Filter frequency-response characteristics.

A bandpass filter is one that combines both high-pass and low-pass concepts (Fig. 13-1C). In this case, the filter rejects all frequencies below F1, and above F2. These frequencies are the upper and lower −3 dB points in the response; gain is compared with the midband frequency, F_c. The bandwidth of the bandpass filter is the difference of F2−F1. The response in Fig. 13-1C is a relatively low-Q type because it has a wide bandwidth. A higher-Q circuit has a narrower bandpass, as in Fig. 13-1D; it admits a smaller range of acceptable frequencies.

A notch filter, also called a stop-band filter, will pass all frequencies except for those clustered around a critical frequency (see Fig. 13-1E). The notch filter is used to take out a single unwanted frequency. A common use for notch filters is to remove 60-Hz interference signals from

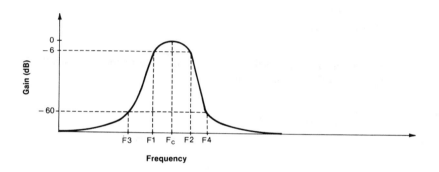

(D) *Narrow bandpass filter.*

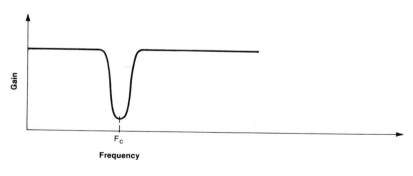

(E) *Notch filter.*

Fig. 13-1—cont. Filter frequency-response characteristics.

electronic instruments. Amateur radio operators sometimes use a notch filter on CW (Morse code) to notch out nearby interfering signals. In this application, the operator tunes the receiver to make the desired signal have a tone of, say, 400 Hz. Interfering signals further away, near 1000 Hz, for example, can be reduced in amplitude with a notch filter. An example of a 1000-Hz notch filter circuit based on a CA3080 OTA is shown in Fig. 13-2. If you desire a 60-Hz notch, then replace the resistors and capacitors with values determined from:

$$F = \frac{1,000,000}{2\pi RC} \qquad \textit{[Eq. 13-1]}$$

where
F is the frequency in hertz (Hz),
R is in ohms,
C is in microfarads

For the 60-Hz model, select a capacitor value in the 0.008-to 0.05-μF range (0.01 μF is a good choice).

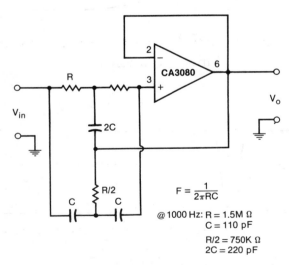

Fig. 13-2. Notch-filter circuit.

High-Pass/Low-Pass Designs

Very simple active filters are shown in Fig. 13-3; a low-pass type is shown in Fig. 13-3A, and a high-pass in Fig. 13-3B. These designs are really

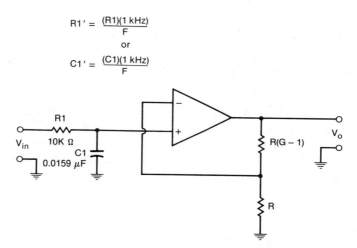

(A) *A 1-kHz normalized low-pass filter.*

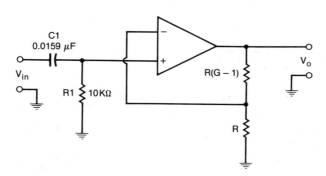

(B) *A 1-kHz normalized high-pass filter.*

Fig. 13-3. Simple active filters.

little more than buffered versions of simple RC passive filters. The values shown in Fig. 13-3 are normalized for 1 kHz. We can find the actual required values (R1′ and C1′) by dividing the strawman values shown by the desired cut-off frequency in kilohertz. For example, suppose we want to change the frequency to 60 Hz (i.e., 0.06 kHz):

$$C1' = \frac{(C1)(1 \text{ kHz})}{F}$$

$$C1' = \frac{(0.0159 \ \mu F)(1 \text{ kHz})}{0.06}$$

$$C1' = 0.265 \ \mu F$$

We must leave one of the values alone, and calculate the other. In the example above, 0.265 μF is not a standard value, but 0.22 and 0.27 μF are standards. Select samples of these for tolerance differences as close as possible to 0.265 μF. Custom selection of capacitors formerly was not too easy, but many modern, low-cost digital multimeters now come equipped with digital capacitor meter functions.

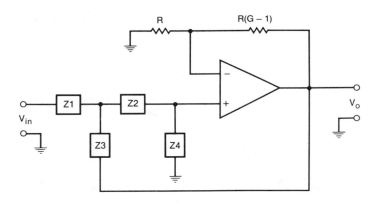

Fig. 13-4. Active filter equivalent circuit model.

A model for the simplistic design of high-pass and low-pass filters is shown in Fig. 13-4. In this generalized case, we have a series of four reactances, labeled Z1 through Z4. These components are replaced with either resistances or capacitances. Examples are shown in Figs.

13-5 (low-pass) and 13-6 (high-pass). Again, the values are normalized for 1 kHz, and we can select actual values using the equations shown.

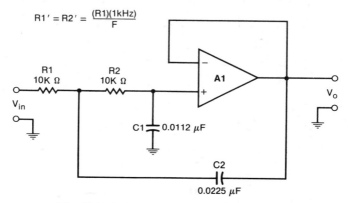

Fig. 13-5. A 1-kHz normalized low-pass filter.

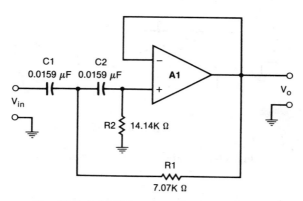

Fig. 13-6. A 1-kHz normalized high-pass filter.

A different form of active filter, the multiple feedback path circuit, is shown in Fig. 13-7. The low-pass version is shown in Fig. 13-7A, and the high-pass in Fig. 13-7B. The values are normalized for 1 kHz, and we find the actual values in the manner described above. Change either the capacitor or the resistor values, but not both. A practical circuit of a multiple function filter is shown in Fig. 13-8. This circuit is set for 1 kHz, and provides both low-pass and bandpass functions.

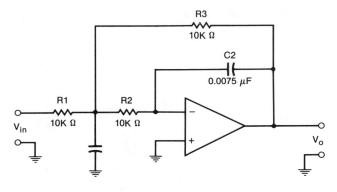

(A) *Low-pass type.*

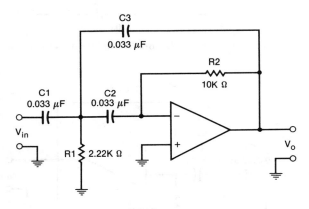

(B) *High-pass type.*

Fig. 13-7. Multiple feedback path active filter.

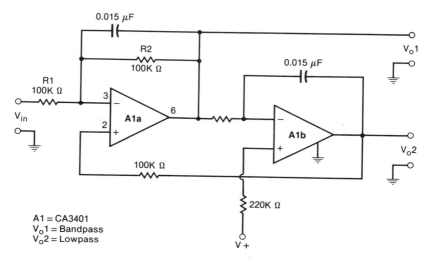

Fig. 13-8. A 1-kHz low-pass/bandpass filter.

For Further Reading

Howard M. Berlin, *Design of Active Filters, With Experiments*, Howard W. Sams & Co.

Donald Lancaster, *Active-Filter Cookbook*, Howard W. Sams & Co.

Frank P. Tedeschi, *The Active Filter Handbook*, Tab Books.

Chapter 14

Digital Electronics: An Introduction for Hobbyists

Digital electronics became easily accessible to all electronics hobbyists with the introduction of integrated circuit logic elements. Prior to IC digital devices becoming available, digital electronics was limited by the nature of the discrete circuits used. The same benefits accorded analog electronics are also available to digital circuits. In fact, the digital circuit fares somewhat better because the devices are available in "families" of devices.

Digital logic families are devices using the same technology and same general circuit elements, designed so that it is easy to interface them using only electrical conductors (e.g., wires and printed-circuit tracks). The interfacing chore is thus eliminated, because we don't need to worry about matching signal levels and impedance values. The two digital logic families that we will consider here are the transistor transistor logic (TTL) and complementary metal oxide semiconductor (CMOS) devices. The TTL devices are based on NPN/PNP bipolar transistors, while the CMOS devices are based on metal oxide semiconductor field effect transistors (MOSFETs). We will discuss these families in greater detail in Chapters 15 and 16. In this chapter we will discuss common logic elements.

How Digital Is Different from Analog

Digital electronics differs from analog electronics in the nature of the signals processed in digital circuits. In analog circuits, the values of the signal can be anything within a certain range. For example, suppose we have an operational amplifier connected as an analog amplifier (as were most of those in this book). Further suppose that the output voltage can swing from a minimum of -12 volts DC to $+12$ volts DC. In an analog circuit, the output voltage can take on any value between -12 volts and $+12$ volts; no values are "forbidden."

In digital circuits, on the other hand, the signals can take on only one of two permissible values—all other values are forbidden. Because only two values are permitted, we say these circuits are "binary" in nature. The two levels are called 1 and 0 (or logical 1 and logical 0), true and false, and high and low. In this book, we will use high and low to denote the different states, except for a few cases where 1 and 0 seem particularly appropriate.

Different families of digital IC devices use different voltage levels for high and low. For example, the TTL family uses +2.4 to +5 volts for high, and 0 volt to +0.8 volt for low. In the CMOS family, on the other hand, it is possible to use anything from 0 to −15 volts for low, and 0 to +15 volts for high. In general, one of two situations is standard in CMOS circuits. Either low is zero and high is +5 volts (when TTL compatibility is needed), or low is a minus voltage (e.g., −12) and high is the same value of positive voltage (e.g., +12).

The terms *positive logic* and *negative logic* sometimes confuse people who are just learning digital electronics. These terms designate relative high/low values. In positive logic systems, the high will be a positive voltage and low will be either 0 volts or a negative voltage. In negative logic systems, on the other hand, high will be a negative voltage while low will be either zero or a positive voltage.

Gates

The most basic digital elements are gates. All other digital elements can be formed from only three basic elements: the NOT gate, the AND gate, and the OR gate. Although these three are the most basic, we also include among basic elements the NOR, NAND, and XOR gates; but more of these in a moment.

Circuit Symbols

Figure 14-1 shows the basic circuit symbols used in digital electronics. The NOT gate, also called an inverter, is represented by a triangle on its side with a circle at the output apex (Fig. 14-1A). The circle used on a lead in any digital electronics circuit diagram indicates inverter action. For example, The standard AND gate (Fig. 14-1B) becomes a NAND gate by inverting its output (Fig. 14-1C). The circuit symbols of Fig. 14-1 are used throughout the rest of this chapter.

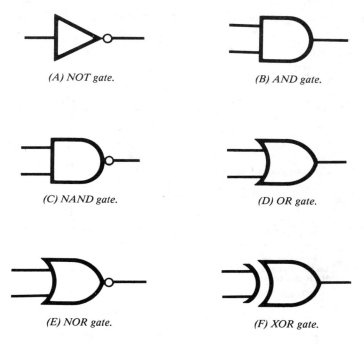

(A) NOT gate.

(B) AND gate.

(C) NAND gate.

(D) OR gate.

(E) NOR gate.

(F) XOR gate.

Fig. 14-1. Symbols used for digital gates.

In the gate descriptions below the rules of operation will be given in four forms. First, we will show you an equivalent switch circuit that operates a lamp. Second, we will describe the action in the text. Third, there will be a truth table (in which 1 = high and 0 = low). Finally, there will be a wave train example. You might want to examine the wave-train examples in order to gain insight on how these gates work in dynamic circuits.

Inverters (NOT gates)

The NOT gate is also called the "inverter." It gets its name from the fact that it produces an output that is opposite of the input level. The usual circuit symbol for the inverter is shown in Fig. 14-2A, while an equivalent circuit is shown in Fig. 14-2B. The rules of operation for inverters are simple: a low input produces a high output, and a high input produces a low output. This circuit action is reflected by the truth table in Fig. 14-2C, and the sample waveform in Fig. 14-2D. In this case, the input is A, while the output is called "NOT-A" (A with an overbar). Every time the input goes high, the output drops low (and vice versa).

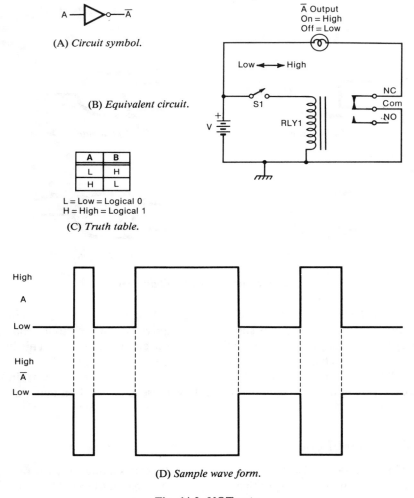

(A) *Circuit symbol.*

(B) *Equivalent circuit.*

A	B
L	H
H	L

L = Low = Logical 0
H = High = Logical 1

(C) *Truth table.*

(D) *Sample wave form.*

Fig. 14-2. NOT gate.

We can sometimes get better insight into a circuit's behavior by looking at the equivalent circuit model. In Fig. 14-2B we saw a simple DC circuit representing the inverter. This circuit is based on the electromechanical relay (RLY1) as the active device, and a switch (S1) as the input device. When S1 is open the input is low, and when S1 is closed the input is high. The output is the lamp, which is on for output = high, and off for output = low. The lamp turns on when the common contact is connected to the normally closed (NC) contact. When the input is low, i.e., switch S1 open, the relay is deenergized so the normally closed contact is connected to the common—the light is on, so the output is high (in other words, a low input produced a high output). But when the input is high (S1 closed), the relay is energized, so the lamp is disconnected, and thus turned off (low)—a high input produces a low output.

OR Gates

An OR gate (Fig. 14-3A) produces a high output if either input is high; in other words, if "A" and "B" are inputs, then the output is high if either A OR B = high, or if both are simultaneously high. Fig. 14-3B shows a simple equivalent circuit of the OR gate. The lamp (output) is on (high) if either switch A OR switch B is high. A truth table is shown in Fig. 14-3C, which can be summarized in the following set of rules:

1. The output is low if, and only if, all inputs are also low.
2. A high on any input produces a high output.

The circuit action of these rules is shown in a practical form by Fig. 14-3D. In this case, both inputs receive a pulse train, and the output reflects the operation of the gate in response to these input levels.

NOR Gates

The NOR gate is a derivative gate made from combining an OR gate with an inverter (note the circle on the output terminal in Fig. 14-4A, and the inset equivalent digital circuit), so it might be called a NOT-OR gate, or NOR. The NOR gate produces a low output if any input is high.

An equivalent switch circuit is shown in Fig. 14-4B. As long as both switches are open, the lamp is on, but if either switch is closed the lamp turns off. The truth table for this type of circuit is shown in Fig. 14-4C, which can be summarized by the following rules:

1. The output is high if, and only if, both inputs are low.
2. The output is low if any input is high.

As in the case of the OR gate, these rules for the NOR gate are represented in practical form in Fig. 14-4D.

AND Gates

The AND gate (Fig. 14-5A) is the inverse of the OR gate. In other words, it produces a high output if, and only if, both inputs are high. The equivalent switch circuit is shown in Fig. 14-5B. Here we can see that the lamp is turned on only if both switch A and switch B are closed. The truth table rules of Fig. 14-5C can be summarized as follows:

1. The output will be low if either input is low.
2. The output will be high only if all inputs are high.

These rules are summarized for dynamic circuits in Fig. 14-5D.

(A) *Symbol.*

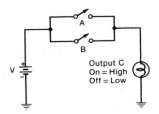

(B) *Equivalent circuit.*

Input A	Input B	Output C
0	0	0
0	1	1
1	0	1
1	1	1

(C) *Truth table.*

Fig. 14-3. OR gate.

NAND Gates

The NAND gate is another derivative gate made from combining an AND gate with an inverter (see Fig. 14-6A). The rules of operation of the NAND gate tell us that the output will be high if either input is low. An equivalent circuit is shown in Fig. 14-6B; if either switch is open the lamp is turned on, and will only go off if both switches are closed. The rules of operation are given in the truth table in Fig. 14-6C, and are summarized below:

1. The output is high if any input is low.
2. The output is low only if all inputs are high.

As in our previous cases, the dynamic application of these rules is given in Fig. 14-6D.

XOR Gates

The last form of basic gate that we will consider here is the Exclusive-OR (XOR). This gate (Fig. 14-7A) is a little unusual, and that fact ac-

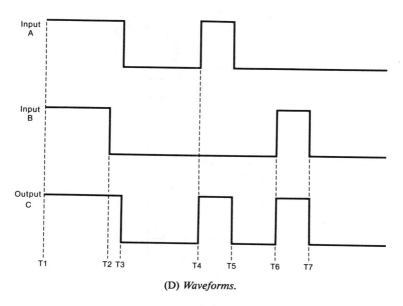

(D) *Waveforms.*

Fig. 14-3—cont. OR gate.

counts for a lot of different applications. The XOR gate will produce a high output as long as the inputs are at different levels, otherwise the output is low. An equivalent circuit is shown in Fig. 14-7B. This switch-

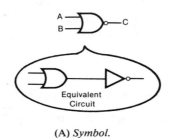

(A) *Symbol.*

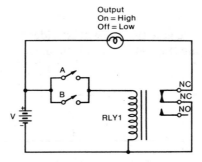

(B) *Equivalent switch circuit.*

Input A	Input B	Output C
0	0	1
0	1	0
1	0	0
1	1	0

(C) *Truth table.*

Fig. 14-4. NOR gate.

ing circuit uses two SPDT switches cross-connected in the manner shown. The truth table (Fig. 14-7C) reveals an interesting behavior:

1. If both inputs are low, then the output is low.
2. If both inputs are high, then the output is low.
3. If one input is high, and the other is low, then the output is high.

In other words, a low output occurs anytime that both inputs are at the same level (regardless of whether high or low). This behavior is summarized in a dynamic situation in Fig. 14-7D.

Some Interesting Combination Tricks

Many different digital IC devices have several functional blocks. For example, the hex inverter contains six inverters; the quad NAND gate (e.g., 7400) contains four two-input NAND gates, and so forth. There

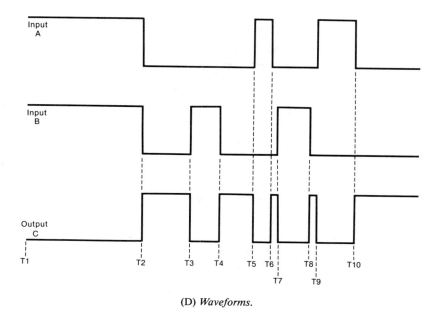

(D) *Waveforms.*

Fig. 14-4—cont. NOR gate.

are a number of other examples, including all forms of gates, flip-flops, and so forth. There are cases where you will only use a single element on a chip, leaving the others wasted and unused, or if you are clever, used in a neat manner.

An example of using other elements as something they are not is shown in Fig. 14-8. Shown here are two NAND-gate and two NOR-gate examples of making an inverter from a spare gate. Both the NOR gate and the NAND gate can be made into an inverter simply by connecting the two inputs together. The NOR gate can also be made into an inverter by grounding one input, and using the other as the inverter input. Alternatively, the NAND gate is an inverter if one input is tied permanently high. These connections are examples of making an inverter from unused gates. I used one of these methods (C in Fig. 14-8) to make a surplus computer keyboard work on my Digital Group computer. My computer wanted to see a positive strobe pulse at bit 8, while the surplus

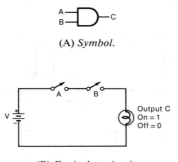

(A) *Symbol.*

(B) *Equivalent circuit.*

Input A	Input B	Output C
0	0	0
0	1	0
1	0	0
1	1	1

(C) *Truth table.*

Fig. 14-5. AND gate.

keyboard used a nonstandard negative-going TTL pulse for that purpose. There was a 7400 quad NAND gate on the printed wiring board (of the keyboard) with one "free" section, so I cut the strobe line, and jumpered it through the unused section of the 7400. The result was a TTL positive-going strobe signal that was usable by my Z80 Digital Group machine.

Figure 14-9 shows how to use unused sections of an open-collector hex inverter as a NOR gate. Simply connect all output lines together and use a common pull-up resistor. In this way, you not only get around the use of another chip where only a single gate is needed (and hex inverters are available), but you also have the ability to make "oddball" NOR gates with up to six or twelve inputs.

Flip-Flops

A flip-flop is a one-bit memory device, although it is rarely thought of as such in this day of 256K memory chips. But flip-flops are still commonly used in digital electronics for various applications that have little or nothing to do with computers. In this section we will discuss some of the more common flip-flops that can be made from gates.

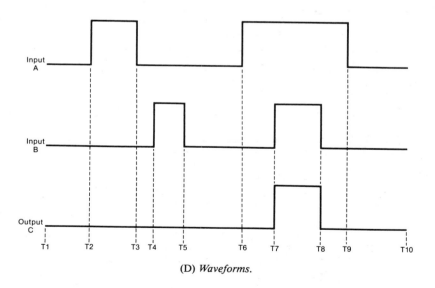

(D) *Waveforms.*

Fig. 14-5—cont. AND gate.

R-S Flip-Flops

The R-S, or reset-set, flip-flop is a circuit that has two inputs. When the reset input is made active, the Q output is forced low (and if a NOT-Q output is available, it is forced high). The set input has just the opposite effect—an active input signal forces the Q output high and the NOT-Q output low. Fig. 14-10 shows some of the common symbols used in circuit diagrams to represent R-S flip-flops. There are two forms of R-S flip-flop—NOR logic (Fig. 14-11) and NAND logic (Fig. 14-12).

The NOR logic flip-flop circuit is shown in Fig. 14-11A, while the truth table is shown in Fig. 14-11B. The NOR logic circuit uses active-

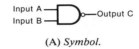

(A) *Symbol.*

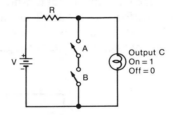

(B) *Equivalent circuit.*

Input A	Input B	Output C
0	0	1
0	1	1
1	0	1
1	1	0

(C) *Truth table.*

Fig. 14-6. NAND gate.

high inputs. In other words, a low on both inputs at the same time will result in no output change. But if either input is made high while the other is low, then the result will be an output state that depends upon whether the set or reset input was made active. The condition of both inputs being simultaneously high is disallowed because results are unpredictable.

The NAND logic circuit (Fig. 14-12A) uses two-input NAND gates instead of NOR gates to form the flip-flop. The NAND gates are of opposite type from the NOR, so we can expect opposite activity—the inputs are active-low instead of active-high. In other words, applying a high to either input (if the other is low) results in an output state consistent with the input selected (Fig. 14-12B). Similarly, applying a high to both inputs at the same time results in no change at all, while a pair of lows is the disallowed state.

Clocked R-S Flip-Flops

One of the problems inherent in the design of the R-S flip-flop is that ambiguity in the arrival of input pulses, and noise on the line, can affect

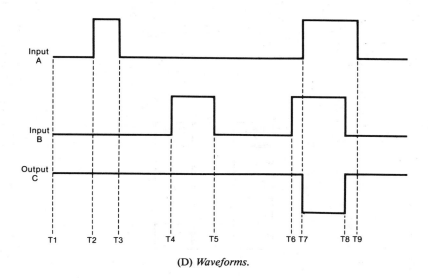

(D) *Waveforms.*

Fig. 14-6—cont. NAND gate.

the operation of the circuit. Also, the R-S flip-flop is asynchronous. In other words, it is not time-dependent and will operate whenever a valid input is applied. A solution to these kinds of problems is the clocked R-S flip-flop circuit of Fig. 14-13.

Gates G3/G4 form a NAND gate logic R-S flip-flop in the same manner as explained for Fig. 14-12A. The inputs of the G3/G4 flip-flop are controlled by the outputs of the other two NAND gates. As long as the clock input remains low, the outputs of both G1 and G2 are locked high, so the R-S flip-flop cannot operate. However, if clock goes high, then the inputs of the R-S flip-flop will respond to inputs applied to the set or reset inputs.

(A) *Symbol.*

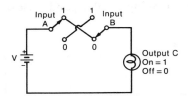

(B) *Equivalent circuit.*

Input A	Input B	Output C
0	0	0
0	1	1
1	0	1
1	1	0

(C) *Truth table.*

Fig. 14-7. Exclusive OR (XOR) gate.

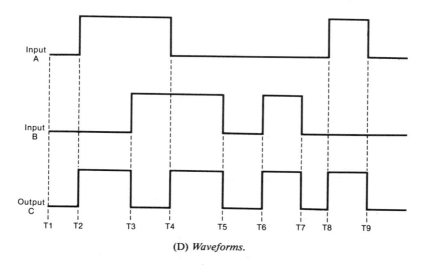

(D) *Waveforms.*

Fig. 14-7—cont. Exclusive OR (XOR) gate.

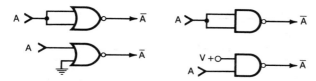

Fig. 14-8. Connecting gates as inverters.

Master-Slave Flip-Flop

The so-called master-slave flip-flop, also called the load-transfer flip-flop, is shown in Fig. 14-14. This circuit consists of two clocked RS flip-flops, designated FF1 and FF2. The circuit is configured such that the outputs of FF1 drive the inputs of FF2. The clock lines of FF1 and FF2 are driven output of phase from a common clock line, now called the load-transfer input.

If the load-transfer line is high, then the clock of FF1 is low and that of FF2 is high. Under this condition, FF2 is active and FF1 is inactive. Whatever levels appear on the outputs of FF1 are automatically transferred to the outputs of FF2 by virtue of Clk2 being high. But when the load-transfer line goes low, FF2 is disabled (but it's outputs

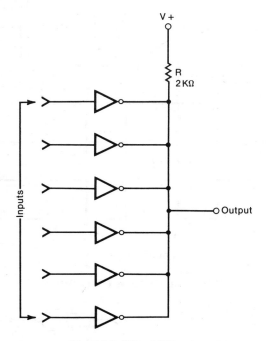

Fig. 14-9. Wired OR gate.

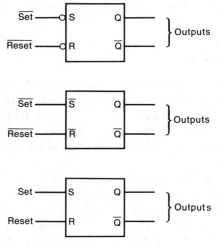

Fig. 14-10. R-S flip-flop symbol.

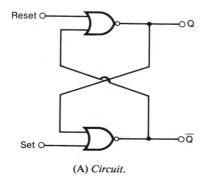

(A) *Circuit.*

Set Input	Reset Input	Q Output	Q̄ Output
0	0	(No Change)	
0	1	0	1
1	0	1	0
1	1	(Disallowed)	

1 = High
0 = Low

(B) *Truth table.*

Fig. 14-11. NOR logic R-S flip-flop.

remain the same), and FF1 is enabled. Any changes on the S and R inputs are reflected on the Q1/NOT-Q1 outputs of FF1. When the load-transfer line goes high gain, these new levels are transferred to the outputs of FF2. The master-slave flip-flop is used where noise or synchronization a problem.

In some flip-flops we see a difference between various types of clock triggering. Figs. 14-15 and 14-16 show the difference between positive and negative edge and level triggering. In level triggering (Fig. 14-15), the circuit action happens when the level is either high (positive-level triggering) or low (negative-level triggering). Edge triggering (Fig. 14-16) occurs when the input signal is in transition from either low-to-high (positive edge), or high-to-low (negative edge).

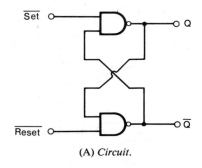

(A) *Circuit.*

Set Input	Reset Input	Q Output	Q̄ Output
0	0	(Disallowed)	
0	1	1	0
1	0	0	1
1	1	(No Change)	

(B) *Truth table.*

Fig. 14-12. NAND logic R-S flip-flop.

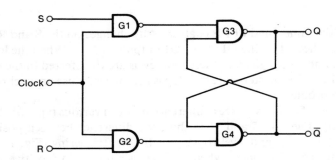

Fig. 14-13. Clocked R-S flip-flop.

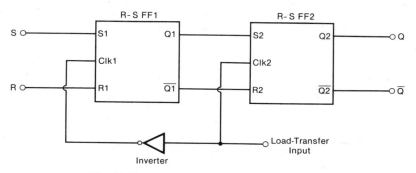

Fig. 14-14. Master-slave (load-transfer) flip-flop.

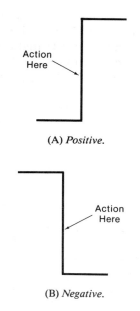

(A) *Positive.*

(B) *Negative.*

Fig. 14-15. Level triggering.

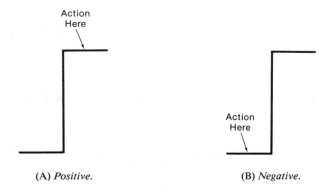

(A) *Positive.*   (B) *Negative.*

Fig. 14-16. Edge triggering

Coming Next

Our discussion of digital electronics continues for the next three chapters. In Chapter 15 we will deal with TTL devices and circuits; in Chapter 16 CMOS is covered; in Chapter 17 digital-device interfacing is covered. Readers are also directed to two other Sams' books: *TTL Cookbook* and *CMOS Cookbook* for details about the operation of specific TTL and CMOS devices.

TTL IC Devices

Of all the IC digital logic families that have appeared on the market over the past 20 years or so, the transistor-transistor logic (TTL, or T²L) is probably the most successful. Although the CMOS family has taken over many applications, TTL is nonetheless still very popular. The TTL devices require more current than CMOS, but also operate at very much faster speeds. Although most TTL devices operate in the 18–25-MHz region, special types are available to speeds of 80 MHz. TTL devices are designated by type numbers in the 74xx and 74xxx series (54xx and 54xxx devices are merely military grade TTL devices). For example, a 7402 is a quad two-input NOR gate. The principal difference between the 54-series and 74-series is the temperature range. The 74-series are commercial grade, and are designed to operate over the range 0 to +70 degrees Celcius; 54-series operate over −55 to +125 degrees Celcius.

Fig. 15-1 shows the operating regions for logic levels and operating potentials. The DC power supply must be +4.7 to +5.2 volts, and must be regulated. Although these "official" limits are well-publicized, it is not recommended to try to operate close to the edges of the range. For example, at +5.2 volts DC the reliability of devices may be compromised. At the other end of the range, +4.7 volts, some complex function devices may become erratic in their operation. As a result, it is probably best to keep the DC power supply in the +4.9 to +5.05 volts range all of the time. In Chapter 19 you will find a DC power supply that will power TTL projects.

The logic levels for TTL are as follows:

high (logical 1): +2.4 volts to +5 volts

low (logical 0): 0 to +0.8 volt

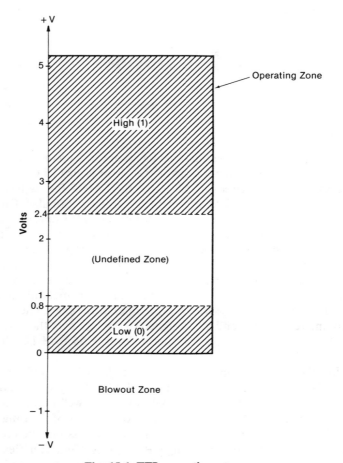

Fig. 15-1. TTL operating zones.

TTL Output Circuits

The output circuit for a TTL device forms a current sink. That is, the output will accept a current from a TTL input (a current source) and route it to ground. Fig. 15-2 shows two popular forms of TTL output. In Fig. 15-2A we see the regular TTL output. This is the approximate circuit in almost all TTL devices. Transistors Q1 and Q2 are an identical pair, and form a *totem-pole* circuit; Q1 is a current regulator, Q2 is the

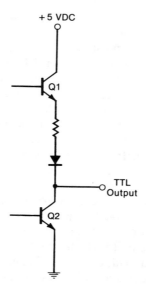

(A) *Regular output.*

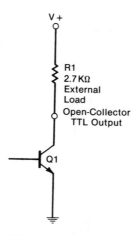

(B) *Open-collector output.*

Fig. 15-2. Forms of TTL output.

output switch. The series diode prevents current flow in the wrong direction. When the output is high, transistor Q2 is turned off, so the current from the next stage is not able to find a path to ground. But when the output is low, transistor Q2 is biased hard on (it is in saturation) so the output terminal is grounded.

Fig. 15-2B shows an open-collector TTL output. In this circuit, there is no current regulator circuit, and that function is taken over by an external pull-up resistor (R1). Depending upon the type of open-collector device, the V+ voltage can be either +5 volts, or anything up to either +15 or +30 volts (see the specifications sheets in Don Lancaster's classic work, *TTL Cookbook*). Open-collector inverters can be used for interfacing to other logic families, other digital devices, or nondigital output devices (relays, LEDs, lamps, etc.). Most open-collector devices are hex inverters.

The TTL output is rated according to the number of standard, 1.8-mA, TTL inputs it will drive. This number is called the *fan-out* of the device. Thus, a fan-out of ten (the usual number for standard devices) means that it will drive up to ten standard TTL inputs. The standard TTL input represents a load, or *fan-in* of one.

Fig. 15-3 shows the relationship between the TTL input and the re-

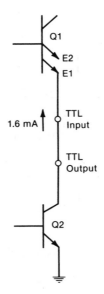

Fig. 15-3. TTL-to-TTL interfacing.

lated output. The input may be a single emitter, as in the case of an inverter, or a multiple emitter; the inputs shown are a dual input as might be found on a 7400 two-input NAND gate, or 7402 two-input NOR gate. The TTL input is a current source, where the TTL output is a current sink.

Power Supply Decoupling

There are several general rules for placing power supply bypassing capacitors in TTL circuits. One of two protocols is generally used:

1. A single 0.001-μF capacitor at each TTL package, or
2. A single 0.01- to 0.1-μF capacitor every second or third device, or every three inches, whichever is closest spaced.

In addition, it is advisable on large projects to place a 50-μF to 200-μF capacitor at the power supply connection for the printed wiring board, and a 4.7-μF unit every 10 to 12 inches along the +5 volt bus (Fig. 15-4).

If you build a really large project, one that draws 4 to 10 amperes from the +5 volt line, you might want to consider one of two power supply schemes. The first type uses a voltage regulator with a *sense* line. This type of DC power supply has a reference voltage sensing line that is connected at the point where you want the voltage to be +5 volts. The DC resistance of the power supply bus causes a voltage drop that can hurt the operation of the circuits. The second type uses distributed regulation. In

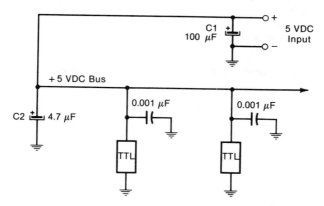

Fig. 15-4. TTL power supply decoupling.

this scheme, the main DC power bus is +8 volts, then each printed wiring board, or several sections of the same board, has its own three-terminal IC voltage regulator. The S-100 microcomputer (the original microcomputer) used this system. Each S-100 plug-in card had one to five 7805, LM340T-05, LM340K-05, or LM309 voltage regulators.

TTL Subfamilies

The overall class of devices called TTL is divided into several subfamilies that are tailored to specified types of applications by differences in operating power, speed, and propagation delay. The ordinary TTL device is called regular TTL, and is typified by power consumptions of about 10 milliwatts per gate, and operates to speeds in the 25–35-MHz region. Propagation delay is on the order of 10 nanoseconds. The other TTL subfamilies include: low-power TTL, high-power TTL, Schottky TTL and low-power Schottky TTL. The type numbers for these devices are modified as follows:

Series	Typical Type Number
Regular TTL	74xx/74xxx
Low-power TTL	74Lxx/74Lxxx
High-power TTL	74Hxx/74Hxxx
Schottky TTL	74Sxx/74Sxxx
Low-power Schottky TTL	74LSxx/74LSx

The operating speeds of the subfamilies are radically different from each other. Typically, 74xx devices operate to 25–35 MHz (with some older samples being limited to 18 MHz); 74Lxx operates to 3 MHz; 74Hxx operates to 50 MHz; 74Sxx operate to 125 MHz; and 74LSxx devices operate to 45 MHz.

The output (fan-out) and input (fan-in) requirements also differ between the families:

Series	Output Sinks (mA)	Input Sources (mA)
74xx	16	1.6
74Lxx	3.6	0.18
74Hxx	20	2.0
74Sxx	20	2.0
74LSxx	8	0.4

Table 15-1 shows how many of which kind of inputs each subfamily drives.

Table 15-1. Subfamily input drives

These Outputs Drive	This Many Inputs				
	74xx	74Lxx	74Hxx	74Sxx	74LSxx
74xx	10	40	6	6	20
74Lxx	2	10	1	1	5
74Hxx	12	40	10	10	40
74Sxx	12	40	10	10	40
74LSxx	5	20	4	4	10

Chapter 16

CMOS IC Devices

Complementary metal oxide semiconductor (CMOS) digital ICs are well known and very available. Found under the "4xxx" series of type numbers (e.g., 4017), the CMOS devices offer extremely low current drain, moderate operating speeds, and low cost. Because of the low current requirements (on the order of a few microamperes), CMOS technology has made possible a wide range of portable products from digital watches, to calculators, to lap-top microcomputers. Because of their properties, CMOS devices also make very useful sensing circuits for a variety of applications that are not always associated with digital electronics. But before getting into the various circuits, let's review the basics of CMOS digital IC devices.

CMOS Digital IC Devices

The basis of the CMOS line of digital ICs is the MOSFET transistor. This device offers an extremely high input impedance by virtue of the fact that the control gate input is isolated from the channel by a layer of insulation (see Fig. 16-1A). There are two polarities of MOSFET transistor, which are determined by the type of semiconductor material used in the channel structure. If N-type material is used, then the MOSFET is an N-channel, while if P-type semiconductor material is used, it is a P-channel MOSFET.

In digital circuits, the MOSFET will be in either of two conditions. When a bias is applied to the gate, the channel resistance is very high (megohms). On the other hand, no bias causes the channel resistance to be very low (200 to 300 kilohms). Although studying MOSFET transistors properly will reveal that this explanation is both not very inclusive of all possible types and somewhat simplified, it will do for the following presentation.

It is useful when examining any digital logic elements to consider

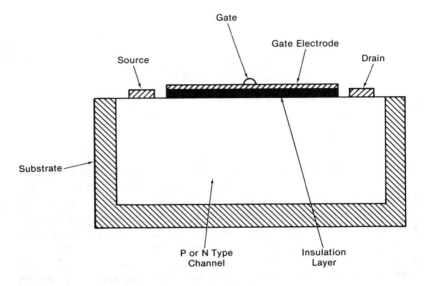

(A) *MOSFET transistor.*

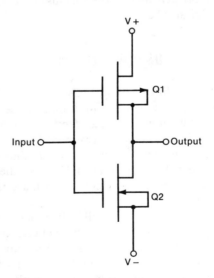

(B) *CMOS inverter.*

Fig. 16-1. Basis of CMOS digital ICs.

the case of the inverter as representative of the whole class. In Fig. 16-1B we see the circuit of a CMOS inverter. This circuit consists of an N-type MOSFET and a P-type MOSFET connected with their respective gates in parallel and their channels in series. The input of the inverter is the gate, while the output is the junction between the P-channel drain (Q2) and the N-channel source (Q1).

There are two DC power supplies shown here: V+ and V−. These voltages are typically −4.5 and +4.5 to −15 and +15 volts DC. In some cases, the V− supply is set to zero, so the V− terminal of the device will be simply grounded.

Because the P- and N-channel MOSFETs are of opposite polarity with respect to each other, one will have a high channel resistance while the other will have a low resistance. The two channels are connected in series, so the overall channel resistance (as measured from V+ terminal to V− terminal) is very high. This resistance is the reason why the CMOS device draws such low current—the power supply sees a resistance in the megohm range. The only time when the CMOS device draws appreciable current is during output transition from high-to-low or low-to-high. At that brief instant, both channel resistances are in a transition region between high and low resistance values.

Fig. 16-2 shows the channel resistance relationship graphically. In both cases (Figs. 16-2A and 16-2B), the total resistance (R1 + R2) is the same even though the relationship of R1 and R2 changes. In Fig. 16-2A we see the situation where the input of the CMOS inverter (Fig. 16-1B) is high. In this case, the resistance of Q1 (i.e., R1) is high, and that of Q2 is low. Thus, the output line is connected through a low resistance to V−. In Fig. 16-2B we see the situation where the input is low. Here, the relationship of R1 and R2 is reversed. In this case, R2 is the high value while R1 is the low value. Therefore, we can see that the output terminal is connected to the V+ supply through a low resistance.

The definition of logical-high and logical-low states is determined by the voltages used. If two potentials are used, then V− is low, and V+ is high. But if the V− is set to zero, then logical-low is zero (grounded), while the logical-high remains at V+. The transition point between high and low (or vice versa) occurs when the input is at a potential halfway between V+ and V−, or, when V− is zero volts, one-half V+.

Electrostatic Discharge (ESD) Damage

The insulated gate of a MOSFET transistor is very thin. The ability to withstand high voltages is directly proportional to the thickness (for any

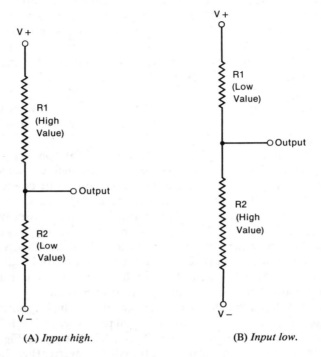

(A) *Input high.*   (B) *Input low.*

Fig. 16-2. Equivalent CMOS inverter circuit.

given material), and with such a thin layer MOSFETs can only handle 50 to 150 volts (80 volts is very common). Greater potentials will pop through the gate insulation, and destroy the device. Potentials up to several kilovolts can be found on the human body, tools, and other implements due to ordinary handling. If you don't believe me, then walk across an ESD-genic carpet on a dry winter day, and then touch a grounded object (ZAPPP!!!).

Unfortunately, the damage from ESD doesn't always take place immediately, but can show up as an unexplained spontaneous failure sometime later. The usual procedure for minimizing ESD damage is to always make sure that the pins are all at the same potential all of the time. This requirement usually means using a metal or carbonized foam working surface, and storing the devices in a conductive container (or on carbonized foam pads). It is also recommended that you discharge the potentials on your body by touching something grounded (but not in the presence of high voltage or AC!) immediately prior to touching the MOSFET or CMOS device. It is also a good idea to avoid handling the device at all unless absolutely necessary to do your work.

A-Series Versus B-Series CMOS

You will find two different types of CMOS device on the market—A-series and B-series chips. The older of the two is the A-series, and these devices are designated either with an "A" suffix on the type number, or no suffix on the type number. For example, both "4013" and "4013A" designate an A-series type 4013 device. The B-series is newer, and some believe improved over the A-series. The B-series devices are always marked with a "B" suffix on the type number (e.g., 4013B).

There are several notable differences between A-series and B-series devices. Perhaps the most well known is the fact that B-series devices are somewhat protected from ESD damage by internal zener diodes to clamp or bypass the high voltage electrostatic potentials. Thus, you will get away safely with handling B-series devices more often than A-series. Note that the occurrences of ESD damage on B-series is not entirely eliminated, but it is very low compared with the A-series.

Another difference is the transition time of the output. Fig. 16-3 shows the transfer function of the two types of CMOS device. The B-series makes the transition more quickly, and thus creates a sharper, faster rise-time pulse. A final difference is that most B-series CMOS devices will drive a larger load than their A-series cousins. In one case, for example, the B-series will drive a load three times heavier than the equivalent A-series device can handle,

CMOS Inverters

Most of the circuits in this article are based on the inverter. There are several inverters in the CMOS line, or you can make an inverter from available NOR or NAND gates. Fig. 16-4 shows how to make an inverter from other logic elements. For both the NOR and NAND gates, connecting the inputs together will cause the element to work. Alternatively, we could make an inverter by grounding one input of a NOR gate, or connecting one input of a NAND gate high. Another alternative is to use a CMOS transistor array such as either the CD3600 device, or the 4017 device. For a potpourri of 4017 circuits, see *Radio-Electronics* for Sept., 1986.

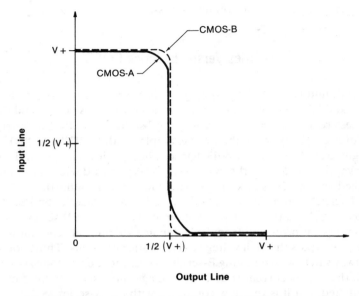

Fig. 16-3. Difference between CMOS-A and CMOS-B series.

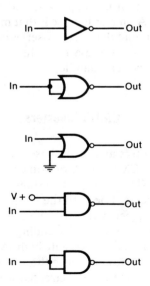

Fig. 16-4. Various inverter configurations.

Universal Sensor Circuit

Fig. 16-5 shows a circuit that can be used with any resistance sensor (e.g., thermistor, photoresistor, etc.). The circuit works on the basis of the ratio between R1 and R2. The voltage at the input of the CMOS inverter (point A in Fig. 16-5) is found from the ordinary voltage divider equation:

$$V_a = \frac{(R2)(V+)}{R1 + R2} \qquad \text{[Eq. 16-1]}$$

The output of the inverter will change state whenever V_a crosses the $(V+)/2$ point. Let's see how this circuit works by considering an example. Suppose we have a photoresistor ("photocell" that has a resistance of 10 kilohms when illuminated by room light, and 220 kilohms when darkened. Assuming the "strawman" value of 100 kilohms for R1 (as shown in Fig. 16-5A), we find values of Va as shown in Fig. 16-5B.

Dark: 0.7(V+), Light: 0.091(V+). Clearly, the dark value places the input in the logical-high region, so the output will be low (remember, the device is an inverter). Similarly, when the photoresistor is illuminated, the input of the inverter is nearly at ground potential (logical-low region) so the output is high. Thus, a low at the output tells the outside world that the photoresistor is in the dark, while a high output tells the opposite tale (photoresistor is in the light).

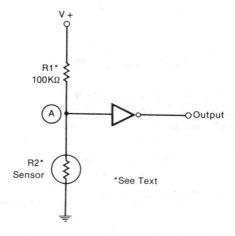

Fig. 16-5. CMOS sensor circuit (see text for sensor types).

We can reverse the operation of the circuit by making R1 the sensor, and R2 the fixed resistor. If the photoresistor is at R1, it will make the CMOS inverter input high when illuminated, and low when darkened.

You can make this circuit do your own job by selecting the most sensible position for the sensor, and by varying the value of the fixed resistor to make the inverter trip point correct for the application. You can also form a sensitivity control by connecting a potentiometer in the circuit at point "A" such that the wiper goes to the inverter input and the two ends are connected to R1 and R2, respectively.

Touch Plate Alarm Indicator

Fig. 16-6 shows a simple circuit that will change output state when a human finger touches the touch plate. Normally, the touch plate is open-circuited, so the inverter input is connected to ground (logical-low) through a 2.7-megohm resistor (R3). The output of the inverter is high under this condition. When a finger touches the touch plate, the resistance of the finger bridges across the gap on the touch plate and connects the V+ line to the inverter input through R1 and R2 (about 100 kilohms each). Thus, the CMOS inverter input goes high so the inverter output snaps low. A high output indicates no touch, a low output indicates that a touch exists.

The output indication of Fig. 16-6 persists only as long as the finger is touching the touch plate. If we want to latch it, then we can follow the inverter output with an RS flip-flop, or a type-D flip-flop.

Liquid-Level Detectors

A liquid-level detector is used to indicate (or sound the alarm) when the level of liquid reaches a certain point. These same circuits can be used to create an alarm for unattended places where water sometimes is, but shouldn't be. An example is a basement that occasionally floods. Another application, sent to me by a reader of another article, was in a fish tank water controller. The fellow had a small electrically operated valve that caused the tank to be "topped off" when evaporation caused the level to drop. Fig. 16-7 shows two basic forms of liquid-level detector circuit.

The version in Fig. 16-7A shows a method using a CMOS inverter and a pair of open electrodes. Normally, when the liquid is below the

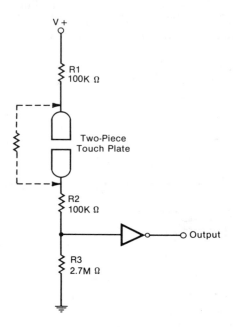

Fig. 16-6. CMOS touch-plate circuit.

critical level, the electrodes are open so the CMOS inverter input is connected to V+ through a 100-kilohm resistor (R1). Thus, the inverter input is high, and the output is low. But when liquid shorts out the electrodes, then the inverter input is grounded (logical-low) and that makes the output snap high.

The same idea is shown in Fig. 16-7B, but in this case the circuit is based on an RCA CA3140 BiMOS operational amplifier. The CA3140 uses MOSFET input transistors, so operates much like CMOS ICs. The circuit configuration is that of an inverting follower with a gain of 120 (12 megohm/100 kilohm). The sensor is the open electrodes as used previously, so when the liquid is below level the input is opened. This situation causes the output of the operational amplifier to see a positive input, so the output goes to V−, or what we will call logical low. But when the sensor is shorted out, the input of the operational amplifier is zero, so the output will be high. The actual output voltage is slightly positive, and is determined by the values of V+, and the two voltage-divider resistors (R3 and R4).

The type of sensor used in these circuits depends partially upon circuit usage, and partially upon materials available. I have used these circuits (or similar circuits) to make level detectors for medical researchers. Where nonchlorinated, nonsalted water was used, then al-

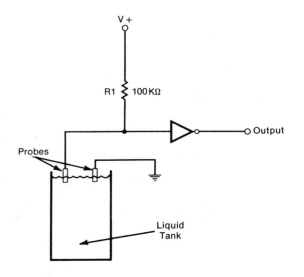

(A) *Electrodes type.*

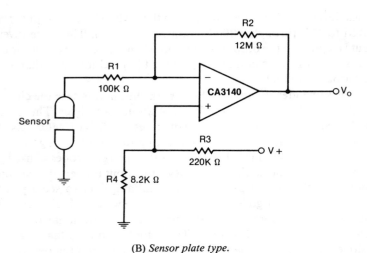

(B) *Sensor plate type.*

Fig. 16-7. Liquid-level alarm.

most any material could be used (copper wire or copper printed-circuit repair foil was popular). Alternatively, brass or aluminum nails or tacks and other similar objects can be used. In my medical electronics days we dealt with body fluids that corroded every common metal they touched, so we used platinum wire, gold wire, or a material called *vitalium* for electrodes. For most common applications, however, one need not appeal to noble or specially made proprietary metals. You can make an etched circuit board by making the grid pattern of Fig. 16-7C. You can make this pattern with a resist pen, or lay it with tape out if you are more picky about neatness.

Fig. 16-8 shows a multiple input liquid-level detector that can interface with a computer. Only six bits were used so that we could fit the circuit into a single hex inverter, or a pair of 4017 devices. Each probe represents a different level of liquid and is connected to a different inverter input. A low condition will exist on the output of each inverter until the liquid reaches its level, at which time the output goes high. A computer input port is connected to the B0 through B5 outputs. A short computer program can be written that tests all six bits for high or low, and indicate to the outside world (or control system) what level exists. In one case, a single probe was fashioned of wires of various lengths (each corresponding to a given level) and the whole bundle dropped into the tank.

Connections

(C) *Printed-grid type sensor.*

Fig. 16-7—cont. Liquid-level alarm.

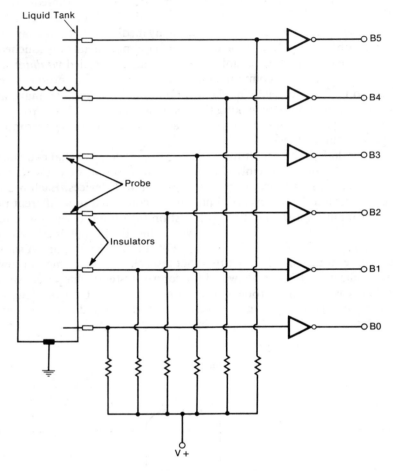

Fig. 16-8. Multiple-level liquid detector.

Touch Plate Pulse Generator

Fig. 16-9 shows a circuit that will produce a 60-Hz train of square waves at the output terminal whenever someone touches the touch plate on the input. Based on the usual CMOS inverter, this circuit responds to the signal injected into the input from the 60-Hz field surrounding the toucher's body. All electrified areas of the country are bathed in 60-Hz energy.

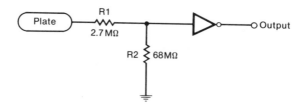

Fig. 16-9. Touch-plate circuit for 60-Hz output.

If you want proof of the 60-Hz field, simply touch the exposed input of an audio preamplifier while listening to the output. A loud hum is produced every time you touch that input. The signal is derived from minute electrical currents that flow in your body because of the 60-Hz magnetic fields produced by the local electrical wiring.

The CMOS inverter of Fig. 16-9 is not biased into linear operation, so the output will assume only one of the two permissible states (high or low) at a time. Thus, the output will snap back and forth at a 60-Hz rate in response to the 60-Hz nearly sine wave at the input.

Linear Operation of CMOS Devices

We can make the CMOS digital IC into a linear device by using appropriate biasing methods. Fig. 16-10 shows two examples of linear operation of a CMOS inverter.

The elementary bias method is shown in Fig. 16-10A. This circuit is quite simple, and consists of only a pair of coupling capacitors (one on input, one on output) and a feedback resistor between output and input. Some degree of control over linearity is possible by varying the 10-megohm value, but not much.

The circuit of Fig. 16-10B is an audio amplifier based on the CMOS transistor array, type 4017. The 4017 array consists of three independent N-channel/P-channel complementary pairs. In this project, we are using a single transistor of the 4017. The bias is derived in a similar manner from the output, but also from the V+ power supply.

The values of input and output capacitance for both circuits depends on the lower −3 dB frequency response desired. This capacitance is set according to the following expression if 10 megohms is used for the resistance seen by the input signal (as in Fig. 16-10):

$$C = \frac{0.1}{2\pi F}$$

[Eq. 16-2]

where

    C is the capacitance in microfarads,

    F is the -3 dB point in the desired frequency response, curve, in hertz

Conclusion

Although CMOS devices are normally thought of as "digital," their unique properties make them also useful in a lot of other applications. Understanding the properties of the CMOS device will allow you to make it work in other than normal circuits.

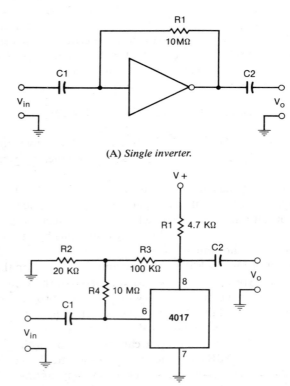

(A) *Single inverter.*

(B) *Using a 4017 device.*

Fig. 16-10. CMOS inverter in linear mode.

Chapter 17

Digital Device Interfacing

In this chapter we will deal primarily with two issues: (1) interfacing digital devices of different families, and (2) interfacing digital devices with "outside world" devices. The problem of interfacing different digital devices comes from the fact that different families use different technologies which are not compatible. For example, TTL and CMOS cannot easily be interfaced without additional components (except in limited cases). Among devices of the same family, interfacing consists of only electrical conductors, but when interfacing different families additional circuit strategies are needed.

TTL-to-CMOS Interfacing

The TTL family uses logic levels of 0 to 0.8 volt for low, and +2.4 to +5 volts for high. The TTL input acts as a 1.8-milliampere current source, while the TTL output is a current sink. (See Fig. 17-1 where Q1 is the TTL

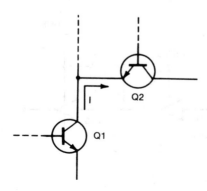

Fig. 17-1. TTL interfacing.

output, and Q2 is the TTL input.) Current flows from ground, through the emitter-collector path of Q1, to the emitter of Q2. As long as only TTL inputs are connected to the TTL output, there is no problem. But when non-TTL devices are connected to the TTL output, we must conspire to make it look like a current source to the TTL output.

Fig. 17-2 shows how to drive a CMOS input from a TTL output. In Fig. 17-2A we see the case for a CMOS device operated from the same +5 VDC power supply as the driving TTL device. In this case, there is a pull-up resistor between the +5 VDC line and the interface connection between the two devices. We want the TTL output to see about 1.8 mA, so for a +5 VDC power supply we use a 2.7-kilohm resistor to pull-up the output. The resistor (R1) acts as the current source required by the TTL output.

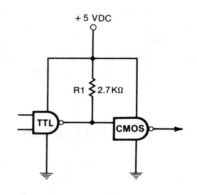

(A) +5 VDC circuit.

(B) Other circuits.

Fig. 17-2. TTL-to-CMOS interfacing.

A similar strategy is used in Fig. 17-2B, but with the exception that the CMOS chip may be powered from sources greater than +5 volts DC. The value of R1 is set to limit the current to a value acceptable to the output of the TTL device. With the 10-kilohm value shown, current will be limited to 1.2 mA in 12-volt circuits, and 1.5 mA in 15-volt circuits. For different values of V+, simply scale the resistance accordingly (keep the value of current—V+/R1—between 1 and 2.5 mA).

CMOS-to-TTL Interfacing

The CMOS output is a low resistance to either V− or ground (low), or V+ (high). In the low condition, when the CMOS device is operated from a single-polarity V+ power supply (in other words, V− is grounded), the CMOS output can act as the current sink required by the TTL input. Thus, some CMOS devices can be directly interfaced to TTL inputs. Fig. 17-3 shows several examples.

In Fig. 17-3A we see a special case for the 4049 and 4050 devices (hex inverter and hex buffer, respectively). These CMOS devices are called TTL-compatible when the 4049 or 4050 package is powered from +5 volts DC. (For the same chips operating at other voltages, this circuit won't work.) The 4049 and 4050 devices will drive two TTL loads—in other words, it has a fan-out of two. Also, when operated from +5 volts, the 4001 and 4002 CMOS devices will directly drive a single TTL input (Fig. 17-3B). Almost any CMOS device will drive a single 74Lxx or 74Sxx device (Fig. 17-3C).

A PMOS gate interfaced to a TTL input is shown in Fig. 17-3D. In this case, a current-limiting resistor is connected from the output of the PMOS device to the input of the TTL device. A 6800-kilohm pull-down resistor is connected to the −12 VDC power supply that serves the PMOS device.

Interfacing Light-Emitting Diodes

A light-emitting diode (LED) is a special PN diode that emits light when it is forward biased. LEDs are used for panel indicators, in sensor circuits, and in other applications. In this section we will learn how to interface LEDs to digital devices. It is possible to control the LED turn on/off operation with a digital logic signal.

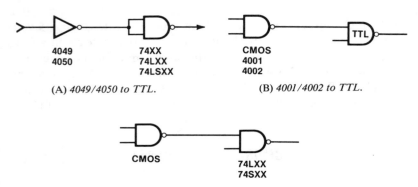

(A) 4049/4050 to TTL.

(B) 4001/4002 to TTL.

(C) Other CMOS to TTL 74L and 74S circuits.

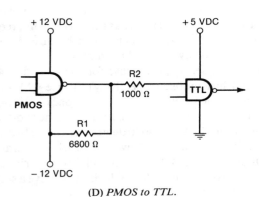

(D) PMOS to TTL.

Fig. 17-3. CMOS-to-TTL interfacing.

CMOS LED Driver

Fig. 17-4 shows a typical CMOS LED driver. Recall from earlier that a CMOS output is always a low resistance to either V+ or V− (or ground). In Fig. 17-4A we see the circuit for turning on an LED with a high input to the inverter (or other CMOS device—inverters are used as examples). When the input is high, then the output of the gate (G1) is low, so LED D1 finds a ground return path. With the output of G1 low, the cathode of the LED is grounded, so it is turned on. The 1000-ohm resistor is for current limiting.

A second circuit, shown in Fig. 17-4B, has just the opposite operation. The cathode of the LED is grounded, and the anode is connected to

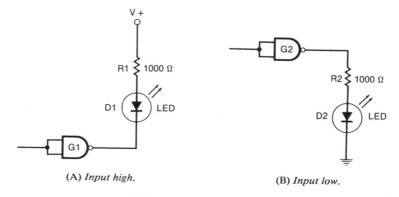

(A) *Input high.* (B) *Input low.*

Fig. 17-4. CMOS-to-LED interfacing.

the CMOS output through a current-limiting resistor. When the output of the CMOS device is low, there is no voltage applied to the LED, so it is turned off. But if the CMOS output is high, a potential is applied to the LED and it turns on. In this case, a low input to the inverter turns on the LED, while in the previous example a high input turns on the LED.

An example of a TTL-to-LED connection is shown in Fig. 17-5. In this case, an open-collector TTL device is needed (ordinary TTL outputs will not work). If the proper TTL inverter is selected, we need not limit the V+ potential of the LED circuit to +5 volts DC (but the TTL device *must* be operated from +5 VDC). Regardless of whether the V+ supply is +5 VDC, or higher, we must set the current-limiting resistor to permit a current flow consistent with the LED specifications. The usual current for "garden variety" LEDs is 15 milliamperes (0.015 ampere).

Example

Find a current-limiting resistor value for a +5 VDC system using a garden variety LED.

$$R = V/I$$
$$R = 5/0.015$$
$$R = 333 \text{ ohms}$$

Because 333 ohms is not a standard value, use 330 ohms (which is standard)—no one will ever know the difference.

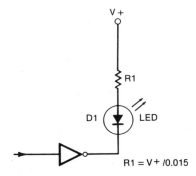

Fig. 17-5. TTL-to-LED interfacing.

Relay and Solenoid Interfacing

The outside world is connected to digital electronic circuits through a variety of devices, but perhaps the most common is the ordinary, old-fashioned, electromechanical relay. These devices use an electromagnet to pull together switch contacts. When the electromagnet coil is ener-

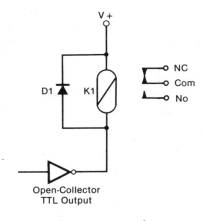

(A) *Low-current relay.*

Fig. 17-6. Relay interfacing.

gized, the relay switch operates. Fig. 17-6 shows several methods for interfacing relays to digital devices.

The circuit in Fig. 17-6A shows the simplest form of interfacing,

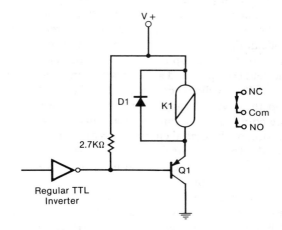

(B) *PNP transistor for high-current relay.*

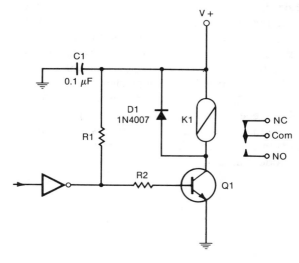

(C) *NPN transistor version of (B).*

Fig. 17-6—cont. Relay interfacing.

and is only useful where the relay current is tiny— on the order of 30 milliamperes or so. The top end of the relay coil is connected to V+, which can be as high as 30 volts if the right TTL inverter is selected. The "cold" end of the electromagnet coil is connected to the output of the inverter. When the output of the inverter is high, the coil has no ground return so it is not energized. If, on the other hand, the inverter output is low, the cold end of the coil is grounded and the relay is energized.

The diode in Fig. 17-6A is used to despike the circuit. When a relay coil is energized, it builds up a magnetic field. When the coil is dee-nergized the field collapses and generates a counter electromotive force (EMF) voltage. Such voltages can reach very high levels, and can potentially damage the device. In any event, whether or not the voltage spike damages the component, it can cause a spurious "glitch" signal that upsets operation of the digital circuit. This diode is a 1000-volt rectifier type, such as the 1N4007. The diode is reverse-biased in normal operation, but when the coil is deenergized it becomes forward-biased and clips the counter EMF spike.

A circuit for interfacing a relay to an ordinary TTL device is shown in Fig. 17-6B. In this circuit we use a PNP transistor (Q1) as an electronic switch to turn on the relay (K1). A PNP transistor is turned on when its base is less positive than the emitter. Thus, when the regular TTL inverter output is low, the transistor is forward biased and the relay is energized. As in the previous case, a 1N4007 diode (or equivalent) is used to despike the circuit. The collector current of the transistor must be sufficient to carry the relay or solenoid coil current.

A similar circuit using an NPN transistor is shown in Fig. 17-6C. In this case, a pull-up resistor is used as a current sink to the TTL output. When the TTL output is high, a bias current flows to transistor Q1 through R1 and R2. Under this condition, the transistor is biased on and the relay is energized. When the output is low, however, bias current is shorted to ground and the transistor is unbiased. This situation makes the transistor turned off and the relay deenergized. Again, a despiking diode is used.

Chapter 18

Waveform Generators and Timers

Almost everyone who dabbles in electronics as a hobby eventually needs to build an oscillator, multivibrator, or digital clock circuit. These circuits are used to produce a variety of electronic waveforms that are needed in many different circuits and applications. A simple oscillator, for example, might be used in a radio transmitter or receiver. Such circuits are generally considered to be sine-wave generators, even though the word oscillator is correctly applied to circuits that produce other waveforms. The multivibrator could produce square waves, triangles, or other waveforms. Similarly, a digital clock is a special case of the multivibrator and/or oscillator that is used in digital logic and computer circuits.

In general, let's keep our jargon straight by adopting the term *oscillator* to cover all three cases, including astable multivibrators and digital clocks. The term oscillator can be defined as a circuit that will produce a periodic waveform (i.e., one that repeats itself). The output waveform can be a sine wave, square wave, triangle, sawtooth, pulse or other waveshape. The important part is that it is *periodic*.

There are two forms of oscillator circuit, relaxation oscillators and feedback oscillators. Some relaxation oscillators use one of several available *negative resistance* devices (e.g., tunnel diode). Such devices operate according to Ohm's law at certain potentials, and contrary to Ohm's law at other potentials. There are other relaxation oscillators using devices that pass little or no current at voltages below some threshold, and pass a large current at voltages above the threshold. Examples of these devices are neon glow lamps and unijunction transistors (UJT).

Feedback oscillators use an active device as an amplifier, and then provide feedback in a manner that produces regeneration instead of degeneration. These circuits account for a large number of oscillators used in practical electronic circuits. We will discuss both forms of oscillator.

Relaxation Oscillators

There are two main devices used in practical relaxation oscillators—neon glow lamps and UJTs. There are also some circuits that are based on SCR-like devices, but these are not common. We also have a class of relaxation oscillators that is based on IC devices such as voltage comparators, integrators, and so forth.

Fig. 18-1A shows a simple relaxation oscillator based on the neon glow lamp. The reason for including it in a book on IC's is to demonstrate the principle of the relaxation oscillator. The neon glow lamp has a low pressure inert gas inside of a glass envelope that also contains a pair of electrodes. When the potential across the electrodes exceeds the ionization potential (V_t in Fig. 18-1B) of the inert gas, the gas gives off light. Popular types of neon glow lamp include the NE2 and the NE51. For these lamps, the threshold potential is somewhere between 40 and 80 volts, although the lamp will maintain its ionized state (and continue to glow) at a somewhat lower "holding potential" (V_H).

The circuit for the relaxation oscillator is shown in Fig. 18-1A, while its operating waveforms are shown in Fig. 18-1B. The frequency of oscillation is set by the ionization and holding potentials, acting in concert with the RC time-constant of the resistor and capacitor. The resistor is connected in series with the lamp, while the capacitor is connected in parallel with the lamp.

We must keep in mind the two states of the neon lamp. When the lamp is not ionized, it conducts no current. This is the situation at all potentials below V_t. At voltages above the threshold, the lamp resistance suddenly drops to nearly nothing (and, in fact, is so low that it will blow the lamp if the resistor is too low a value). When the circuit is turned on, the capacitor begins to charge and the capacitor voltage (V_c) begins to build up. When the voltage across the capacitor reaches the threshold potential, the lamp ionizes and takes on a very low resistance. Since this low resistance is across the capacitor, the capacitor discharges. But the discharge only continues until V_c reaches the holding potential. When this potential is reached, the lamp goes out and reverts to its high resistance state. The cycle continues, with the capacitor voltage varying between threshold and holding potentials. The frequency of oscillation is determined by the difference between these potentials and the values of R and C.

Negative Resistance Devices

There are several semiconductor devices on the market that have a so-called negative resistance property. What does this mean? Regular, or

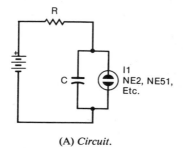

(A) *Circuit.*

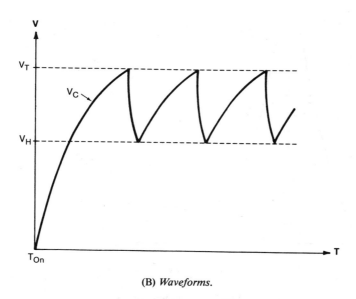

(B) *Waveforms.*

Fig. 18-1. Simple relaxation oscillator.

"positive resistance," operates according to Ohm's law. When the voltage across the circuit is increased, the current in the device increases proportionally; when the voltage is decreased, the current decreases also. In a negative resistance device, however, exactly the opposite is found. An increase in voltage will produce a decrease in current, and vice versa.

An example of a negative resistance device is the tunnel diode (also called an Esaki diode after the inventor), the symbols for which are shown in Fig. 18-2A. The I versus V curve for the tunnel diode is shown in Fig. 18-2B. In the positive resistance zone (PRZ), the tunnel diode operates much like other Ohm's law devices. But in the negative resistance zone (NRZ), it behaves just the opposite from Ohm's law.

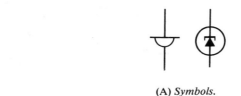

(A) *Symbols.*

(B) *Current versus voltage curve.*

Fig. 18-2. Tunnel diodes.

Relaxation oscillators are simple, and are good circuits for students and beginning hobbyists to build (if only to learn how they work). Most other applications, however, will use one or another feedback oscillator circuits.

Feedback Oscillators

A feedback oscillator consists of an amplifier and a feedback network (see Fig. 18-3). It is called a "feedback oscillator" because the output signal of the amplifier is fed back to the amplifier's own input by way of the feedback network. We call the gain of the amplifier A_{vol}, and the transfer function of the oscillator B. The overall gain of this circuit is given by the relationship:

$$A = \frac{A_{vol}}{1 + A_{vol}B}$$

[Eq. 18-1]

The amplifier can be any of many different devices. For some cases, it will be a common-emitter bipolar transistor (NPN or PNP devices). In others it will be a junction field effect transistor (JFET) or metal oxide semiconductor field effect transistor (MOSFET). In older equipment it was a vacuum tube, most often operated in the common cathode mode. In still other cases, it will be an integrated circuit operational amplifier, or other form of IC amplifier. In most cases, the amplifier will be an inverting type, so the output is out of phase with the input by 180 degrees.

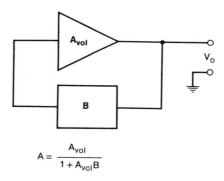

Fig. 18-3. Block diagram of a feedback oscillator.

The feedback network will provide a sample of the output signal to the input of the amplifier. This network may be LC, RC, or RLC. Rarely is it a simple resistance network, because such networks are not frequency selective. They will produce oscillation, however, but at some frequency that is not controlled. The problem is that there are distributed (stray) circuit capacitances in the circuit, and these act with the resistance to produce an RC time constant at some unspecified frequency—that is rarely a frequency that you want!

This circuit will oscillate if two conditions are met: (1) the loop gain is greater than unity, and (2) the feedback signal is in phase with the input signal. Since the typical amplifier inverts the signal (180 degrees), and since we need a total phase shift of 360 degrees (in order to have an in-phase feedback signal), the feedback network must provide an additional phase shift of 180 degrees. If the network is designed to produce this required phase shift at only one frequency (as in an LC or RC network), then the circuit will oscillate at that frequency.

In the rest of this chapter, we will discuss several forms of oscillator circuits in which the active element is either an analog or digital integrated circuit.

Sine-Wave Oscillators

Sine-wave generators produce an output signal that is sinusoidal in nature. Such a signal is very pure, and, if a perfect waveform, will contain only a fundamental frequency with no harmonics. The harmonics of nonsinousoidal waveforms are what give it a characteristic shape. The active element in all of these circuits is the ordinary operational amplifier.

Wien Bridge Oscillators

Figs. 18-4A and 18-4B are examples of Wien bridge oscillators. The elementary form is shown in Fig. 18-4A. The operating frequency in the general case is:

$$F = \frac{1}{2\pi\sqrt{R3R1C1C2}} \qquad \textit{[Eq. 18-2]}$$

Or, in the special case where R1 = R2, R3 = R4, and C1 = C2:

$$F = \frac{1}{2\pi R3C1} \qquad \textit{[Eq. 18-3]}$$

In the above equations, the resistances are in ohms, the capacitances are in farads and the frequency is in hertz.

A problem with this oscillator is the fact that the output amplitude varies, especially as the frequency is changed. We can overcome that problem in part with the rearranged circuit in Fig. 18-4B. In this circuit we place an incandescent lamp in one of the bridge arms to overcome the variable amplitude problem. As the amplitude of the output voltage increases, so does the current in lamp I1 (a #1869 lamp is used for I1). This reduces its resistance, thereby lowering the gain of the amplifier. This relationship is easier to see in the redrawn circuit. The operating frequency is found from:

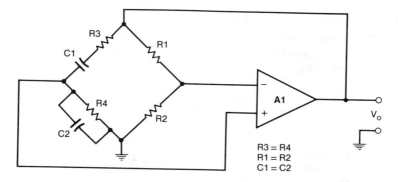

(A) *Classic version.*

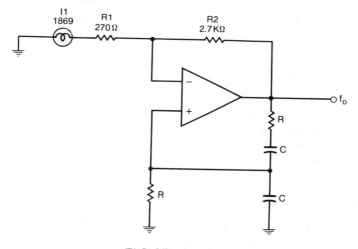

(B) *Stabilized version.*

Fig. 18-4. Wien bridge oscillator.

$$F = \frac{1,000,000}{2\pi RC}$$

[Eq. 18-4]

where

F is in hertz (Hz),
R is in ohms,
C is in microfarads (μF)

Twin-T Oscillators

A twin-T network is a two-branch RC circuit as shown in Fig. 18-5A. There are two T networks in this circuit: R1/R2/C3 and R3/C1/C2(Fig. 18-5B). The required 180-degree phase shift is created by this circuit at the frequency defined by:

$$F = \frac{1,000,000}{2\pi RC} \qquad \text{[Eq. 18-5]}$$

where
F is in hertz,
R is in ohms,
C is in microfarads (μF)

Diodes D1 and D2 (Fig. 18-5A) are used to clip the output if the gain is too high, but that event should be limited by adjusting the ratio R_f/R_{in}.

Bridged-T Oscillators

A variant of the twin-T oscillator is the bridged-T of Fig. 18-6. In this circuit, one of the T circuits is replaced with a single resistor bridging the remaining T network. A variant on the circuit reverses the roles of all the elements. In that circuit, R2 and R3 are capacitors, while C1 and C2 are resistors; the principles are the same, however.

Phase-Shift Oscillators

Fig. 18-7A shows a phase-shift network consisting of three resistors and three capacitors. Each resistor-capacitor combination (R1-C1, R2-C2 and R3-C3) produces a 60-degree phase shift at the resonant frequency. When combined, the overall phase shift is 180 degrees—which is exactly as required for oscillation.

Fig. 18-7B shows an oscillator circuit based on the phase-shift network. The active element is an operational amplifier, while R1-R3/C1-C3 form the feedback network. The operating frequency is found from:

$$F = \frac{1,000,000}{2\pi\sqrt{6}\ RC} \qquad \text{[Eq. 18-6]}$$

or, when all of the constants are collected into one:

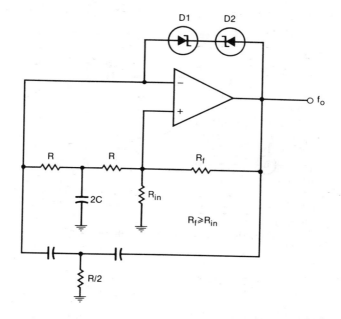

(A) *Active oscillator.*

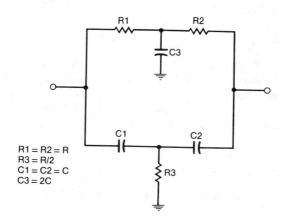

R1 = R2 = R
R3 = R/2
C1 = C2 = C
C3 = 2C

(B) *Twin-T networks.*

Fig. 18-5. Twin-T oscillator.

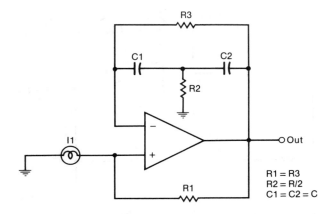

Fig. 18-6. Bridged-T oscillator.

$$F = \frac{64{,}975}{RC}$$

where

    F is in hertz (Hz),
    R is in ohms,
    C is in microfarads (μF)

(Provided that R1 = R2 = R3 = R, and C1 = C2 = C3 = C).

The overall gain of the circuit of Fig. 18-7B is the sum of the forward gain of the amplifier (R4/R1) and the "gain" of the feedback network. The feedback network gain is a loss of about 1/29 at the resonant frequency, so the ratio R4/R1 must be at least 30R in order to make up for the loss and permit oscillation (recall the criteria for feedback oscillators).

Nonsinusoidal Waveform Generators

All nonsinusoidal waveforms contain a fundamental frequency plus a collection of sine and cosine harmonics of the fundamental. In fact, all mathematical functions, whether waveforms or not, can be made up from a series of harmonically related sine and cosine waves. The only difference between waveforms is the specific harmonics present, and

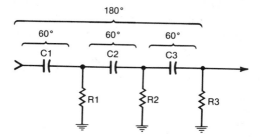

(A) *A 180-degree phase-shift network.*

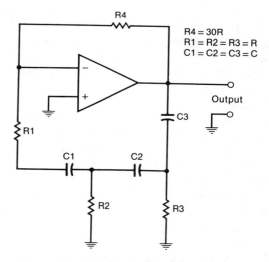

(B) *Active phase-shift oscillator.*

Fig. 18-7. Phase-shift oscillator.

their relative amplitudes and phases. In this section we will discuss square wave, triangle wave, and sawtooth wave generators.

Square Wave Generators

Fig. 18-8 shows two examples of simple square wave generator circuits. Although these circuits produce waveforms with poor rise and fall time characteristics, they are simple enough to merit our attention. Fig. 18-8A shows a circuit based on the RCA CA3048 amplifier. The circuit is simplicity itself, with only a capacitor from the inverting input to ground, and a feedback resistor from the output to the noninverting input. The frequency is found very approximately from:

$$F \cong \frac{1,000,000}{2\pi RC}$$ *[Eq. 18-7]*

where
  F is in hertz (Hz),
  R is in ohms,
  C is in microfarads (μF)

The second circuit, Fig. 18-8B, is based on the CMOS Schmitt trigger device. A Schmitt trigger output snaps high when the input voltage crosses a specified threshold potential in a positive-going direction, and drops low again only after the input voltage crosses a second threshold potential in a negative-going direction. The inverting Schmitt trigger offers a high output until the first threshold is crossed, and a low after the threshold potential is reached.

At turn-on, capacitor C is discharged, so the voltage at the input of the 4584 is zero. This potential is below the triggering threshold, so the output remains high. The high output charges capacitor C through resistor R. When the capacitor voltage (V_c) reaches the Schmitt trigger point, the output of the 4584 drops low. Now that the output is low, the capacitor begins to discharge through R, and when it reaches the second trip point the output snaps high again. The high/low seesaw continues as long as power is applied.

An operational amplifier square-wave generator circuit is shown in Fig. 18-9. The description of the operation of this circuit is similar to that for Fig. 18-8B, except that an operational amplifier is used. The "trip points" are set by the feedback resistors, R1 and R2. The general case gives us a 50-percent duty cycle square wave with a period of:

$$T = 2R3C1LOG\left(\frac{1 + B}{1 - B}\right)$$ *[Eq. 18-8]*

where
  T   is in seconds (s),
  R3 is in ohms,
  C1 is in farads (F),
  B   = R1/(R1 + R2)

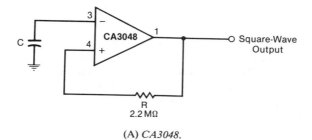

(A) *CA3048.*

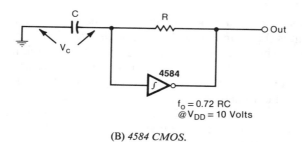

(B) *4584 CMOS.*

Fig. 18-8. Square-wave oscillators.

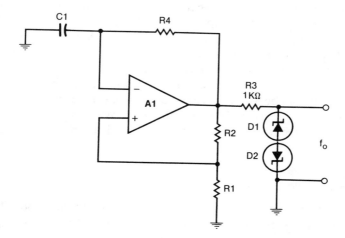

Fig. 18-9. Op amp square-wave oscillator.

A special case for the above equation occurs if B = 0.46 which we can force by making R2 equal to 1.17R1. (Example: R1 = 15000, and R2 = 18000 comes close to this ideal using standard value resistors.) If this criteria is met, then T = 2R3C1. In either event, the operating frequency is the reciprocal of the period: F = 1/T.

The diodes (D1 and D2) in Fig. 18-9 are used to limit the output voltage to a value less than V− and V+. Operational amplifiers tend to saturate when the output hits the supply rail, at least for a short period. As a result, the rise and fall times are adversely affected.

Square Waves from Sine Waves

Fig. 18-10 shows the method for converting sine waves to square waves. The circuit is shown in Fig. 18-10A, while the waveforms are shown in Fig. 18-10B. The circuit (Fig. 18-10A) is an operational amplifier connected as a comparator. Because the op amp has no negative feedback path, the gain is very high; with typical op amps, gains of 20,000 to 2,000,000 are not uncommon. Thus, a voltage difference of only a few millivolts across the input terminals will saturate the outputs. From this behavior, we can understand the operation of the circuit, and the waveform in Fig. 18-10B.

The input waveform is a sine wave. Because the noninverting input is grounded (Fig. 18-10A), the output of the op amp is zero only when the input signal voltage is also zero. When the sine wave is positive, the output signal will be at $-V_o$; when the sine wave is negative, the output signal will be at $+V_o$. The output signal will be a square wave at the sine-wave frequency, with an amplitude of $(+V_o)-(-V_o)$. An output level control, variable gain post-amplifier stage, or an attenuator network can be used to reduce the signal to a usable level.

Earlier we discussed textbook integrator circuits. We learned that these circuits can be used as (1) low-pass filters, (2) to generate quadrature sine-wave signals, and (3) to generate triangle waves out of square waves. In this section we will look at some practical circuits that use the integrator.

Sawtooth Generator Circuit

I recently had a need for a sawtooth generator circuit. The "Poor Man's Spectrum Analyzer" by *Science Workshop* (which I am building) required a sawtooth from an oscilloscope. But the designer of the original circuit used a 30-year old Heathkit— modern oscilloscopes don't have a sawtooth output. My oscilloscope is a modern triggered sweep model

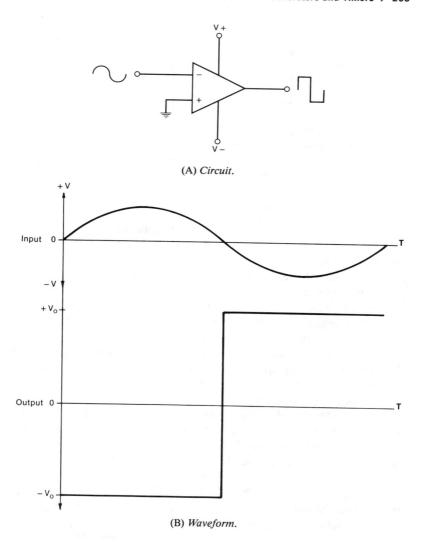

(A) *Circuit.*

(B) *Waveform.*

Fig. 18-10. A sine wave to square wave converter.

with X-Y capability. Although I eventually bought the *Science Workshop* sweep board, I decided to look into sawtooth generator circuits. Because they are based on the integrator circuit, I decided to include them here.

Fig. 18-11 shows one attempt at designing a sawtooth-generating

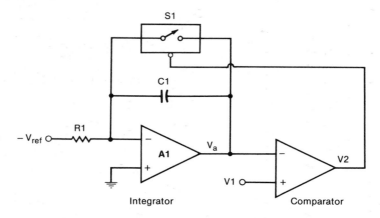

Fig. 18-11. Trial sawtooth oscillator.

circuit. It consists of an integrator (A1) followed by a voltage comparator; the output of the comparator drives the control input on an electronic switch (which is active-low). At turn-on, the charge on capacitor C is zero, so voltage V_a is zero. Because voltage V1 is positive, the output of the comparator (V2) is positive. Under this circumstance the control line of S1 is inactive, so S1 is open.

At turn-on, the stable reference voltage $-V_{ref}$ causes the output of the integrator to ramp upwards. At the point where $V_a = V1$, the output of A2 drops low, forcing S1 to close. This discharges C, forcing the output voltage (V_a) close to zero.

Fig. 18-12 was derived from a circuit given in one of Graeme's classic op-amp books.[1] The ramp generator circuit is the integrator formed with A1, C1, and R3 (being driven by $V-$). The output voltage ramps up until it reaches the threshold of comparator A2. This comparator uses positive feedback and a reference voltage (V_{ref}) provided by a potentiometer. The trip threshold is $V_{ref} + V1$ (which is set to 0.7 volt greater than the zener voltage of D1/D2, assuming that these diodes are identical). When the output voltage hits the threshold voltage, the comparator output snaps positive and forward biases diode D3. If the value of resistor R2 is very much less than R3, C1 will discharge very rapidly, resulting in the classical sawtooth waveshape. The reset time, T2, will be very much shorter than period T1, if R2 << R3.

Another means of generating a sawtooth waveform is to use a special function generator chip, such as the Exar XR2206 (which is available from *Jim-Paks* and others. Although in another circuit the XR2206

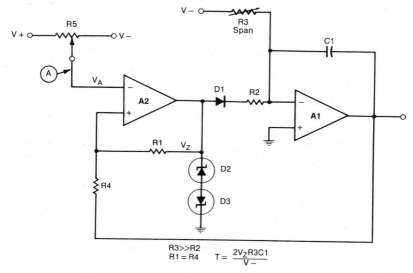

$$R3 \gg R2$$
$$R1 = R4 \qquad T = \frac{2V_Z R3 C1}{V-}$$

Fig. 18-12. Classical op-amp sawtooth oscillator.

will generate sine/square/triangle waveforms, in the circuit of Fig. 18-13A the chip generates a sawtooth and a short duty factor (D.F.) pulse.

The frequency of this sawtooth generator circuit is set by resistors R1 and R2, plus capacitor C2:

$$F = \left(\frac{2}{C1}\right)\left(\frac{1}{R1 + R2}\right) \qquad \text{[Eq. 18-9]}$$

where
  F is in hertz,
  C1 is in farads,
  R1 and R2 are in ohms

The duty factor (D.F.) is found from:

$$D.F. = \frac{R1}{R1 + R2} \qquad \text{[Eq. 18-10]}$$

Jim-Pak makes a circuit board "function generator" kit for less than $20 that creates the sine wave, square wave and triangle wave signals. It can be easily modified for sawtooth applications. The sawtooth and pulse output waveforms of Fig. 18-13A are shown in Fig. 18-13B.

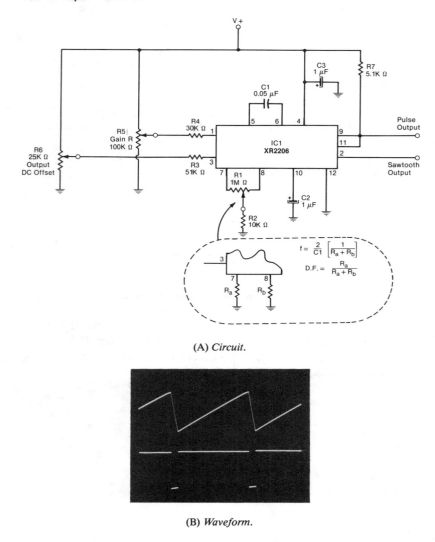

(A) *Circuit.*

(B) *Waveform.*

Fig. 18-13. Exar XR2206 pulse/sawtooth oscillator.

The same Exar XR2206 device can also be used for generating sine-wave and square-wave signals. Fig. 18-14 is the circuit for this application. Switch S1 determines whether the signal at pin 2 is a sine wave or a triangle waveform. This circuit is similar, but not identical, to the Jim-Pak function generator circuit. The operating frequency is:

$$F = \frac{1}{RC1}$$

[Eq. 18-11]

where

F   is in hertz (Hz),
R   is in ohms, and is the sum of R1 + R2,
C1 is in farads (F)

The amplitude and DC offset of the output waveform are adjusted using trimmer potentiometers R6 and R7.

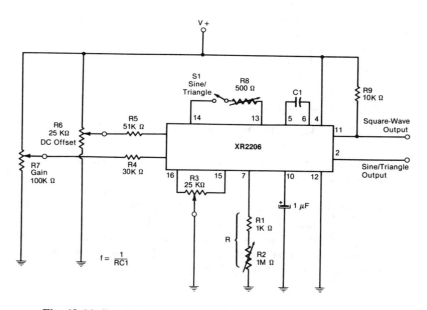

Fig. 18-14. Sine/triangle/square wave oscillator using an XR2206.

Digital Waveform Generators

Modern digital electronics technology can be used to make purely analog waveforms. This type of circuit is the basis for many electronic music projects today. Fig. 18-15 shows generally how this job is accomplished. The heart of the circuit is a digital-to-analog converter (DAC). The output current of the DAC0806 is converted to a voltage by amplifier A1, and then filtered to remove the digital quantization steps

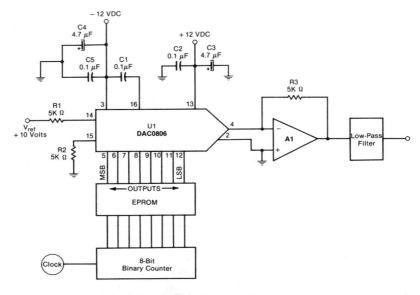

Fig. 18-15. Digital sawtooth generator.

in a second-order low-pass filter. We select the waveform by changing the binary input to the DAC.

If we need a sawtooth, then it is merely necessary to connect the eight-bit DAC inputs to the outputs of an eight-bit binary counter. As long as the clock runs, the output will oscillate back and forth as a sawtooth with a frequency equal to the clock frequency divided by 256. The binary patterns for other waveforms can be stored in an erasable programmable read only memory (EPROM).

Timers

A timer chip is a device that can be used as a monostable multivibrator (one-shot) or astable multivibrator, and is timed with a resistor-capacitor network (Figs. 18-16 and 18-17).

The monostable circuit of Fig. 18-16A will produce a single output pulse of duration T for each input pulse. The input trigger pulse must drop from the high (close to $V+$) to a value less than $V+/3$ in order to "fire" the circuit. The relationship between the trigger input pulse and the output pulse is shown in Fig. 18-16B. The output pulse duration is given by:

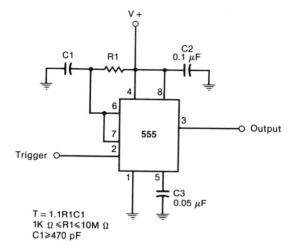

(A) *Circuit diagram.*

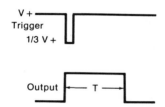

(B) *Input and output pulses relationship.*

Fig. 18-16. LM555 monostable timer circuit.

$$T = 1.1 \ R1C1 \qquad \textit{[Eq. 18-12]}$$

where
    T   is in seconds,
    R1 is in ohms,
    C1 is in farads

The astable configuration shown in Fig. 18-17A produces a pulse of square-wave nature shown in Fig. 18-17B. The total period is the sum of high time (T1) and low time (T2):

$$T = T1 + T2 \qquad \textit{[Eq. 18-13]}$$

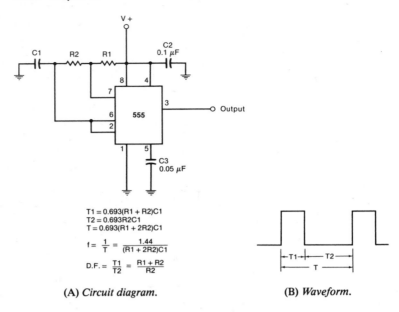

(A) *Circuit diagram.*　　　　**(B)** *Waveform.*

Fig. 18-17. LM555 astable timer circuit.

where
$$T1 = 0.693 \, (R1+R2)C1,$$
$$T2 = 0.693 \, R2C1$$

Therefore,

$$T = 0.693 \, (R1+2R2)C1 \qquad \textit{[Eq. 18-14]}$$

The frequency is found from:

$$F = \frac{1.44}{(R1+2 \, R2)C1} \qquad \textit{[Eq. 18-15]}$$

Reference

1. Graeme, Jerald G.; *Designing With Operational Amplifiers: Applications Alternatives*, McGraw-Hill Book Company (New York, 1977), pp. 159-162.

Chapter 19

A DC Power Supply for Hobbyists

Almost all electronic hobbyists eventually need a bench power supply to carry out their construction projects and experiments. In this short chapter you will find a typical DC power supply (Fig. 19-1) that should meet the needs of 99.99 percent of the readers. It has a +1.25 to +30 volt, 1-ampere adjustable power supply, a +5 volt DC, 1-ampere power supply for digital projects, and a pair of +12 volt 1-ampere DC power supplies.

Fig. 19-1. DC power supply project for the hobbyist.

All outputs on this power supply are floating, that is, they are not referenced to chassis ground. Thus, the outputs can be series-connected to increase the output voltage, or parallel-connected to increase the current capacity. Alternatively, the various outputs can be ground referenced if you so desire.

Note that the 12-volt DC power supplies are both floating. With this design, we can connect the positive (RED) terminal of one power supply, and the negative (BLACK) of the other power supply to form a common, or ground connection. The remaining outputs thus form a −12 volt and +12 volt supply for linear ICs, or CMOS devices. We could have built a single −12-volt, + 12-volt, dual-polarity power supply, but that would have reduced our flexibility. With the design shown, we can make (1) two independent + 12 volt power supplies, (2) two independent − 12 volt power supplies, (3) a single − 12 volt, + 12 volt dual-polarity power supply, or (4) a single +24 volt power supply. These various configurations are selected simply by jumpering or not jumpering the output terminals.

The circuits for the four different power supplies are shown in Fig. 19-2. In Fig. 19-2A we see the circuit for the fixed-voltage power supplies (5 volt, 12 volt), while in Fig. 19-2B we see the adjustable voltage power supply.

The circuit in Fig. 19-2A is a universal design based on the 78xx and LM340T-xx three-terminal IC voltage regulators (see inset to Fig. 19-2A). The voltage rating of the device is given by replacing the "xx" in the type number. For example, 7805 and LM340T-05 are +5 volt regulators, while 7812 and LM340T-12 are + 12 volt regulators.

The transformer used in the power supply depends upon the voltage and current ratings selected. For the +5 volt power supply, select a 6.3-VAC (rms), 1-ampere, transformer. The + 12 volt power supplies use a 12.6-VAC (rms) transformer with a current rating of not more than 1 ampere (I used 300-mA versions for my power supply.)

The rectifier is a bridge rectifier rated at 100 volts PIV (peak inverse voltage) at 1 ampere of forward current. Some of these rectifiers can be quite small, so don't be surprised when you see it. One popular type is in the form of a 4-pin mini-DIP IC package, while another (found at *Radio Shack*) is a small dime-sized disk.

Capacitor C1 is the main filter capacitor. It is rated (approximately) at 2000 μF/ampere, with a 1000 μF minimum. The working voltage rating must be not less than 35 WVDC. Capacitors C2 and C3 are 0.1-μF/25-WVDC bypass capacitors, and are used to prevent high-frequency noises from interfering with the operation of the regulator. These capacitors must be mounted as close as physically possible to the body of the regulator, or they won't be as effective as possible. The output capacitor, C4, is optional, and is rated at 100 μF/ampere and 25 WVDC. The purpose of this capacitor is to smooth out variations in load requirements. When the circuit demands a sudden blast of current, the capacitor supplies it for a few microseconds until the regulator automatically readjusts.

If you opt to use capacitor C4, a good idea by the way, you must also use diode D1. In fact, because your load might be capacitive, I would recommend diode D1 in any event. The diode is connected in the reverse bias mode, so that it does not affect normal operation. When the

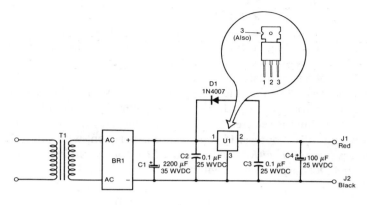

(A) *Three-terminal circuit for +5 VDC and +12 VDC supplies.*

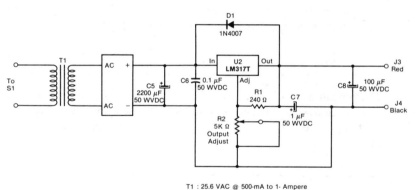

(B) *Adjustable voltage supply.*

Fig. 19-2. DC power-supply circuits.

power supply is turned off, however, there is a transient point at which the C4 voltage is larger than the C1 voltage, which could damage the regulator IC. Diode D1 will shunt the current stored in C4 harmlessly around U1. Do not ground either side of the circuit in Fig. 19-2A, for reasons explained above.

The adjustable power supply is shown in Fig. 19-2B. This circuit is functionally the same as Fig. 19-2A, except for the regulator, so we will not repeat the description of the capacitors and diode D1. The only difference is the voltage ratings of the capacitors (see the ratings in the figure).

The voltage regulator is the LM317T. It will produce output voltages as low as 1.25 volts, and as high as 35 volts. With the values shown and the transformer selected, the output voltage upper limit is 30 volts. The transformer is selected because it is commonly available at *Radio Shack* and other sources. If you wish to experiment with other transformers (see the *Digi-Key* and *Newark Electronics* catalogs), then the expected DC output voltage will be:

$$V_{dc} = (V_{rms}) \, (1.414) \, (0.9) \qquad \textit{[Eq. 19-1]}$$

where
   V_{dc} is the DC output voltage,
   V_{rms} is the rms rating of the transformer

Of course, if you want to select a transformer from a known DC output requirement, then rearrange the equation to the form:

$$V_{rms} = V_{dc}/(1.414) \, (0.9) \qquad \textit{[Eq. 19-2]}$$

The output control, 10-turn potentiometer R2, is mounted on the front panel, and is used by the operator to set the output voltage level. As was true in the fixed-voltage case, do not ground either side of the circuit.

Getting It All Together

Fig. 19-3 shows how all of these circuits are interconnected. Construct four power supplies on one board (see Fig. 19-4): an adjustable supply using Fig. 19-2B; two 12-volt supplies and a +5-volt supply using Fig. 19-2A. The respective output terminals are in the form of red and black 5-way binding posts. Although the gold-plated professional types are expensive (horribly so, given their simple construction), they don't corrode and they do last longer.

An optional meter switch is provided. A pair of 5-way binding

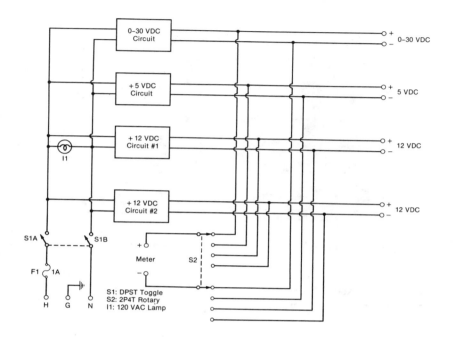

Fig. 19-3. Block diagram for overall supply.

posts on the rear panel is used to connect the outputs to a digital multimeter. If money is no object, buy a digital panel meter with the correct ranges and place it on the front panel. Not being made of bucks, however, I opted for using my bench meter occasionally when I feel it is needed. For many applications, incidentally, it is possible to get away with using a single digital or analog DC voltmeter for the adjustable supply and just trust that the fixed-voltage supplies are accurate.

Fig. 19-4 shows the construction of the DC power supply. It was constructed in a Hammond metal cabinet, although that is optional for you. It is, however, essential that you select a rugged cabinet in order to keep the power supply in good shape. The transformers for the two 12-volt supplies and the adjustable supply are mounted on the perforated circuit board, while the heavier transformer for the +5-volt supply is mounted on the chassis.

WARNING!!! This DC power supply operates from 110 volts AC, which can be dangerous. Always disconnect the AC power cord from the wall when working on the supply. In construction, be absolutely cer-

Fig. 19-4. Internal construction of power supply.

tain to keep the AC line from being accidentally grounded, even if the cabinet is flexed. Place the fuse or circuit breaker as close as possible to the AC line entrance point, and don't even think about deleting the fuse/breaker.

Index

John D. Lenk's Troubleshooting & Repair of Microprocessor-Based Equipment
John D. Lenk

This text provides a simplified, practical system of troubleshooting for the many types of microprocessor-based electronic devices. Concentrating on the basic approach to troubleshooting, the book includes numerous procedures and "tricks" that can be effective in diagnosing, isolating, and locating faults in microprocessor circuits.

Topics covered include:

- Microprocessor Test Equipment
- Problems in Troubleshooting Microprocessors
- Troubleshooting the Gate and IC
- Stimulus-Response Testing
- Vcc and Ground Shorts from Unexpected Causes
- Flip-Flop Troubleshooting
- Register Troubleshooting
- Current Flow Analysis
- Wired-AND and Wired-OR Troubleshooting
- Using the Logic Analyzer
- Step-by-step Procedure for Troubleshooting the VCR

176 Pages, 8½ x 11, Softbound
ISBN: 0-672-22476-3
No. 22476, $21.95

Understanding Microprocessors, Second Edition
Cannon and Luecke

This book provides insight into basic concepts and fundamentals. It explains actual applications of 4-bit, 8-bit, and 16-bit microcomputers, software, programs, programming concepts, and assembly language. The book provides an individualized learning format for the newcomer who wants to know what they do and how they work.

With numerous illustrations and examples, the author discusses how to apply microprocessors to specific problems, the steps necessary in programming a system, and how to choose the right microprocessor for each application.

Topics covered include:

- The World of Digital Electronics
- Basic Concepts in Microcomputer Systems
- How Digital Integrated Circuits Provide the Functions
- Fundamentals of Microcomputer System Operation
- A System Application with SAM
- Programming Concepts
- An 8-Bit Microprocessor Application
- A 16-Bit Microprocessor Application

288 Pages, 7 x 9, Softbound
ISBN: 0-672-27010-2
No. 27010, $17.95

Understanding Digital Troubleshooting, Second Edition
Don L. Cannon

Digital electronic systems are more reliable than the systems they replace, yet, at some point, they will need repair and maintenance. This book provides an insight into this high technology world in a language that both technicians and non-engineers can understand. It presents the basic concepts and fundamental techniques needed to locate faults in digital systems and how to repair them.

Starting with digital system fundamentals and proceeding through advanced system timing techniques, the book is an excellent tutorial providing basic troubleshooting techniques in an easy-to-understand, easy-to-learn format.

Topics covered include:

- Digital System Fundamentals
- Digital System Functions
- Troubleshooting Fundamentals
- Combinational Logic Problems
- Sequential Logic Problems
- Memory Problems
- Input/Output Problems
- Basic Timing Problems
- Advanced Techniques

268 Pages, 7 x 9, Softbound
ISBN: 0-672-27015-3
No. 27015, $17.95

Advanced Digital Troubleshooting
Alvis J. Evans

Technicians ready to expand their skills to include advanced digital troubleshooting can learn quickly with this practical, illustrated how-to guide. Detailed coverage of microprocessor service and repair, instructions explaining how to maintain digital systems, and several successful approaches to troubleshooting make this book a valuable tool for the service professional.

Practical troubleshooting of digital equipment is explained at the board and component level. The author also briefly reviews digital circuits.

Topics covered include:

- Electrical Characteristics of Digital Systems
- Digital Troubleshooting Methodology and Approaches
- Microcomputer Fundamentals
- Meet the Main Chips
- Software and the Diagnostic Program
- Using Basic Digital Troubleshooting Instruments
- The Logic Analyzer
- An In-Circuit Emulator
- Signature Analysis
- Preventive Maintenance and Repair Checkout

208 Pages, 8½ x 11, Softbound
ISBN: 0-672-22571-9
No. 22571, $19.95

Visit your local book retailer, use the order form provided, or call 800-428-SAMS.